**Adventures
in
Video**

Adventures in Video Series

Adventures in Video

A Guide to the Best Instructional Videos

by
Patricia A. Wendling

Arden Press, Inc.
Denver, Colorado

Library of Congress Cataloging-in-Publication Data

Wendling, Patricia A., 1939-
    Adventures in video : a guide to the best instructional videos /
by Patricia A. Wendling.
        p.   cm. -- (Adventures in video series)
    Includes index.
    ISBN 0-912869-19-4. -- ISBN 0-912869-20-8
    1. Video tapes in education--Catalogs.   2. Self-culture--Video
catalogs.   3. Videocassettes--Catalogs.   I. Title.   II. Series.
LB1044.75.Z9W45   1995
371.3'35--dc20   95-25834
                                                               CIP

Typography and design by AK Graphics, Inc.

Published in the United States of America

Arden Press, Inc.
P.O. Box 418
Denver, Colorado 80201

*This book is dedicated
in loving memory
to my best friend and companion,
Andre Vanyo,
who gave me the support
and confidence to complete this book.*

He is truly missed.

Contents

INTRODUCTION

The "video revolution" that started in the late 1970's is rapidly approaching full-blown maturity, and the penetration of VCR's into the home has long since passed the fifty percent mark. The instructional video product, using this broad definition to distinguish it from movies and musical performance videos, is evolving as a popular market product. Major distributors are now producing tapes for the general public covering a vast array of subjects. In recent years, video has become an accepted and important teaching tool, and instructional tapes cover the gamut of skills, as basic as baking a cake to as complex as tapestry weaving, offering many unique and fascinating learning opportunities.

Adventures in Video is an invaluable aid in building a video library. Instead of searching through numerous vendor catalogs, just browse through the chapters of this book. From the literally thousands of videos that are available, more than 2,000 have been selected based on their content, presentation and overall quality. The better instructional videos are both educational and entertaining. They are worth watching again and again. Like a good book, a good video can end up as a lifelong companion.

Collecting videos is surprisingly affordable. A video is comparable in price to a book and certainly less expensive than taking a class or hiring a private instructor. In the privacy and comfort of your own home, you can learn a new hobby or enhance skills at your own pace with your own "video tutor." Difficult concepts can be mastered by rewinding the tape and repeating as often as necessary. What better way to learn than by actually observing the experts in their fields of expertise.

Each of the first ten chapters covers a general subject area, enabling you to quickly locate material related to your specific interests. But don't limit yourself. Open your mind and explore other areas, too. A new hobby or skill you haven't pursued before because of the time or expense involved could now be feasible just by a touch of a button on your VCR. Like a good library, there's something for everyone—from toddlers to grandparents.

For your ordering convenience, Chapter 11 lists the sources for all videos detailed in this book, along with their addresses and phone numbers. Make your selections from this fast-growing list of how-to tapes, order your videos and you'll discover exciting new learning opportunities that will enhance and enrich your life.

CHAPTER 1:

AROUND THE HOUSE

DECORATE LIKE A PRO - DO-IT-YOURSELF HOME IMPROVEMENT - GREEN THUMB TECHNIQUES - HOME, SAFE HOME - LET'S GET COOKING - PARTY TIME - TAKE THE DRUDGERY OUT OF HOUSE-WORK - YARD/LAWN SHAPE-UP - SOURCES

DECORATE LIKE A PRO

Whether a modern condominium, a house in the suburbs or an old-style farm house, our home is where we try to make a distinct statement about our personality and our life style. Successful professional decorators always take their client's needs and personality into consideration when planning the perfect room. With the aid of one of the excellent videos available on the subject, you can achieve the same results—but with much less expense and much more fun.

DECORATING COURSES

For a comprehensive decorating course, viewing the **NEW AMERICAN HOME** (CEP) tape is an informative and worthwhile undertaking. This program not only covers interior decorating but expands into home design and innovative building products. Starting with the development of the floor plan, the viewer is presented ideas and information on various aspects of interior design, including color and methods of creating an atmosphere of character and charm to personalize the home. You'll be given tips on how to customize a home within a planned community and will see the newest in architecture and home-building products. Whether tackling a small or large project or simply updating your current home, this video has a house full of ideas for you.

Guaranteed to be a time- and money-saving resource for years to come is the **ART OF INTERIOR DECORATING** (CEP). This tape allows you to learn professional decorating at your own pace. You'll learn to make individual design statements in an economical way that reflect your individual tastes and needs. While discovering how to create and implement a decorating plan, you'll also get invaluable information on selection and arrangement of furniture and accessories and how to get the most from a limited budget. This is an excellent tape not only for use in your own home but also for preparing you to offer your decorating talents to others.

Starting with a vacant house? Wondering what to do first? That's easy. Pop **DESIGN FOR LIVING** (CEP) into your VCR and learn how to turn a

1

vacant house into a comfortable, livable home. This is a live-action video hosted by a professional interior designer who guides you through the entire design process. You start with traffic patterns and room functions, utilizing the reproducible floorplans and furniture template that are packaged with the tape. Tips on furnishings, wall coverings, color choices and more will help turn those naked rooms into a home you'll be proud of.

FINISHING TOUCHES

One of the first things to be installed in a room just might be your carpet, and for help in making a wise decision in this area **DECORATING: SELECTING THE RIGHT CARPET** (DIY) is both helpful and informative. While this program is basically dedicated to explaining how to make the right choice in carpets, it does go a step further. Your video host also takes you through each room you are carpeting and discusses the basic decorating and design concepts to consider to make your house feel like a home.

The carpet/tile is laid and the walls are prepared. In comes the furniture, but where do you put it? Get professional advice via video on shaping up any room in the house. **ROOM ARRANGING DO'S AND DON'TS** (BHG) is an entertaining and helpful video on furniture arranging for comfort, need and your own particular life style. It's like having the best decorators in the world go to work for you.

FINISHING TOUCH (CEP) is a video that teaches you just what its title implies. This is a light-hearted yet educational lesson on personalizing each room. Full of before and after shots, it contains professional advice on using accessories such as plants and art objects to accent a room. A very illuminating section on lighting tips is particularly useful for creating a special atmosphere. While this video is an excellent do-it-yourself aid, it also contains a segment on what questions to ask professionals and what to expect from a pro hired to do your decorating.

An exceptional decorating video by the people at House Beautiful is **HOUSE BEAUTIFUL: DECORATING WITH SHEETS** (CEP). Practical and creative ways to use sheets to decorate with a minimum of expense might be just the creative solution you're looking for. The program demonstrates many simple, easily executed projects that can be completed in less than two hours. Armed with your choice of sheets and this video, you can create many beautiful decorating projects in your living room, bedrooms and child's room that are sure to add a distinctive touch to your home.

****

After you've learned the basics of decorating and put them to good use, you might want to learn a few other skills that can be incorporated into your decorating schemes. The HOBBIES, CRAFTS & MORE chapter contains many creative skills via video that can be utilized in producing special accents for each room. Also of interest to the home decorator are the topics in the DO-IT-YOURSELF HOME IMPROVEMENT section below.

DO-IT-YOURSELF HOME IMPROVEMENT

Home improvement is one of the most prolific areas of how-to videos. From a comprehensive beginner's course in home repairs to very specialized tapes, videos abound that can be invaluable to those tackling their own home improvement projects. Whether you're on a limited budget or just want the satisfaction of doing it yourself, an investment in a video may be the way to go. You'll be pleasantly surprised at how easy a seemingly complicated repair can be when taught by your video instructor. And once you get the basics under your belt, you can go on to more complicated and intricate projects. Your VCR will enable you to learn at your own pace and then put your new-found knowledge to good use.

SHOP TOOLS AND TECHNIQUES

One of the most important preparatory steps to be taken before tackling any building/repair/remodeling project is learning about the use and care of basic tools. **BASIC CARPENTRY** (DIY) is an excellent introduction to choosing the necessary tools for any task. This tape is an overview of the general use of various tools, including a tape measure, combination square, power saws, drills and sanders. It is a very informative tape for the beginning do-it-yourselfer. Another valuable reference video for becoming familiar with various tools is **HAND AND POWER TOOLS** (CEP). This comprehensive guide to tools teaches how to work with measuring and layout tools, how to use various types of saws and how to choose the correct hammer for your project and provides information on the correct use of drills, chisels, planes and routers.

Power tools can help any do-it-yourselfer achieve a professional finished project easily and effectively if used correctly. There are videos available on many different types of power tools that show correct techniques for usage as well as safety tips. **MASTERING YOUR TABLE SAW** (TAU) demonstrates a variety of techniques to get the most out of the table saw. **MASTERING YOUR BANDSAW** (TAU) will teach the viewer some extraordinary bandsaw tricks and techniques. **WORKING WITH YOUR RADIAL ARM SAW** (MWP) provides shortcuts, safeguards and shop tips on this important shop tool. For basic router handling, **ROUTER JIBS AND TECHNIQUES** (TAU) teaches dozens of efficient ways to use this tool. And **SHOP PLANES** (MWP) teaches the viewer how to choose, use and sharpen planes and discusses various special planes that can be utilized.

BASIC HOME REPAIRS/REMODELING

For a basic reference video on common home repairs, several excellent tapes are available that you'll be sure to turn to time and time again. **HOME REPAIR** (DIY) clearly explains a wide variety of common home repair projects. Subjects in this program include replacing a faucet and toilet, unclogging drains, caulking a tub, replacing light fixtures and switches, repairing lamps and many, many more repair projects that you'll learn to handle yourself instead of calling for expensive help. **DO-IT-YOURSELF HOME REPAIRS** (BHG) is another invaluable reference tape to help master common household repair jobs. Viewing this tape will enable you to tackle such problems as a dripping faucet, replacing a screen, patching damaged walls, repairing broken tile and countless other repair jobs around the house. And for step-by-step instructions for fourteen time- and money-saving projects, join PBS hosts Bob Vila and Norm Abram in **THIS OLD HOUSE** (RHV). This popular program covers doors, floors, electrical work, plumbing and more and provides a handy video index.

If you dread calling a plumber because of the cost, you may want to invest in a video that will teach you the basics of doing your own plumbing work. **PLUMBING** (DIY) covers many plumbing projects and repairs that you can learn to tackle yourself. Detailed explanations and demonstrations will enable you to install toilets, vanities and sinks, tubs and showers and a washer and dryer, among other projects. The tape also provides you with information on safety codes along with instructions on necessary tools and materials to help you with all your fundamental plumbing jobs. Another area where videos can be extremely cost effective is electrical repairs. **ELECTRICAL** (DIY) will provide you with everything you need to know to do basic electrical repairs. This tape also stresses safety codes and provides instructions on using the proper tools and materials you'll need to run new wiring and install lights, switches and circuit breakers.

Many homeowners have tackled the job of painting and/or wallpapering a room only to find the job a little more than they bargained for. By investing a little time beforehand with a video, you can learn to paint and wallpaper like a pro. **WALLPAPER LIKE A PRO!** (BHG) is a worthwhile investment. This tape is a complete course in wallpapering. You'll learn everything you need to know to get professional results. Another comprehensive tape on this subject is **INTERIOR PAINT AND WALLPAPER** (DIY), which contains many money-saving tips. Starting with wall repair and preparation, you'll learn wallpaper planning and hanging, how to paint walls, ceiling and trim, as well as professional tips and techniques. There is also detailed discussion on the tools and materials that you will need for your projects. As an alternative to paint or paper, you may be contemplating paneling as a wallcovering. To get the best results from your efforts, take a look first at **PANELING** (DIY). This program teaches all the skills and tips you need to panel over new or existing walls. You'll learn trim techniques and how to install various types of paneling to fit your particular situation.

Ceramic tiles lend themselves to a variety of uses in a home, and the do-it-yourselfer can easily complete attractive projects utilizing the knowledge available in various videos. **CERAMIC TILE: WALLS** (DIY) contains step-by-step instructions for using ceramic tiles in the kitchen or bath. You'll learn the professional method of wall preparation, establishing working lines, spreading adhesive and laying the tile. **TILING WALLS** (MWP) will also teach you all the basics including how to handle out-of-plumb walls and maneuver around plumbing. In addition, you'll be able to choose the proper tile for the project and install trim and accessories such as soap dishes and towel racks. If it's a ceramic tile floor or countertop you have planned, **CERAMIC TILE: FLOORS AND COUNTERTOPS** (DIY) will lead you step by step through the process. Again, you'll learn all the basics plus many professional tips and techniques to complete the job. **TILING**

COUNTERTOPS (MWP) is a perfect introduction to tiling for countertop jobs. You'll receive detailed instructions on working with a backer-board and mortar-bed substrate and learn how to lay tile around a sink.

Hardwood flooring can be a beautiful foundation for any home. Whether you're planning on installing a complete new floor or want to beautify an existing one, there is a video that can teach you everything you need to know. **LAYING HARDWOOD FLOORS** (MWP) is an excellent basic tape for installing a complete new floor. You'll learn how to prepare and install a tongue and groove oak floor from selecting stock to laying to finishing. This program contains many tricks of the trade that will enable you to do a really professional looking job. For existing hardwood floors that need a pickup, **HARDWOOD FLOORS** (DIY) is a very informative program that discusses repairing, sanding and refinishing existing hardwood floors. There is also a segment on installing prefinished parquet and plank flooring. Another video to help you refinish your existing flooring is **SANDING AND FINISHING HARDWOOD FLOORS** (MWP). This comprehensive video includes sanding techniques that give optimum results and finishing for a durable and beautiful floor. The segment on types of equipment to rent is especially helpful.

Perhaps the most used room in anyone's home is the kitchen. If you'd like to update your kitchen but don't know where to start, start with a video. **KITCHENS** (DIY) will definitely get you on the right track and keep you there. You'll learn how to plan and design an entire kitchen that will fit your life style. Design to finished project can be accomplished by following this program's step-by-step instructions for removing old cabinets, plumbing and appliances and preparing the new design you want to create. It also includes everything you need to know for the plumbing and electrical hookups and instructions on how to trim and finish your new cabinets. **MAKING KITCHEN CABINETS** (MWP) is a useful guide to making your own cabinets using tools found in most home workshops. You'll get details of layout, joinery, drawers, doors and more. A segment of this program is devoted to installing your finished cabinets.

DO-IT-YOURSELF EXTERIOR PROJECTS

Exterior painting or siding can be an expensive undertaking. If you're thinking of tackling this project yourself, you can ensure your success by first gaining a thorough knowledge of just what is involved. **EXTERIOR PAINTING** (CEP) explains how to paint the exterior of a house from priming to painting the trim. The tape discusses color selection, types of paint available and the correct brushes and applicators to be used. You'll learn to prepare the outside surface using traditional methods plus the advantages of electrical scrapers, heatguns and pressure washers. Safety is stressed with detailed discussion on extension ladders and scaffolding. If siding is your choice of exterior finish, **SIDING** (CEP) is an excellent guide to doing the job right. You'll learn about the necessary tools and how to correctly estimate the material you need. Detailed instruction will show you how to tear off old siding and/or replace existing sheathing. The correct flashing and caulking to finish the job is also demonstrated.

Most homeowners at some point are faced with having to replace their home's roof. If you've decided to try this project yourself, **ROOFING** (CEP) will aid you in correctly tearing off old shingles and preparing for new ones by installing underlayment and flashing. You'll learn to install the new shingles for professional looking results that are sure to improve your home's appearance. And since you're already on the roof, you might be interested in installing a skylight or two. **SKYLIGHTS** (DIY) will teach you how to plan, locate and cut openings for attractive skylights. Techniques for installing flashing and insulation and for finishing the frame opening will ensure an attractive finished project.

There are many other exterior projects that can be completed by the do-it-yourselfer. A useful tape that is a good general reference for miscellaneous projects is **EXTERIOR PROJECTS** (DIY). This program covers installing a lockset and deadbolt, a garage door opener and a door threshold, building a deck and more. For detailed instructions on doors and windows, **INSTALLING DOORS AND WINDOWS** (MWP) is an excellent way to learn from the experts. The tips and techniques on this tape will have you installing doors and windows expertly and quickly. If your needs include a garage, **GARAGES** (DIY) will help you design, plan and lay out your own garage. You'll learn how to frame the walls and how to install the roof, windows and doors. You'll be able to professionally finish your new garage by installing siding, trim and even a garage door opener. If it's a new deck that's on your wish list, **BUILDING A DECK** (BHG) is the video you need. This program shows the entire process of deck building from basic planning and design to assembly and includes many tips on professional finishing touches. Another important video for any homeowner is **ENERGY CONSERVATION** (DIY). This informative program discusses weatherstripping, programmable thermostats, batt insulation and vapor barriers. In addition, you'll learn how to conserve energy through proper caulking and water heater insulation.

MISCELLANEOUS DO-IT-YOURSELF PROJECTS

The number of do-it-yourself projects around the home is limited only by your imagination. If you can imagine it, there is probably a video available that will teach you how to do it. For starters, **EASY TO BUILD WOODWORKING PROJECTS** (DIY) includes several easy projects for the beginner. This program will teach you to make bandsaw boxes, a towel rack, cassette racks and turning bowls. **SMALL SHOP PROJECTS** (TAU) contains great ideas for all those lovely bits of wood you can't bear to throw out. Other small object projects can be found in **MAKING OVAL SHAKER BOXES AND CARRIERS** (MWP). You'll learn how to cut, bend wood and fit tops and bottoms. This program is all about making beautiful and functional shaker boxes. And a really useful and fun program is **PICTURE FRAMES** (DIY). Learn to choose stock, design cutting profiles, bevel cuts, assembly and finishing touches for beautiful wood frames.

If you feel ready to graduate into some large projects, several videos may be of interest. **MAKE A BLANKET CHEST** (MWP) shows the step-by-step procedure using hand and power tools in the making of a blanket chest. This is a novel hands-on approach video. Another unique project you may wish to tackle is to **BUILD A SHAKER TABLE** (MWP). This tape covers the entire process of making a leg-and-apron table from stock preparation to final sanding. All the procedures are explained, and a list of alternative tools is included. Other tables can be yours for the making by viewing **BUILDING TABLES** (DIY). This tape will aid you in building a variety of table styles, taking you through all the necessary steps up to the finishing touches. If bookcases are what you need, try your hand at building them. **BUILDING BOOKCASES** (DIY) will teach you everything you need to know, starting with the design and choosing the stock. You'll be guided through the entire process to a professional looking finished product. Another unique video you may want to consider is **CHAIRMAKING** (MWP). You'll learn how to construct an oak rocking chair using spokeshaves, drawknives and more. Included is a segment on weaving chair seats.

There are some interesting videos available on outdoor projects. If you have the right spot in your yard for a picnic table, consider building your own. **HEXAGONAL PICNIC TABLE** (DIY) will help you choose the proper stock and gather the necessary tools. You'll see step-by-step detailed instructions on cutting and building a lovely picnic table that will be a useful and decorative addition to your yard. If your yard is populated by children, you might want to consider the **CHILDREN'S PLAYSETS** (CEP) video. You'll learn how to design a playset that utilizes the necessary safety considerations and materials that will give a long-lasting exterior use. Details on various types of playsets will help you plan and design a unique, personalized play area in your yard that will delight the youngsters.

Various other tapes exist that are sure to be of interest to the do-it-yourselfer homeowner. **CEILINGS** (DIY) will teach you all the techniques and tricks needed to install suspended ceilings or ceiling tiles. You'll learn safety tips, how to plan ahead and what tools and materials are needed. **VINYL FLOORS** (DIY) will prove invaluable in helping you lay a new vinyl floor by first spreading adhesive or using self-adhesive tiles. Lots of tips are included on proper tools and materials and tricks of the trade for cutting border tiles and curves. And for the really ambitious, **ATTIC CONVERSION** (DIY) may be the help you need to add additional living space to your home. Starting with the insulation, you'll proceed to applying and finishing drywall, preparing the floors and even installing skylights.

****

Much of the knowledge and many of the techniques learned through the above videos can be applied to various specialized skills. Take your newfound skills along and browse through the FURNITURE REPAIR\REFINISHING and WOOD CARVING sections of the chapter on PRACTICAL, VOCATIONAL & UNUSUAL SKILLS.

GREEN THUMB TECHNIQUES

The "Green Thumb" species among us can thrive under many different conditions. Whether you're situated in the middle of ten acres, own a small plot of land around your house or are limited to patio gardening, there are videos available for your entertainment and education. Flower growers can expand their knowledge to produce beautiful, unique bouquets as well as the standard varieties. Videos can help the vegetable farmer produce a bumper crop under all conditions. For those confronted with landscaping projects including trees and shrubs, videos have been produced to impart all the knowledge you'll need to be successful. And if your green thumb wants to stray beyond the usual gardening area, tapes on specialized gardening projects also exist.

THE WORLD OF BEAUTIFUL FLOWERS

The most successful, abundant flower garden should begin with a basic design. To achieve this first step, **HOW TO DESIGN A FLOWER GARDEN** (ACB) is a great introduction to the basics of flower garden design. Always keeping the end result in mind, you'll learn how to choose a site, create a design and select the annuals and perennials that will best produce the flowering garden you have in mind. This informative program also provides the viewer with a good foundation for preparing the soil, irrigating, mulching and much more necessary to produce a spectacular flowering area. An added bonus of interest to many gardeners is a special segment on how to make your own high-quality compost.

Other videos are available that are sure to delight and inform both the beginning flower gardener and the more experienced grower. **FOOLPROOF FLOWER BEDS** (BHG) is a very basic tape that teaches how to create the garden of your dreams. It includes valuable tips and techniques for keeping your dream garden beautiful for years to come. A practical tape for the flower grower is **HOW TO GROW FLOWERS** (ACB) from the Yardening Series. You'll learn how to start your own seedlings and then properly transplant them. The tapes in this series are very informative and include practical tips on correct planting techniques, mulch, water, feeding your plants and protecting your flowers from pests and diseases. A bonus segment on this video addresses how to create long-lasting floral displays.

If you've always yearned to create an unusual garden that will be the envy of your neighbors, **CREATING THE ROMANTIC GARDEN** (ACB) is a delightful exploration of a "cottage" garden. Ryan Gainey, one of America's foremost cottage gardeners, takes you on a tour of his exquisite Atlanta gardens. During the tour you'll be treated to intriguing insights into the entire creative process of flower gardening and learn how a brilliant designer tends his own romantic garden. This program also includes a reference list of all the plants featured on the tape.

Flowers are typically designated as either perennial or annual, and there are tapes dedicated to each of these species. To discover the world of perennial gardening, a very informative video, **PERENNIAL GARDENING** (ACB), guides you through the entire perennial garden process. All the information in this tape is geared specially to perennials and includes soil preparation, plant selection, planting techniques, maintenance, propagation and more. A "Planting Guide" for perennials is featured for your reference. If annuals capture your fancy, **ANNUALS AND HANGING BASKETS** (ACB) is the video to watch. You'll learn the basics of growing beautiful annual flowers that will be the envy of all. The tape also dedicates a segment to creating eye-catching hanging baskets utilizing decorative annuals. A highlight of this program is a visit to the beautiful Butchart Gardens in British Columbia.

One of the most widely cultivated and popular flowers in the world is the rose. **FOR THE LOVE OF ROSES** (ACB) is an invaluable video for both the novice and the experienced rose grower. This program shows you exactly how to grow roses like a pro, no matter where you live. The detailed tape instructs on rose care season by season and carefully explains all the tips and techniques needed to produce this magnificent flower. Another video of interest to the rose grower is **HOW TO GROW ROSES** (ACB). This program provides step-by-step instructions that you can use to create a spectacular rose garden. You'll learn how to plant, mulch, water and prune for professional results. Also featured is a segment on tips for creating long-lasting displays with your own cut roses.

For those who have ever tried their hand at growing orchids or would like to, **ORCHIDS: JEWELS OF THE RAINFOREST** (ACB) is an excellent video guide for beginning orchid growers. The program explains all the major orchid types and shows you how to select varieties that will do well in your environment. Practical demonstrations are given for potting these unique flowers and the general care they require. With this enjoyable program as your guide, you'll discover that orchids can be surprisingly easy to grow.

BOUNTIFUL HARVEST

As anyone who has ever undertaken the growing of a vegetable garden will attest, there is no greater satisfaction than harvesting your own vegetable crop. And if that crop is bountiful, that satisfaction can be viewed on the table throughout the year. **THE VICTORY GARDEN** (RHV) is a step-by-step, comprehensive crash course in vegetable gardening. This program is useful for the beginning gardener but also contains invaluable tips for the experienced grower. For the viewer's convenience and reference, the tape has onscreen indexing by subject matter that lets you find, in a matter of seconds, tips and techniques on growing a particular vegetable.

To view your own video seminar on the basics of vegetable gardening, take a look at **BLUE RIBBON VEGGIES** (ACB). This program is hosted by gardening expert Ed Hume, who takes you into his backyard to demonstrate a step-by-step approach to producing an outstanding vegetable garden. The topics discussed in this informative program include soil preparation, fertilization, watering, pest control and more. Many of the more popular crops are featured in detail, such as beans, peas, corn, tomatoes, potatoes and asparagus. This is a worthwhile addition to your gardening library.

Because of today's emphasis on the environment, many gardeners and would-be growers are increasingly interested in learning more about organic gardening. A program to help build a healthy vegetable garden from the ground up is **ORGANIC GARDENING** (ACB). You'll learn about selecting

9

and starting seeds, constructing raised beds and making your own compost in addition to soil testing, pH adjustment and soil deficiencies. This tape keeps a keen eye on the environment while teaching the basics of producing a healthy and abundant crop.

The National Gardening Association has endorsed two excellent videos that are sure to help you get the most out of your vegetable or herb garden all season long. From the Yardening Video Series, **HOW TO GROW WARM WEATHER VEGETABLES** (ACB) instructs the viewer on selecting the right crops to grow during the warmer time of the year. The latest techniques are explained in detail, and additional segments give tips on transplanting, trellis systems, mulching and weed control, watering methods and pest control. And if you'd like to extend your growing season by several months, you can enjoy an extra crop by viewing **HOW TO GROW COOL WEATHER VEGETABLES** (ACB). Learn which vegetables to plant, how to protect them from cool temperatures and how to control pests. You'll be amazed at the additional harvest that can be yours as you learn the tricks of the trade from this informative tape.

HEALTHY, HAPPIER PLANTS

Potted plants can be spotted almost everywhere we go. They're used to decorate homes, offices, stores and the neighborhood mall. If your green thumb needs a little help in the area of plants, there are videos available that show the latest methods for growing beautiful plants in your home, sunspaces or greenhouses. One of the most informative programs is **HOW TO GROW HEALTHY HOUSEPLANTS** (ACB). Whether you're interested in plants to decorate your home or office, this tape will teach you how to select the right container, how to mix potting soil and how and when to water and fertilize. Most importantly, it also addresses one of the biggest problems plant growers encounter, which is finding the best location to ensure that your plant stays healthy and thrives.

If you're lucky enough to have a garden room or even a room or two with sufficient sunspaces, you'll want to take a look at **HOW TO GROW PLANTS IN SUNSPACES** (ACB). This tape is packed full of tips for evaluating light, temperature and humidity to find the right spot for each plant. You'll also discover how to keep your plants healthy and happy by avoiding watering mistakes and preventing pests and diseases.

For the serious plant grower who is contemplating a home greenhouse, **HOW TO GROW PLANTS IN A GREENHOUSE** (ACB) contains the latest advances in home greenhouse design and maintenance. This program is packed with practical advice on greenhouse technology. Detailed information is given on plant selection, watering and fertilizing especially for greenhouse plants. This tape teaches everything you need to know to get the most from your home greenhouse and ensure continuous displays of luxuriant foliage.

GREEN THUMB POTPOURRI

DISCOVERING GARDENS (RDM) is an exciting video series of six volumes sure to delight serious green thumbers. Via video you are taken on a tour of England's finest gardens while top gardeners offer tips, historical anecdotes and hard-to-find information. Travel through Cornwall, Devon, Somerset, Wiltshire and the Isles of Scilly and learn about the spectacular flowers shown in this stunning series.

Whether growing flowers, vegetables, herbs or exotic crops, **HOW TO GROW AND NURTURE SEEDLINGS** (ACB) will help you get your seedlings off to a great start. Learn to select the proper containers, prepare the potting medium, germinate seeds and protect the new seedlings from insects and disease. This program will teach you how to promote faster, healthier growth using indoor grow lights and get you off to a great start.

You can have a beautiful garden with a lot less water than you may have thought possible. **WATERWISE GARDENING** (ACB) gives the viewer a hands-on demonstration of how to match plants to your climate, analyze watering needs, efficient and effective use of sprinklers and mulches and much more. To discover how to control pests in your vegetable garden without poisons or toxic chemicals, view the informative **NATURAL PEST CONTROL** (ACB). You'll learn how to select and use disease resistant varieties, which insects are really beneficial and how to use companion plants.

One of the most satisfying and fun gardening projects is growing your own herbs. **HOW TO GROW AND COOK HERBS** (ACB) is a delightful and informative video to view whether you plan an extensive herb garden or a few windowsill pots. You'll learn how to select, grow, harvest and store your own fresh herbs. And the program goes a step further by showing you how to add zest to any meal with the delicious herb recipes you'll discover in this tape.

If you'd like to try your hand at an unusual form of gardening to beautify your yard, take a look at **NATIVE WILDFLOWERS OF WOODLAND AND PRAIRIE** (ACB). While this video is basically a fascinating exploration of wildflowers, it also includes suggestions on species that can be adapted in your garden landscape. As an added bonus, you'll learn medicinal and culinary folklore of the many plants described. Another type of gardening that is becoming more popular all the time is water gardening. Learn how you can create your own water garden with the help of **SUCCESSFUL GARDEN POND** (ACB). From selecting the right location for your water garden to stocking it with aquatic plants and fish, this tape will give you all the basics for getting started in this fascinating garden area. You'll also learn tips that will be helpful in maintaining your pond once it is installed.

A great way to interest children in nature and stir their creativity is to introduce them to the joys of gardening. **GET READY, GET SET, GROW!** (ACB) is a delightful introduction to gardening. This program is based on more than seventy years of experience at the Brooklyn Botanic Garden. It uses imaginative techniques to show children and their parents how to create successful vegetable and flower gardens. It is sure to enthrall the youngsters in your home and can be the beginning of a rewarding family project.

****

*M*any of the vegetables and herbs you'll learn to grow in abundance with the above videos can be put to good use in your kitchen. The LET'S GET COOKING section of this chapter is full of delicious recipes you can use to put your bountiful harvest to maximum use. In addition

11

to beautifying your yard and patio, the superb flowers you'll learn to grow can be utilized in many ingenious ways that you'll discover through the videos discussed in the CREATING WITH PLANTS & FLOWERS section of the HOBBIES, CRAFTS & MORE chapter.

HOME, SAFE HOME

We all like to think of our home as a secure place to be. Viewing one or more of the following videos would be time well spent in ensuring that your home always remains a safe haven.

SAFE & SECURE

CONSUMER REPORTS: HOME SAFE HOME (CEP) is a comprehensive guide to keeping your home safe and secure. This video will help you find hidden safety hazards and teach you how to correct them. You'll get valuable tips on fire prevention and security systems that will protect your property. Topics covered in this program include electrical safety tips, child-proofing your home, emergency plans and kitchen safety.

HOME SECURITY (DIY) teaches you just what its title implies. You'll learn to install a locking door knob, a deadbolt and anti-jimmy devices in a door. Instructions are given on installing locking devices on windows and electronic alarm systems. A home security survey is included.

RADON INFORMATION

RADON—A HOMEOWNER'S GUIDE (ACN) is a complete introduction to radon gas, a major American health concern. This program explains where radon gas comes from and demonstrates testing options, proper testing techniques and guidelines for interpreting test results.

Another good video on this subject was produced with the support of the U.S. Environmental Protection Agency. In **RADON FREE** (XJX), TV family man Dick Van Patten leads the way through this special homeowner's guide as you learn what radon is, how it affects your health and how to test for and eliminate it. This program will help you determine just how safe your home and family are.

****

In addition to making your home secure with the above videos, you can further prepare yourself for any emergency by taking a look at some of the videos listed in the SAFETY & FIRST AID section of the HEALTHY LIVING chapter.

LET'S GET COOKING

Utilizing the VCR, beginners and expert chefs alike can now enjoy a one-on-one cooking class. Enroll in a basic course with a famous food guru. Pick a food category and learn to prepare hundreds of delicious recipes for any "mealtime" situation. Become a master at preparing unusual and ethnic foods. Cooking videos abound for everyone's taste, pocketbook and particular situation. Kids around the house? Let the VCR introduce them to the delightful world of cooking. A family of one or a virtual Brady Bunch? There's a video available just for you. Want to put that microwave to more use than just heating a frozen dinner? There's a video for you, too. Do you have an abundance of garden vegetables or herbs? Use your VCR to learn how to put them to good use. And just as important as the actual cooking, let's not forget the skills needed in wise and economical food purchases. Let your VCR teach you to be a wise shopper.

COOKING LESSONS

Both novices and gourmet cooks will benefit from a cooking school series produced by some of America's most famous chefs. America's favorite cooking teacher, Julia Child, shows the viewer how to master the basics of good cooking as she demonstrates a wealth of superb recipes in her video series **THE WAY TO COOK WITH JULIA CHILD** (RHV). This cooking course is a series of six videos, each devoted to a particular culinary category. **POULTRY** teaches how to cook a variety of poultry with variations of the recipes demonstrated using mushroom sauce, a melange of sweet peppers, tomatoey Provencal flavors and more. To learn how to sauté steaks and how to cook hamburgers, pork chops and many more varieties of meat, try viewing Ms. Child's **MEAT** video.

VEGETABLES provides instruction on how to cook twenty-five different vegetables, from asparagus to zucchini, with tricks for maximizing tenderness and flavor and preserving color. To learn how to make delicious soups from a French onion to a Mediterranean fish soup, view the **SOUPS, SALADS & BREAD** tape, which also gives the viewer a complete lesson in making French bread. **FISH AND EGGS** not only demonstrates the techniques of broiling, sautéing and oven-poaching fish, but includes techniques for making custards, quiches, mayonnaise, hollandaise and a spectacular souffle. To begin your meal with a flourish and end with a bang, **FIRST COURSES & DESSERTS** discusses perfecting the tart crust for tantalizing appetizers and savory, sweet-filled crepes.

Though better known as the king of comedy than the king of the kitchen, Dom DeLuise, in his **EAT THIS** (CEP) series, takes the viewer on a cooking spree through his kitchen and demonstrates some delicious recipes inspired by his mamma, Vincenza DeStefano DeLuise. Spend a delightful and educational time with the DeLuise family through this four-tape series as they shop for traditional Italian ingredients, observe mozzarella cheese being stretched and pulled by hand, visit a store where dough is transformed into every kind of pasta imaginable and visit a meat store where pork is transformed into delicious Italian sausages. Each of these videos contains a variety of recipes in assorted categories and introduces fun into the art of cooking.

Craig Claiborne's **NEW YORK TIMES VIDEO COOKBOOK** (CEP) is a good choice for novices or experienced gourmet chefs. Mr. Claiborne, the *New York Times* food expert, presents twenty new gourmet recipes from preparation to completion in easy-to-follow steps. Entries range from

13

appetizers to desserts. The video is supplemented with a mini-cookbook and seasoned with helpful hints to make appropriate side dishes and sauces. Also included are the expert's tips for attractive table settings and garnishes. This video is a complete "how to" on becoming a gourmet in your own kitchen.

Another celebrity chef who is also a restaurateur, Wolfgang Puck, shares an imaginative collection of irresistible recipes inspired by the cuisine of Hollywood's famous Spago restaurant in his video **COOKING WITH WOLFGANG PUCK** (CEP). Join co-hosts Kate Capshaw, Christina Ferrare, Vincent Price, Joel Grey and Robert Townsend for a sampling of Puck's thoroughly original and enjoyable recipes. Sections of this video include Appetizers, Pastas and Pizzas, Entrees and Desserts.

America's hottest new chef, Chef William Neal, brings his outstanding cuisine to your home via his **FIVE STAR COOKING** (CEP) video. For the beginner as well as the expert, this tape provides the ingredients for mastering the techniques of five-star chefs around the world. Follow the step-by-step creation of such creative dishes as field greens and wildflowers, miniature BLT's, sweet golden pepper and garlic soup, giant sea scallops, cheese puffs and many more delectable recipes.

If you're interested in mastering the culinary techniques of a particular food category, Chef Harold Alexander provides the viewer with practical, how-to-cook-it **COOKBOOK VIDEOS** (ALW). These videos highlight one food subject on each tape, with short, practical, easy-to-learn segments. Each recipe segment features a dish that even a novice can easily duplicate successfully. Subtitles and video graphics reinforce verbal instructions. Chef Alexander shows the fundamentals of cooking while suggesting how to be creative by adding and changing ingredients. In the meat, fish and poultry category, the viewer can learn the techniques of preparing **LAMB CHOPS, FILLETS OF SOLE, HAMBURGER, SAVORY VEAL DISHES, BASIC CHICKEN SAUTE** and **ROAST TURKEY** along with **POULTRY DRESSINGS** and **EASY SLICED TURKEY GOURMET DISHES.** For appetizing vegetable dishes, try a tape devoted to preparing **BROCCOLI, CAULIFLOWER, ARTICHOKES** or **ASPARAGUS.** Videos to satisfy your sweet tooth include **CHOCOLATE MOUSSE, DELICIOUS DROP COOKIES** and **BASIC CAKES.** These videos are an informative and entertaining cooking class on tape that can be reviewed as often as needed.

ETHNIC COOKING

The delectable culinary world of ethnic cooking is available through your VCR in a comprehensive array. Join Jeff Smith, better known as "The Frugal Gourmet" as he prepares foods from around the world and dishes that have been savored throughout history. His easygoing style is not only educational, but also informative and easy to follow. As he prepares his sumptuous cuisine, Smith presents the history of the foods, tools and spices he uses and provides a unique and fun way to learn about history along with new and exotic dishes. These videos will be enjoyed by beginners and expert chefs alike. **THE FRUGAL GOURMET: INTERNATIONAL COOKING I** (CEP) is a series of videos that introduce you to **FOODS FROM GREECE, HUNAN TREASURES, AFRICAN DISHES, THE POLISH KITCHEN** and **EDIBLE ITALIAN HISTORY**. **THE FRUGAL GOURMET: INTER-NATIONAL COOKING II** (CEP) covers food preparation in **THE ITALIAN KITCHEN, THE CHINESE KITCHEN, THE JAPANESE KITCHEN, THE FRENCH KITCHEN,** and **THE SPANISH KITCHEN.** For old world recipes, **THE FRUGAL GOURMET: ANCIENT CUISINES FROM CHINA, GREECE, AND ROME** (CEP) introduces dishes that have been savored throughout history, including appetizers, soups, sauces, desserts and religious dishes.

Continuing in the fascinating world of international cuisine, use your VCR to learn how to prepare your own healthy and economical Chinese meals. **THE ART OF CHINESE COOKING** (CEP) consists of two video programs showing step-by-step lessons on how to prepare a variety of Chinese meals. Cook along with a professional chef who shows the ingredients, preparation and serving of a number of authentic Oriental dishes. Volume I includes won ton soup, moo goo gai pan, snow peas with shrimp and more. Volume II will teach you how to prepare such Oriental specialties as lobster Cantonese, chicken chow mein and many other dishes. To really get into Chinese cooking, learn the quick, easy and healthy way of the wok. Two videos that show you how to utilize a wok to prepare many dishes are **WOK ON THE WILD SIDE** (CEP) and **WOK BEFORE YOU RUN** (CEP). These videos are entertaining, informative and can be followed by individuals with no experience in wok cookery.

Other countries are represented in the videos from **THE VIDEO COOK-ING LIBRARY** (CEP), including **BASIC ITALIAN CUISINE, BASIC MEX-ICAN CUISINE** and **BASIC MIDDLE EASTERN CUISINE.** These videos teach the tricks and techniques from expert chefs through step-by-step demonstrations to allow the viewer to cook an authentic ethnic meal with confidence. For a truly delightful introduction to Jewish cooking, **THE JEWISH MOTHERS' VIDEO COOKBOOK** (ERG) reveals the secrets of traditional Jewish cooking, previously passed on only from mother to daughter. The tape leads you step by step through sixteen delicious kosher recipes, including appetizers, side dishes, main courses and desserts. **EENIE'S KITCHEN** (ERG) introduces the viewer to the preparation of traditional foods associated with particular Jewish holidays, including Hanukkah and Passover.

Not to be overlooked in international cooking are those foods and recipes indigenous to America. **THE FRUGAL GOURMET: TASTE OF AMERI-CA** (CEP) series is a delightful trip through culinary America. Start with **EARLY AMERICAN CUISINE** and **THE COLONIES.** Travel the food trail through **NEW ENGLAND,** the **SOUTHWEST, NEW ORLEANS** and **PHILADELPHIA.** Learn the traditional recipes of the **PENNSYLVANIA DUTCH** and the **SHAKERS** and enjoy an **AMERICAN BREAKFAST.** Continue your journey through the **VIDEO COOKING LIBRARY** (CEP) as you learn to prepare **HEARTY NEW ENGLAND DINNERS, BASIC NEW ORLEANS CUISINE** and **SOUTHERN DESSERTS & DELIGHT.** For a side trip into Cajun Creole cooking, **CHEF PAUL PRUDHOMME'S LOUISIANA KITCHEN** (CEP) teaches how to cook a complete Cajun meal featuring blackened redfish and other Cajun dishes. To complete your Americana course, a viewing of **AMERICAN BARBECUE AND GRILLING** (CEP) explains the difference between barbecuing and grilling and how to get the most out of each cookout method. This video covers meats, marinades and sauces; woodchips and briquets; and grills and utensils, along with a tasty collection of tidbits packed with information and expert advice. You'll not only be better informed on historical America but in the process will learn to be a great American chef.

DELICIOUS VEGGIES

In today's health-conscious environment, vegetables often take the spotlight. For the gardener with an abundant crop of vegetables, Marian Morash demonstrates her favorite recipes for freshly harvested vegetables in **VICTORY GARDEN RECIPES: FROM THE GARDEN TO THE TABLE** (RHV). For the vegetable lover, Chef Kurma, renowned throughout his Australian homeland as an epicurean chef, presents **COOKING WITH KURMA** (CEP). This is a three-tape series in which Chef Kurma brings wit and authentic Indian techniques together for an entertaining exploration of gourmet vegetarianism. In **DELICIOUS VEGETABLE ENTREES** (CEP), Marilyn Diamond demonstrates low-fat, zero-cholesterol recipes from her successful *American Vegetarian Cookbook*. Chef Diamond shows how vegetables, normally used as side dishes, can become principal players in nine easy-to-prepare main courses. As the name implies, **MOUTHWATERING MEATLESS MEALS** (CEP) is a vegetarian's guide to scrumptious entrees. This Video Cooking Library tape is also a valuable aid to those chefs who just want to prepare an occasional meatless meal.

DELECTABLE DESSERTS

Kids of all ages love desserts, and many chefs are revered for their "sweet tooth" recipes. **CHOCOLATE & OTHER DIVINE DESSERTS** (CEP) from The Everyday Gourmet series demonstrates fast, easy and delicious recipes that require little time, energy and money. From simple cookings to sinfully rich chocolate desserts, these gourmet recipes are easy, affordable and fun! For chocolate lovers, **CHOCOLATE** (CEP) is a gourmet cooking lesson that guides you from simple chocolate-dipped strawberries to truffles to an elegant frozen chocolate mousse. The videos provide a wealth of information for novice cooks and experienced chocolatiers. Time-saving techniques in preparing desserts can be learned easily by viewing **FESTIVE DESSERTS** (CEP) from the Too Busy To Cook Series. Learn detailed preparation of some great desserts from French chocolate cake to tarte d'abricots.

And to top off your newfound dessert expertise, try your hand at cake decorating. **SISTERS CAKE DECORATING MADE FUN & EASY** (CEP) is an entertaining, step-by-step introduction to cake decorating. Techniques are easily learned through good close-ups of the procedures described. The program covers the basic equipment, ingredients and techniques for producing a variety of cakes, including a birthday cake, doll cake, bridal shower cake, Halloween cake, Santa face cake and petite fours. Also included are shortcuts, do's & don'ts and details for making borders, flowers and much more. For a really ambitious undertaking, turn your attention to the **SISTERS WEDDING CAKE DECORATING** (CEP) video. Sisters Wagner and Ellison demonstrate the techniques necessary for making beautiful wedding and anniversary cakes. You'll learn about the tools used and many tricks of the trade for creating these edible masterpieces.

FAST FOOD TECHNIQUES

Food preparation in today's fast-paced world can often take second place to other activities. Why struggle through "trial and error" by yourself when you can learn to be a creative, gourmet cook in a minimum of time through videotapes. **COOKING MADE MICROWAVE EASY** (BHG) demonstrates in clear, step-by-step instructions how great meals can be fast and easy, as well as delicious. This program covers beginning methods to advanced techniques. **MICROWAVE MIRACLES** (CEP) will teach you to use your microwave with confidence as you transform simple meals into special occasions. You'll learn everything needed—from ingredients to equipment—through the clear explanations of microwave cooking techniques. To take the mystery out of microwaving and replace it with reliable information, **MICROWAVING SECRETS** (CEP) will teach you how to cook food, use covers and wraps, defrost in minutes and achieve browned meats and poultry. You'll learn successful use of temperature probes and how to cook complicated dishes easily by using varied power settings.

Other videos are available that will help the chef reduce preparation time without sacrificing the end result. **TRUCS OF THE TRADE** (CEP) takes the viewer into the kitchens of forty-eight of America's finest chefs to see their favorite *trucs* (French for "tricks")—the special techniques and shortcuts they've developed over the years. Learn how to cook fish in paper, remove the bite from garlic, salvage burned rice, tenderize meat with corks, use plastic wrap as a sausage casing and many more genuinely helpful trucs. Cook better, faster, healthier and have more fun in the kitchen. The "Clever Cleaver Brothers," America's funniest chefs, illustrate eleven simple but elegant complete meals that take less than twenty minutes to prepare in their video **COOKING FOR COMPLIMENTS** (CEP). From stir-fry chicken to fettucini Alfredo, they make you laugh as you learn with their upbeat, light-hearted style. **THE SHORT ORDER GOURMET** (CEP) presents hands-on advice from experts on all the basics of food preparation and delivery. With the techniques shown by some of America's greatest chefs, even the busiest people can enjoy the satisfaction of preparing and presenting great food. This video is a great crash course in cooking essentials.

CULINARY POTPOURRI

Just as the traditional hardcover cookbook comes in many sizes, shapes and subjects, cooking videos cover a vast array of culinary subjects. In **HOW TO GARNISH** (CEP), Chef Harvey Rosen helps you acquire a new skill that you'll enjoy putting to use for the rest of your life. You'll learn how to use special garnishing tools and how to create beautiful designs.

In **COOKING WITH EDIBLE FLOWERS & CULINARY HERBS** (ACB), you are taken on a delightful tour packed with recipes and hands-on cooking demonstrations. The viewer visits world-class restaurants and discovers how top chefs prepare and cook with edible flowers and herbs. A unique video, **EDIBLE WILD PLANTS** (NUQ), takes you on a field trip

17

foraging for useful wild botanicals. In addition to informative details on wild plants and medicinal herbs, you'll discover new recipes using wild plants and how to make herbal teas and "berry-delicious" desserts. Discover dozens of delightful recipes, as well as folk medicine lore and little-known health tips, in the video **TREES, SHRUBS, NUTS & BERRIES** (NUQ).

If bread baking is your forte, let videos expand your horizons. **LET THE FLOUR FLY** (CEP) presents a fun approach to baking bread. The tape starts from scratch and takes you through each stage, highlighting critical steps. You'll learn to bake Swedish rye, crunchy oatmeal bread, quick & easy French bread, Grandma's rolls, and traditional white breads. The Video Cooking Library's tape **BASIC BREAD BAKER** (CEP) is a comprehensive guide to the basic techniques of preparing mouthwatering homemade breads. **DELICIOUS BREADS** (CEP) from the Deliciously Simple Series presents quick and easy techniques for the beginning baker and many helpful hints that surprise even the experienced cook. The tape also teaches buying, cleaning and storing tips as well as nutritional information. Here is an opportunity to learn techniques that are almost impossible to master through books.

HEALTHY COOKING

Caught in the dilemma of wanting to provide your family with both nutritional menus and gourmet flavor? **LYNN FISCHER'S LOW CHOLESTEROL GOURMET** (CEP) tape from the Discovery Channel is a good solution. Learn how to prepare quick and easy meals that are low in salt, sugar and calories but still delicious and appetizing. **DELICIOUS LOW CHOLESTEROL/LOW CALORIE COOKING** (CEP) is a complete cooking course in healthful food preparation. While the ingredients are based on their low-cholesterol/low-calorie content, the end results are high in taste.

A truism making headlines today is that Americans have too much fat in their diets. Just how it gets there is examined in the informative video **LOW FAT COOKING** (EVN). The viewer will also get advice on quick and healthy home-cooked alternatives to the "fat" problem, and the recipes included are a bonus in this educational package. Another rather unique video in the healthful cooking category is **LIGHT & FRESH COOKING** (CEP) from the Too Busy To Cook series. The viewer learns to prepare a complete Oriental meal as well as an after-the-workout meal.

There's no need to feel guilty anymore if you crave good Italian food. **ITALIAN COOKING FOR A HEALTHY HEART** (FSV) features delicious, low-fat, low-cholesterol gourmet recipes. This easy-to-follow program by nurse-author Joanne D'Agostino will show you the secrets of easy-to-prepare proven recipes for a healthy heart. These recipes use low-fat substitutes for fatty food, but there is no substitute for the great-tasting results.

KIDS CAN COOK, TOO!

If you have kids around the house, get them involved early in the intriguing world of culinary feats. **KIDS IN THE KITCHEN** (SMV) teaches children to prepare delicious, nutritious things to eat for themselves or as a surprise for the family. This tape comes with a smudge-resistant, stand-up recipe book and a measuring spoon set and wire whisk. For the age five and up crowd, introduce these first-time chefs to cooking through **MY FIRST COOKING VIDEO** (SMV). Simple instructions show children how to make bread animals, decorated cookies, picture pizzas and lots of other tasty things to eat.

To help youngsters learn and understand the importance of food and nutrition, try **KIDS GET COOKING** (SMV). Presented by talented young actors using folksy puppets, comedy and song, this video is sure to shape a healthy interest in culinary skills. For a special treat the whole family can enjoy, **BUILDING A GINGERBREAD HOUSE** (ALW) is a delightful experience for people of all ages. This visual demonstration of the art of building gingerbread houses is an entertaining, well-organized and easy-to-follow program. Step-by-step instructions guide the viewer through the creation of gingerbread houses for special occasions as well as decorating tips that develop creativity.

WISE FOOD SHOPPERS

Just as important as the actual preparation of food is the gathering of ingredients. Here again, videos can be both informative and entertaining. **SUPERMARKET SAVVY** (CEP) takes the viewer on an informative tour through the grocery store and details facts about each food group. Its main thrust is on the discussion of labels and how not to be misled, in addition to tips for purchasing food for special diets. This program is an aisle-by-aisle nutritional tour of a supermarket. Put this video on your shopping list and begin eating smarter.

SURVIVING THE CHECKOUT: WISE FOOD BUYING (CEP) helps today's food buyer save money and become aware of techniques used by stores and manufacturers to entice consumers. This entertaining video shows how to make wise food-buying decisions in a trip to the supermarket. Learn about labels, brands, unit prices, USDA grading and many more wise shopper tips. This program is packed with useful information for beginners as well as "seasoned" shoppers. Another video that takes the viewer into the fluorescent jungles of the supermarket is **WINNING THE GROCERY GAME** (CEP). Learn about store layouts and merchandising tricks that increase impulse buys in addition to great tips on buying real value instead of convenience foods that aren't. To save money at the meat counter, a **CONSUMER'S GUIDE TO MEAT** (CEP) will amaze you with knowledge of general butchershop practices that will revolutionize your shopping. You'll learn how to get better cuts and quality of meat and save up to fifty percent on the meat portion of your grocery bill with the helpful tips in this video program.

****

*S*o rev up the VCR, don your apron and GET COOKING! You might also want to take a browse through the PARTY TIME section of this chapter to supplement your newly learned culinary skills. And for further information on healthy eating, check out the available videos in the NUTRITION & WEIGHT MANAGEMENT section of the HEALTHY LIVING chapter.

PARTY TIME

Does the idea of entertaining throw you into a panic? Are you in awe of those gracious hosts who keep their cool while serving up memorable, seemingly flawless events? Is the family descending on your house this year for the holidays? If leaving town is not a viable solution, pick up a video to turn any entertaining event into a fun, stress-free and successful adventure.

GENERAL ENTERTAINING

There is a wide selection of videos available to fit your entertaining needs. One of the most "entertaining" series stars the famous chef Jeff Smith, better known as "The Frugal Gourmet." This delightful chef is famous for his easy cooking style and unusual cooking techniques, and he applies these traits to the serious business of entertaining. His videos cover the entire process of entertaining—from selecting and purchasing ingredients to garnishing the final product to dazzling your guests. Pick a tape to fit your particular situation, and let "The Frugal Gourmet" help you plan the entire event. If a buffet is your choice of operation, there are several videos available that you may want to consider. **THE SANDWICH BUFFET** (CEP) and **THE PASTA BUFFET** (CEP) both offer recipes, tips and complete step-by-step preparation to lay out a scrumptious feast for your guests with a minimum of fuss and expense. For a buffet with variety, try **CASSEROLES FOR THE BUFFET** (CEP). Or if your entertaining is to be a bit more formal, follow the step-by-step preparation plans in **THE SIT-DOWN DINNER** video as "The Frugal Gourmet" helps you from start to finish to stage a truly remarkable dining experience for your guests.

Entertaining videos that stress fast, easy and stylish entertaining without spending a lot of time, energy or money are yours for the viewing. You might want to try a different twist and treat your guests to a **TABLETOP COOKING** (CEP) production that is sure to be entertaining and deliciously edible. Or take a look at the tapes from The Everyday Gourmet Entertaining series. These tapes contain practical suggestions on everything from shopping and hospitality to decorating and cleaning up. In addition to providing appealing recipes for two to twenty, these tapes help the host/hostess to create classic centerpieces suitable for the occasion and offer tips on stylish ways to dress up a dinner. **WINNING WAYS TO FEED A CROWD** (CEP) will help you produce a stress-free, delightful culinary event for as many guests as your home will hold. **TERRIFIC BRUNCHES FOR 2 TO 20** (CEP) teaches just what its title implies and could earn you the title of "Brunch Gourmet." If your entertaining schedule calls for a more formal affair, **AN EASY & ELEGANT DINNER PARTY** (CEP) will put you on the right path. Again, follow the step-by-step instructions from start to finish to create an elegant dinner table and a delicious menu and to earn a reputation as a gracious host or hostess.

Instead of hiring a professional "party giver," let Martha Stewart, America's most famous hostess, assist with your next party. Martha's videos contain simple techniques for everything from easy appetizers to full-course meals. She'll help you create the perfect party with a touch of elegance. **SECRETS FOR ENTERTAINING** (RHV) is a comprehensive entertainment guide that goes behind the scenes to show a real pro at work. Follow Stewart from the kitchen, where she shows how to prepare delicacies for your parties, to the dining room, where she demonstrates tips on hospitality. For a memorable party, try an **ANTIPASTO BUFFET** (RHV). This video will help you prepare more than a dozen antipasto recipes, including marinated grilled seafood and focaccia with toppings. Learn to make puff pastry and bread dough that will impress your guests. As in all of Martha's tapes, she takes it a step beyond the kitchen and helps you decorate a truly spectacular buffet table.

Another excellent video from Martha featuring buffet entertaining is **BUFFET FOR FAMILY/FRIENDS** (RHV). In addition to delicious and attractive culinary offerings, such as decorated poached salmon and filet of beef with leek bows, there is a section devoted to decorating your buffet table. Martha demonstrates with china and glassware inventive ways to design an impressive and eye-catching buffet setting. The formal dining tape in this series is for the host or hostess who is contemplating a very formal, elegant dinner party. **FORMAL DINNER PARTY** (RHV) shows how to create a black-tie dinner for six complete with champagne and hors d'oeuvres. Again, Martha demonstrates setting an elegant table and shows complete instructions for creating an equally elegant menu with the choice of two entrees.

For a more general overview of entertaining, two videos are available that put the emphasis on easy, simple entertaining. From the Too Busy To Cook Series and the editors of *Bon Appetite* magazine comes **EASY ENTERTAINING** (CEP). This is a live-action video that shows many time-saving techniques for preparing several great meals. And you'll still have time to talk to your guests. As an added bonus, this video comes with recipe cards. Another video for parties in general that is worth a viewing is **DELICIOUS AND SIMPLE PARTIES** (CEP). This program is geared toward quick and easy techniques for the beginning cook and also contains many helpful hints that will surprise even the experienced chef and partygiver.

SPECIAL ENTERTAINING SITUATIONS

Entertaining for children can be a special dilemma. Turn a potentially frustrating experience into a fun event by utilizing the tape **MAKE YOUR PARTIES FUN** (DIY). This program will make your children's party fun to plan and execute. There are ideas for creating three memorable theme parties for children: a clown party, a western party and a teddy bear picnic, but the techniques and tips given can be applied to all children's parties. Unique to this program are directions for getting the children involved in making invitations, centerpieces, favors and placemats for the big day. And as an added bonus, in addition to recipes, suggestions are given for games to fit the occasion. This tape is certain to get a lot of use, as it is adaptable to many different children's parties. Or to delight the very young children, let **BIG BIRD'S FAVORITE PARTY GAMES** (SMV) be your guide. *Sesame Street's* popular Big Bird and his friends know lots of party games that everyone can play, including musical games and a special "Oscar Says."

While the thought of entertaining usually conjures up a picture of a room full of people, entertaining for two can also be a challenge. Several videos are available to help you plan a special event just for two. The easy-going style and unusual cooking techniques of Jeff Smith, "The Frugal Gourmet," are not just for feeding a crowd. **ENTERTAINING FOR TWO, JUST TWO** (CEP) will help you create an appealing and intimate setting for "just two." And if "just two" is intended to be a romantic evening, be sure to get help from **CANDLES, CHAMPAGNE & ROMANCE** (CEP). This tape is full of ideas from the menu itself to the champagne to serve and the atmosphere to create.

For the fine points of any **EVENT PLANNING** (EMG), this informative video is worth a view. Experienced planners will show you how to develop themes and create fancy centerpieces and other props. You'll also learn the skills needed to get your own business up and running, including designing a professional portfolio. This tape is sure to aid you in planning trouble-free parties and other events.

HOLIDAY ENTERTAINING

Holidays are usually special occasions and the times of the year we entertain the most. From Martha Stewart's entertaining series, **HOLIDAY FEASTS** (RHV) is chock-full of ideas for festive entertaining for Thanksgiving, Christmas and other holidays. As in all her tapes, Martha takes you from start to finish with delicious recipes and entertaining tips. This unique program also contains ideas for making fruit and vegetable gifts to incorporate into your holiday menu. And what holiday is complete without some special treats? **HOLIDAY COOKIES & TREATS** (CEP) and **HOLIDAY GIFTS FROM YOUR KITCHEN** (CEP) are worth viewing for recipes and ideas to spice up the holidays for family and friends.

To keep you sane when hosting a family get-together for a particular holiday, start your planning by viewing **FAMILY GATHERINGS & CELEBRATIONS** (CEP). From The Everyday Gourmet series, this program stresses ways to entertain that are fast and easy yet sure to delight even the most critical family guest. This is a great tape to make family gatherings both affordable and fun with crowd-pleasing buffet menus and special centerpieces to catch your guests' attention. And whether your Thanksgiving holiday is for only a few family members or is expanding to include an extended family gathering, **THANKSGIVING DINNER** (CEP) from the Video Cooking Library is a basic program you should view. This tape will teach you tricks and techniques from expert chefs through step-by-step demonstrations to transform your meal into a feast deserving of thanks.

If you're Jewish or plan to entertain Jewish friends, there are two invaluable videos devoted to the introduction of Jewish holidays and observances. These programs are designed for the entire family to watch and include: **SABBAT TRADITION** (ERG) and **THE FOUR SONS: A GUIDE TO PASSOVER** (ERG). These informative tapes explain the rituals and significance of Jewish holidays and how to prepare the traditional menus. These are entertaining and instructional guides to Judaism's important festivals.

THE ART OF NAPKIN FOLDING

The videos on the subject of napkin folding all contain delightful ideas for special occasions. **THE ART OF TABLE NAPKIN FOLDING** (CEP) demonstrates how to make twenty-three decorator shapes that will charm your breakfast, lunch, dinner or party gathering. Along with the special napkin shape, you'll be shown an attractive place setting and ideas for special occasions. You can learn with just a little practice how to shape a napkin for every holiday season, every mood and every occasion. Another tape on this fascinating art is **FOLD-ALONG NAPKIN ART** (NUV). The step-by-step demonstrations in this program make it incredibly easy to create napkin shapes for affairs of the heart and for affairs of state, for picnics and for elegant banquets. Most of the designs shown look great made from paper as well as cloth, and many can be combined in group arrangements for dramatic centerpieces. A unique section of this video features eight designs especially for children and the young at heart.

TABLE MANNERS

No matter how simple or how elegant the setting, it takes special knowledge to truly enjoy the offering. **TABLE MANNERS FOR EVERYDAY USE** (EVN) is a humorous program great for kids of all ages as well as adults. It shows proper etiquette for breakfast, lunch and dinner, both at home and in restaurants. Whether the video is viewed for social or business occasions or just at home with the family, the knowledge it imparts will be beneficial to everyone.

****

If you're contemplating entertaining, you'll also want to take a look at the LET'S GET COOKING section of this chapter for some inspiring recipes. The HOBBIES, CRAFTS & MORE chapter will give you great ideas on party decorations, and be sure to take a look at the FUN & GAMES section for some great entertaining videos.

TAKE THE DRUDGERY OUT OF HOUSEWORK

Yes, there are videos available to help take the drudgery out of housework. **IS THERE LIFE AFTER HOUSEWORK?** (CEP) is a useful, informative and funny video all about housework. Learn step by step exactly how to clean every area of the house faster, better and for less money. Learn an effective system for getting rid of junk, what equipment is needed and dozens of ways to prevent housework in the first place.

QUICKER CLEANING: FOR EVERYONE WHO HAS BETTER THINGS TO DO THAN HOUSEWORK (CEP) is another truly delightful tape. Don Astlett, the nation's number one house cleaner, presents tips on cleaning with your head, not your hand. Learn how to wash down a whole room in less than thirty minutes and never have a drop of dirty water in your bucket. Wash enormous windows in seconds. Once you know these cleaning secrets you'll wonder how you ever got along before.

23

****

*A*nd now that you have all that free time you used to spend doing housework, put it to good use. Try a unique exercise video from the FEEL FIT/LOOK GOOD chapter or a new adventure from the GREAT OUTDOORS chapter.

YARD/LAWN SHAPE-UP

If outside yard work is taking up too much of your time, let videos help you gain the knowledge you need to spend less time working in your yard and more time enjoying it. Whether you're starting with a bare plot of land or need to enhance and/or improve an existing lawn, there are tapes available that will provide invaluable help. Videos can help you cultivate a lawn that will be the envy of the neighborhood and help you discover unique ways to dress up your yard. If shrubs and trees threaten to take over your outdoor space, let the tapes discussed below help you get a handle on effective tree/shrub maintenance, including those fruit trees that need a boost to produce.

PICTURE-PERFECT LANDSCAPING

A good basic landscaping program presented on an introductory level is **BASIC LANDSCAPING** (ACB). This tape is geared toward the new lawn and starts with teaching how to plan and design a landscape. You'll learn how to prepare your site, lay out the flowerbeds and plant shrubs and trees that you have already laid out on paper. Tips and techniques on using simple landscaping tools are also included, along with a "Hometime Project Guide" that is an excellent reference aid. Not every plot of land is perfectly suited to easy landscaping, and many sites can, at first glance, seem impossible. **SOLVING LANDSCAPING PROBLEMS** (BHG) addresses many common landscaping problems and offers viable and attainable solutions. Whether you need to handle steep slopes, ugly foundations or overgrown plantings, this program can help. Before you give up on your yard, try viewing this tape for some unique solutions.

Depending on the size and condition of your lawn, you may be spending an inordinate amount of time and money trying to create a new lawn or renovate an old one. **HOW TO CARE FOR YOUR LAWN** (ACB), endorsed by the National Gardening Association, is a very upbeat, informative tape. Through precise explanations and graphics, you'll be shown how to use the latest advances in lawn care. The baffling array of grass varieties is explained so you will be able to make a wise decision for your particular site. You'll also learn the best way to water your lawn, mow it, fertilize it and control pests.

Another ideal solution for difficult landscaping problems is **GROUND COVERS** (ACB). There are a wide variety of ground-cover plants available, including ivy, juniper, hebe, boxwood, heathers and succulents. This program discusses these varieties and more and demonstrates how to use them in your particular situation and how to care for them to ensure continued healthy growth.

While sitting in the shade on a hot summer day may be an ideal way to spend an afternoon, shade can be the bane of many a lawn. **MADE IN THE SHADE** (ACB) shows you how to create a beautiful shade garden that enhances the environment and practically takes care of itself. Easy-to-follow instructions for growing a lush, natural moss lawn could be just what you need to update your yard. You'll learn how to use low-maintenance plant materials, control any weeds and much more. If shade is your problem, this video is your solution.

PERFECT PRUNING

An excellent video program from the University of Idaho, **PRUNING YOUR OWN SHRUBS AND SMALL TREES** (ACB) is an invaluable reference tool for anyone confronted with pruning chores. This tape teaches the correct methods for pruning deciduous shrubs and trees, coniferous shrubs and trees and broadleaf evergreens. You'll also receive expert advice on tools, pruning techniques, pests and diseases. This video could be as helpful as your pruning shears. To demystify the pruning process, see **PRUNING** (ACB), a hands-on program that explains why pruning is important. Watch as professionals demonstrate the proper use of pruning tools. Learn how, when and where to prune to achieve the maximum beauty of your prized shrubs and trees.

If you're contemplating planting fruit trees in your yard or already have an orchard in place, you may need some expert advice on the basics of fruit tree care. **EASY STEPS TO FRUIT TREE PRUNING** (ACB) is well worth viewing and will provide some very basic knowledge as well as professional tips and techniques. See how to prune your fruit trees the right way with the help of this practical, down-to-earth program. In addition to providing instruction on the correct use of tools, this tape gives details on open centers, central leaders and espaller training systems to ensure healthier, more fruitful trees. There is also a helpful segment on how to handle old and neglected trees to turn them into hardy producers.

****

*O*nce you've gotten your yard into shape, you'll want to use it more often. The DO-IT-YOURSELF HOME IMPROVEMENT section of this chapter contains some practical, easy-to-do outside projects. Or take another look at THE WORLD OF BEAUTIFUL FLOWERS, also in this chapter, for some great ideas on beautifying your yard.

SOURCES

(See Chapter 11 for a complete alphabetical listing of all sources with addresses and phone numbers.)

ACB	-	A.C. Burke & Co.
ACN	-	Acorn Media
ALW	-	Alwhit Productions
BHG	-	Better Homes & Gardens
CEP	-	Cambridge Educational Products
DIY	-	Do-It-Yourself Inc.
EMG	-	Entrepreneur Magazine Group
ERG	-	Ergo Media Inc.
EVN	-	Educational Video Network
FSV	-	Fusion Video
MWP	-	Manny's Woodworking Place
NUQ	-	New & Unique Videos
NUV	-	Nuvo Ltd.
RDM	-	Rand McNally Videos
RHV	-	Random House Inc.
SMV	-	Schoolmasters Videos
TAU	-	Taunton Press
XJX	-	Xenejenex

CHAPTER 2:

HOBBIES, CRAFTS & MORE

ART INSTRUCTION - CRAFTS FOR FUN & PROFIT - CREATING WITH PLANTS & FLOWERS - FUN & GAMES - KIDS' CRAFTS & ACTIVITIES - SEW LIKE A PRO - COLLECTING - SOURCES

ART INSTRUCTION

To learn a new hobby or enhance your artistic techniques, you can now study with some of the world's leading art instructors. They will show you how to simplify the painting process, remove the fear and mystery and make painting fun. For both beginning and advanced painters, these videos are designed to increase confidence and skills needed for growth as an artist as you rewind and review at your own pace.

DRAWING & SKETCHING

Drawing *can* be taught! The Art Smart Drawing series is designed specifically for those who decided long ago that they couldn't draw but also for those who already love drawing. In **FUNDAMENTALS OF DRAWING** (CEP), artist Carroll Erlandson demonstrates still-life drawing. The viewer is introduced to the elements and principles of art through the use of inspiring narrative and graphic effects. Live-action demonstrations will soon have you filling your drawing pad. **FIGURE DRAWING** (CEP), as the title implies, will introduce you to drawing figures. This tape will give you a good basic background in figure study via an instructor and several clothed models. To expand your knowledge, view the tape **PORTRAIT DRAWING** (CEP), which begins with a historical introduction to portrait drawing and continues with straightforward examples of the three basic poses. The demonstrating artist in this program will teach you about design, mood texture and form within a portrait.

An excellent basic drawing video is **DRAWING COURSE** (CEP), which features three drawing programs within one tape. The first section, Drawing with Charcoal and Pastels, is an innovative approach to creating art work through the use of colored paper, smudging, blending, lifting, collage and much more. Drawing with Mixed Media, the second segment, concentrates on drawing a 3-D object and using mixed media such as pencils, ballpoint pens, colored pencils, colored markers and paint in drawing. In the third section, Drawing with Markers, the viewer will learn about the use of markers to create line, texture and tone in executing a drawing.

For further basic drawing instruction, two more programs are available. **PENCIL DRAWING** (CEP) is a useful tape to learn to draw individual subjects like fruit or plants while learning about contour line, values, form and texture. You'll be able to combine all these skills to produce an impressive still life. For some unusual and effective drawing techniques, take a look at **DRAWING METHODS** (CEP). Artist and teacher Gail Price shows how to use wax crayons, India ink, watercolor wash and other interesting methods that can be used on a variety of papers.

An effective video series providing instruction on the basics of sketching is the **SKETCHING TECHNIQUES SERIES**. These tapes teach critical drawing principles that will enable you to draw any subject realistically and adeptly. Each series contains several tapes dedicated to reinforcing a special drawing principle. The tapes available in the **PEOPLE SERIES** (CEP) include **HANDS IN ACTION, SKETCHING EYES WITH EXPRESSION** and **CARICATURE.** For learning special sketching techniques, the **TECHNIQUES SERIES** (CEP) teaches a variety of different techniques including **DRAWING IN THREE DIMENSION, CREATING MOOD** and **SPECIAL EFFECTS IN SKETCHES**. If you have a particular subject in mind you'd like to sketch, the **SUBJECTS SERIES** (CEP) lets you pick from many titles such as **SKETCHING FLOWERS, STILL-LIFE SKETCHES** and **ANIMALS**. And for special sketching styles, be sure to view a tape from the **STYLE SERIES** (CEP) where you can pick from such programs as **DRAWINGS BY THE CLASSIC ARTISTS, SKETCHING FOR COMMUNICATION** and **SKETCHING IN ARCHITECTURE**.

If you're looking for something a little beyond basic drawing, **DRAWING: LEARNING PROFESSIONAL TECHNIQUES** (AVP) is an excellent choice. Artist Tony Couch demonstrates contour drawing, gesture drawing and more as he uses basic shapes and shading to create three different landscapes. The **LIFE DRAWING SERIES** (AVP) with artist Ruth Block is a comprehensive set of nine tapes that provide the viewer with both male and female models in excellent poses. The experienced and enthusiastic instructor provides exercises and encouragement that will challenge you to draw and keep drawing. And for a condensed and clear overview of the process leading from figure drawing to finished illustration, try **THE ILLUSTRATED FIGURE** (VTX). This program will show you step by step how to turn sketches into finished illustrations such as full-color posters, newspaper ads or book illustrations.

LEARNING TO PAINT

If you want to learn to paint and can't get to a teacher, have the teacher come to you via your VCR. **PAINT!** (CEP) is a straightforward introductory tape that shows the viewer how to use artistic materials and media to achieve varying effects. Demonstrations utilizing a simple still life and two landscapes will teach you the basic techniques and different ways to approach a subject for your painting experiment. Or with a minimum amount of supplies and the **STARTING TO PAINT** (EVN) video, the beginning artist can learn about basic brushes, strokes, mixing colors and other skills and then produce a painting.

If your artistic visualization includes a lovely watercolor, the **WATER-COLOR WORKSHOP** (EVN) program can make it a reality. Art teacher Guy Corriero takes the viewer on a step-by-step exploration of watercolors and shows how to attain the best results with this delicate medium. Another good beginner's tape is **BASIC WATERCOLOR TECHNIQUES** (EVN). This live-action program demonstrates the initial steps and essential procedures for creating a watercolor painting. And to expand a little on the watercolor theme, take a look at **WATERCOLOR AND COLLAGE** (CEP). Artist Gerald Brommer demonstrates a watercolor and collage landscape painting from conception to finished work. His techniques will aid you in bringing a unique look to your own canvases.

Beginners are often intimidated by the thought of trying their hand at oil painting, but the only way to learn is to do it. Start with a basic oil painting course such as **STARTING TO PAINT** (FIN), designed for the beginning artist. This program will introduce you to the basics and show exactly how to apply oil paints to the canvas. Using an enclosed 8" x 10" transfer sketch, you'll learn how to mix colors and complete a small simple painting in a short time. Or you can bring one of California's leading artists, Anita Wolff, into your home. Via **OIL STILL LIFE** (EVN), Wolff provides the oil painting student with detailed instructions in this medium. To learn how to create an explosion of color in an oil still life, take a look at **ABSTRACT OIL: BOB TAPIA** (EVN). The artist's knife and brush method is a wonderful way to create texture and mood.

A must for the serious artist is **OIL PAINTING TECHNIQUES** (FIN). This tape packs literally dozens of lessons into one invaluable program. Artist William Palluth demonstrates his fascinating techniques from wood textures, shadows and reflections to soft edges, wet-on-wet and glazes. The skills acquired through this tape will allow you to put a higher form of realism into your works. You can also follow along with this noted landscape artist as he takes you step by step through painting believable, vivid landscapes. His **WORKSHOP IN OILS** (FIN) series contains four progressively more challenging tapes that will help you create your own masterpiece at your own pace. In each tape the artist takes you from roughly sketched outlines to beautiful finished works as you learn proper techniques and skills. Starting with an **AUTUMN LANDSCAPE**, you can paint your way through a **WINTER LANDSCAPE** and a **SUNSET** and crown your journey with a spectacular **MOUNTAINS** oil painting.

PORTRAIT IN OIL: BERNARD (AVP) is a unique video by well-known portrait painter Daniel Greene. The tape begins with an extensive discussion of the artist's palette and goes on to explain every aspect of executing a portrait in oils. You'll learn how to select materials, prepare the painting surface, position and light the model and compose the picture itself. Frequently during the program, a split screen image will show simultaneously the model and the artist as he paints.

Numerous mediums are used to create a work of art, and each brings its own rewards. **ACRYLICS** (CEP) is a great way to learn the techniques of painting with acrylics. Through sequential demonstrations, the viewer will complete a painting using the tips and techniques described throughout the program. To create a watercolor look with acrylics, see **WATERCOLOR**

TECHNIQUES WITH ACRYLICS (ACV). This program provides good descriptions of the necessary supplies, including brushes, and a helpful explanation of the different types of paper available.

A great find for the beginning painter who wants to learn about the versatile medium of pastels is **PAINTING WITH PASTELS** (EVN). Art instructor Guy Corriero guides the viewer from blank paper to a finished work as he teaches the basic techniques and tips in pastel painting. And for a step-by-step explanation of the process of creating a pastel portrait, try viewing **PASTEL PORTRAIT: ANITA WOLFF** (EVN). This live-action tape will help you to easily master this art medium.

WATERCOLOR TECHNIQUES

Watercolor is an art medium that lends itself to an unlimited array of special techniques and executions. **WATERCOLORING PAINTING: LETTING IT HAPPEN** (VTX) is a two-tape series by artist Judy Howard that will help the viewer develop new insight into this unique medium. Part One, **WET AND SPONTANEOUS**, introduces the materials needed and presents an excellent demonstration on color theory. You'll complete two beautiful landscapes in a free and wet style without ever drawing a single pencil line first. Be sure to progress on to Part Two, **TAMING THE WET MEDIUM**, where the artist will help you apply your new insight into the color shadings of fruit, flowers and grass and to get special effects with a wet-into-wet technique.

For some truly exciting videos on watercolor painting, invite noted artist Irving Shapiro into your home via video. In his videos, Mr. Shapiro shares a wealth of information about the conception and execution of watercolor. His enthusiastic and well-organized running commentary will inspire you to greater artistic heights. In **MOUNTAIN STREAM** (AVP), you will follow him as he starts with a photograph, develops a pencil sketch and then creates the painting. This same exciting and informative method of teaching watercolor is employed in other tapes of Shapiro, which include **GLOUCESTER HARBOR, AMERICAN COUNTRYSIDE, FRESH COLOR OF SNOW and QUIET BEAUTY OF STILL LIFE.**

Several other noted artists are available via video. **FRANK WEBB PAINTING** (AVP) is an energetic and adventurous program in which the artist aids you in creating two landscapes. You'll enjoy Webb's rare combination of scholarly interest in aesthetics and contagious enthusiasm for painting. Learn from an artist known for her exciting interplay of spontaneity and masterly control in **BARBARA NECHIS PAINTING** (AVP), which imparts new ideas to stimulate your own painting. A brilliant flower form watercolor will be your reward for watching and learning from this video. And to witness a beautiful still life emerge from contour drawing to last brush stroke, take a look at **FLOWERS IN WATERCOLOR** (AVP). Artist Charles Reid is a pleasure to watch and learn from as he discusses his philosophy, his techniques and his materials.

Watercolor can also be used to create portraits. **PORTRAITS IN WATERCOLOR** (VTX) by artist James Kirk is a two-tape series that teaches the processes and skills necessary for portrait painting in this medium. Part One, **THE ELEMENTS OF DESIGN**, stresses the understanding of artistic content over depiction of reality and leads directly into painting a portrait. Be sure to go on to Part Two, **THE MAGIC OF LIGHT AND DARK** (AVP), where the artist explores a variety of different approaches. By implementing the techniques demonstrated in these tapes, you'll be able to artistically capture the essence of your subject.

To learn some special and exciting techniques in the medium of watercolor, view three inspiring tapes featuring well-known painter and educator Gerald Broomer. In **WATERCOLOR IN ACTION, RESPONDING TO NATURE** (AVP), the artist is shown working on location. He demonstrates how to capture the "feel" of a specific place, from the first laying in of shapes to the moment of completion. **EXPLORING WATERCOLOR, FROM LOCATION TO STUDIO** (AVP) will help the watercolor artist add details and enhance values without losing the initial freshness and energy of a painting. And **IMAGING IN WATERCOLOR** (AVP) will enable the viewer to recall visual elements and use them to construct a strong and vivid composition.

ARTISTIC POTPOURRI

THE ABC'S OF COLOR - KEEPING IT SIMPLE (BWV) leads a student step by step through the basics of color theory. This excellent video was designed by color theorist Barbara Watson to teach color theory regardless of the media used. A must-see for all artists, this program shows ways to control values and intensities, choose color schemes, create color dominance and much more. For additional demonstrations on the importance of color in effective painting, **COLOR CONCEPTS** (AVP) is worth a viewing. Artist Stephen Quiller will show you how to develop five different color schemes: monochromatic, complementary, analogous, split complementary and triad.

The principles of design are important subjects for both novice and experienced artists. **THE VISUAL LANGUAGE OF DESIGN** (EVN) starts with the basic elements of art and explores how works are created and how the design of various parts contributes to the whole. The video also contains a brief, informative history of western art. To learn how shapes can create balance or how color can provide gradation, be sure to take a look at **ELEMENTS AND PRINCIPLES OF DESIGN** (AVP). In this informative video, artist Tony Couch uses diagrams and masterworks to graphically explain how elements of design are combined.

Two more programs featuring artist Tony Couch are available to enrich your artistic skills portfolio. **DRAWING AND SKETCHING WITH MARKERS** (AVP) teaches basic marker techniques. You'll learn three basic values as you watch Couch sketch and draw a nautical scene and then create a still life. To teach the viewer basic methods with pencil and ink, in **DRAWING LANDSCAPE WITH PENCIL AND INK** (AVP) the artist draws a coastline in pencil and then demonstrates an ink drawing over a loosely painted watercolor wash.

The **ART IS...VIDEO SERIES** contains some exceptional single-concept instructional videos with artist Stephen Quiller. **COMPOSITION** (AVP) teaches the viewer how to use shapes and values effectively, and **COLOR** (AVP) introduces an overview of color concepts. To learn how to see subject matter more creatively, **VISUALIZING WHAT YOU PAINT** (AVP) is a worthwhile video. And if you're open to experimentation, be sure to take a look at **EXPERIMENTAL WATER MEDIA** (AVP). As a viewer, you'll get to explore imaginative new ways to add interest to your paintings with this easy-to-follow program. Learn to create new effects by combining watercolor with pastels, collage, color pencil and oil pastels.

For some other unusual combination techniques, there are several videos you may wish to view. **WATERCOLOR AND GOUACHE** (AVP) contains short lessons by artist Stephen Quiller on how these two mediums can be used together for interesting effects. In another tape, the artist combines **ACRYLIC AND CASEIN** (AVP) to create transparent and opaque washes and impasto textures. **EASY TO DO INK AND WASH METHOD** (ACV) is a fun video to view. Artist Nancy Wekarchuk does an excellent job explaining shading and highlighting by combining an ink and wash method.

If flowers are your thing, see **ROSES—DELANE'S WAY** (ACV), which does an excellent job of demonstrating each stroke needed to paint roses. The practice pattern included for this tape is a beautiful bouquet of roses and lilacs. Viewing **ROSES & POSIES: AN EASY METHOD** (AVP) will help you create beautiful, full-blooming flowers that are as easy to paint as they are stunning to look at. And for a fun to use and easy to do technique, take a look at **WILDFLOWER SPONGE TECHNIQUES** (ACV). The sponge techniques learned in this video will enable you to create realistic wildflower bouquets that can be applied to many different projects.

Another program that will prove valuable in your artistic endeavors is **FUN AND REALISTIC FUR TECHNIQUES** (ACV). This challenging video shows you how to overcome problems with painting furry creatures. It is well worth getting this video just to learn how to create incredible and realistic animal eyes as well as animal fur. And the program **FACE TECHNIQUES** (ACV) teaches how to take a simple base form and change it into a face with great warmth and personality. The techniques you'll learn in this video will be very helpful for any projects that feature faces.

****

"Art" is not limited to just canvas and paint. There are many expressive ways to be artistic and creative. CRAFTS, CREATING WITH PLANTS & FLOWERS and SEW LIKE A PRO are all sections of this chapter that provide a glimpse of some of the countless ways you can funnel your artistic bent. And for more videos that will help you express yourself, take a look at THE WORLD OF MUSIC, DANCE & THEATRE chapter.

CRAFTS FOR FUN & PROFIT

Traditional and contemporary craft techniques are the subject of numerous videos. These tapes can make learning fun, easy and successful. What a great way to learn by seeing someone actually doing it. Whether you're interested in learning a craft for your own enjoyment or you have a market in mind for your creations, there is sure to be a video available in your chosen craft field. From basic knitting techniques to basketmaking to Victorian-style lampshades, there is a video workshop that will provide you with an in-depth study opportunity.

QUILTING AND APPLIQUE PROJECTS

A unique and informative video for beginners and experienced quilters alike is **A VIDEO GUIDE TO QUILTING** (VVP). Hosted by nine members of The New England Quilters Guild, this program teaches the intricacies of patchwork quilting and is an excellent video workshop. Another program geared to both the beginner and the seasoned quilter is **SNOWBALL QUILT SIMPLIFIED: A QUILT IN A DAY** (NNL). The patterns in this informative tape provide an easy beginner project with the basic snowball quilt. Experienced quilters will enjoy learning many variations of these basic patterns that can also be applied to wallhangings and swags.

You have probably seen evidence of the popularity of patchwork quilts at craft fairs and shops as well as around many homes. A good video workshop devoted to this versatile craft is **MASTERING PATCHWORK** (VVP). The viewer will learn how to make templates, how to choose and combine different prints and colors and how to estimate yardage. Many more tips and techniques are shared to produce the basic blocks of this quilting method. An interesting variation is demonstrated in **AMAZING MOSAIC PATCH-WORK** (VVP). These designs are fun and easy to make, and this unique video will teach you step by step how to make a desert landscape. The technique can be utilized easily when you try one of the seventeen different projects shown in the book that accompanies this video.

The techniques and methods of quilting are many and varied, and videos are available for each specific design and method. **TRIP AROUND THE QUILT VIDEO** (NNL) will guide you through the process of creating a magnificent geometric masterpiece. And for both beginners and experienced quilters, **FLYING GEESE QUILT** (NNL) is unique. Using contemporary tools and vertical rows of rectangular geese blocks, you can have your flying geese quilt finished in days.

To create a treasured keepsake, be sure to look at **LOVER'S KNOT VIDEO** (NNL). The lover's knot quilt portrays the close bond with loved ones through two intertwined wedding bands. The pattern is fun to piece together, and step-by-step instructions are given for assembly. And to make use of all the scraps and strips of material you've managed to collect, **SCRAP QUILT, STRIPS AND SPIDER WEBS** (NNL) is a great way to reduce the scrap bag. Recycle those favorite fabrics and rejuvenate your decor with a new quilt.

Applique is the process of stitching one or more layers of fabric to a ground fabric to create a design. To learn hand applique techniques that can be applied to machine applique, **APPLIQUE—TRADITIONAL, STAINED GLASS AND SHADOW** (VVP) is an informative instructional tape. The techniques demonstrated can be used for creating unusual clothing, pillows, quilts or wall hangings. Patterns are included for three projects that utilize three different techniques.

KNITTING AND CROCHETING TECHNIQUES

CROCHET—FROM START TO FINISH (VVP) shows just what its title implies. This video is an excellent instructional workshop for beginners. You'll learn all the basics and many functional uses for each stitch. The accompanying booklet includes sixteen projects that will have you using your

33

new-found skills in no time. If you already have an understanding of basic crochet, a fun tape you may wish to watch is **HOW TO CROCHET WITH YARN & FABRIC** (VVP). This program includes information on blending yarn, selecting materials and joining techniques. You'll also want to try the different gift ideas included.

Perhaps you're interested in making an afghan. Even if you've never picked up a crochet hook before, **LEARN TO CROCHET THE MILE A MINUTE WAY** (VVP) is the way to go. This tape will teach you all the basics as you create your very own afghan. The mile-a-minute technique will let you work up your projects in easy-to-carry strips. You'll probably enjoy this method so much you'll want to go on to view **CROCHET AFGHANS— LOOP 'N LACE** (VVP). This program teaches the way to lace the strips together in seconds instead of sewing up long seams. The lacing forms a lovely cable pattern, and it's as easy as lacing a shoe.

A unique crocheting method involving a two or more color motif, **TAPESTRY CROCHET** (VVP) is both fun and easy. Also known as jacquard, mosaic or hard crochet, this method enables the crafts person to create clothing accessories, baskets and intricate wall hangings with unique texture and color motifs. The viewer is certain to be inspired and delighted by this technique, which can be carried over into many different projects. This would be a worthwhile addition to your video craft library.

BASIC KNITTING TECHNIQUES (VVP) answers many of the questions encountered by both the beginning and intermediate knitter. Starting with the cast-on technique, the viewer will learn all the basics plus many expert tips and techniques. A comprehensive reference booklet packaged with this video is an added bonus. And after you've learned all the basics, be sure to go on to **KNITTING: MULTI-COLOR TECHNIQUES FOR HANDKNITTERS** (VVP). This intermediate/advanced video knitting course teaches the viewer many processes, including how to create multiple and single rows of stripes for a lovely gradation of color. Many more expert techniques are shown, plus tips on incorporating beads. A must for every handknitter.

The last but very important step in a knitting project is proper assembly. **FINISHING HAND KNITS** (VVP) is a comprehensive video teaching all the proper finishing methods, including invisible seam weaving and sewing bound-off edges, set-in sleeves and more. Tips on crocheted edges, button-making and handwash blocking make this an excellent video to have on hand. Another tape you should consider adding to your library is **KNIT REPAIR TECHNIQUES** (VVP). You'll learn a process for repairing knits that makes the repair invisible to the eye. Learn to "rob yarn," choose correct repair tools, clear the hole and repair the worn or eaten area. This informative program also includes an explanation of types and styles of knit garments and their construction.

BASKETMAKING

Baskets come in all sizes, shapes, colors and designs, which makes basketmaking a fascinating and challenging craft that invites use of the imagination. A two-tape video course in basketmaking is a worthwhile investment for those who want to master this skill. **SPLINT BASKETRY- I** (VVP) is an educational, award-winning tape that begins with a bit of historical background on styles, shapes and materials. The program goes on to teach the viewer how to weave an Appalachian egg basket and a melon basket. Various rim, handle and finishing techniques are demonstrated for both left and right handers. Moving on to **SPLINT BASKETRY- II** (VVP), the viewer will learn to weave two distinctly different baskets, one round and the other square or rectangular. Finish your video course by learning several techniques for creating lovely handle decorations.

Another tape that is both informative and instructional is **SHAPING IN PLAITING: FOOTED BASKETS** (VVP). Basic plaiting techniques are detailed step by step with instructions for many different footed baskets, including six-footed, eight-footed and six-footed plaited with a center star design. **SHAPING IN PLAITING: HANGING BASKETS** (VVP) also teaches the basics of plaiting. However, the viewer will learn these techniques using a variety of material, including paper veneer, flat reed, lauhala, braided bamboo and pink palm. This video will help you create some very unique and creative baskets.

John McGuire is a noted basketmaker, author and historian in the field of American basket forms, and his video, **TRADITIONAL NEW ENGLAND BASKETMAKING** (VVP), is an excellent production. John first teaches you how to prepare the materials and then takes you step by step through the process of making a traditional New England basket from start to finish. The information is concise and easily translated into your own basket designs. Another worthwhile addition to your crafts video library.

RUG-MAKING TECHNIQUES

Even a beginner can produce a respectable rug after watching a special video, and **CUT PILE RUG WEAVING** (VVP) is special indeed. This video begins with a little history and then solves the mystery of knot tieing. The next step the viewer learns is how to build a small frame loom strong enough to support a tight warp, which is necessary for this type of weaving. Detailed, step-by-step instructions will show you how to warp the loom, weave and finish your rug. The end result is a beautiful Oriental cut-pile rug. In addition to the design used in the demonstration, many ideas are provided to aid the viewer in preparing future designs. A great video to get you started in rug weaving.

Traditional handhooked rugs are made from strips of wool fabric with the hook used to pull the wool strip to the surface, forming a loop. **HOOKING & BRAIDING** (VVP) is a comprehensive video that teaches the basic techniques of this age-old method of handhooking rugs, from planning to completion. Additional information on color, finish and backing and ways to dye fabrics will help you produce your very own unique finished rug. You'll also learn some basic rug-braiding tips in this informative video. Or if you prefer the punch technique for making rugs, which uses a variety of yarns and other fibers, **HOOKING RUGS** (VVP) is a useful and educational program. This process can be used to create delightful rugs, attractive wall hangings and even art to wear. The tape includes an interesting segment on using unusual materials in original designs.

If you have just the spot for a braided rug, consider several videos by Verna Cox, a noted author in the field of rug braiding. In each of her videos, Cox guides you step by step through the process. You'll learn all the basics of braiding plus techniques unique to the style of rug you are constructing and expert tips to turn your project into a beautiful finished work. Depending on the configuration you have in mind for your new rug, you can pick from **RUG BRAIDING: OVALS** (VVP), **RUG BRAIDING: RECTANGULAR RUGS** (VVP) and **RUG BRAIDING: ROUND RUGS**. Or add all three videos to your library and fill your home with your own creations.

Rag rugs are very easy to make, and joining strips is a snap. There is no sewing involved if you follow the simple procedure presented in **TOOTH-BRUSH RUGS** (VVP). The program will teach you techniques you might like to use with other rag methods including how to calculate the size of a rug and how to strip a whole bolt of fabric in just a few minutes. This program also includes the plastic needle that is used by the instructor on the tape, or you can make one out of an old toothbrush! Hence, the name.

THE WORLD OF WEAVING

Handweaving is perhaps the most functional craft of all. And now you can learn how to weave at home via video. If you've never woven before, start with **INTRODUCTION TO WEAVING** (VVP). This video introduces you to the tools, yarns, vocabulary, projects, types of weaving and equipment that will aid you in choosing many different types of weaving projects. As you continue to explore weaving, you will often refer back to this tape. It is truly a prerequisite to all other weaving courses for those who are new to weaving.

Next, expand into the particular type of weaving you think you might want to try. **CARD WEAVING** (VVP) is a technique that allows you to weave without a loom. The video teaches the basic techniques, including how to measure the warp, thread the cards and set up and weave patterned bands. Or if you always wanted to weave on a loom but don't have much space, **RIGID HEDDLE WEAVING** (VVP) is a great way to get started. Using a small, inexpensive and very portable rigid heddle loom and this video, the viewer will be guided through the process of weaving a beautiful wool scarf. All the techniques you'll learn are easily adaptable to countless other projects.

Tapestry is a pictorial weaving technique that can be woven on any type of a loom, even a simple self-constructed frame loom. Instructions for making such a loom are included in **TAPESTRY WEAVING: LEVEL I** (VVP). This video course includes technical considerations as well as many tapestry techniques to build a solid foundation for any further tapestry exploration. The skills you'll learn as you complete three projects will enable you to create your own unique tapestry work. And if you enjoy this tape, be sure to continue your education with **TAPESTRY WEAVING: LEVEL II** (VVP). The additional weaving knowledge you'll gain through this tape will set you firmly on your way to becoming an expert weaver.

For those of you with some weaving experience and fortunate enough to own a standard size loom, be sure to look at **TIPS, TRICKS & PROBLEM SOLVERS FOR THE HANDWEAVER** (VVP). One picture is worth a thousand words holds true here. The expert host points out many potential problems encountered in the handweaving process and then offers a variety of practical, successful solutions. As you proceed through the sections, you will learn wonderful tips and problem-solving solutions that are guaranteed to make your weaving easier and more successful. Another video well worth adding to your crafts library.

POTPOURRI

If you're in the market for a unique gift item you can create yourself, take a look at **GIFT BASKET SERVICE** (EMG). You'll learn to create beautiful baskets with various types of containers, color combinations, ribbons, flowers and even nesting material. As an added bonus, this informative video will teach you how to shrink-wrap your newly created baskets for a great finishing touch.

If you're interested in adding beads to your own craft creations or making beautiful jewelry, you're sure to enjoy the several beads videos available. **COMPREHENSIVE BEAD STRINGING** (VVP) is a three-tape series that will introduce you to the art of beading and enable you to become extremely adept at utilizing beads in numerous projects. Volume I starts with a look at types of beads, historical information and materials to pick from. You'll also learn about tools, planning appropriate lengths for necklaces and bracelets and design arrangement ideas. The hands-on part of the process is shown in Volume II as you learn all the various techniques of bead art. To round out your education, Volume III covers more advanced techniques. This is a fascinating craft that has countless applications.

One application that is sure to be of interest is **BEAD WOVEN NECK-LACES** (VVP), a video workshop you won't want to miss. You'll learn the entire process from design considerations to finishing techniques as you make a beautiful beaded necklace from the accompanying pattern. Or to update your garments with your own unique creativity, **BEAD EMBROI-DERY** (VVP) is an excellent technique to learn via your VCR. The viewer is taught how to embroider buggle, seed beads and sequins onto fabric plus sewing machine techniques for machine-made beaded tassels. You'll learn many more expert tips that you can adapt to other craft projects.

If you've often admired garments embellished with beautiful lace stitches but didn't know how to do it, take a look at **NEEDLELACE: MEDAL-LIONS** (VVP). All you need to follow along with the instructions in this video are various threads, a needle and an embroidery hoop. It's a fun, fast and easy way to elegantly decorate clothing. And if you love lace, you'll definitely want to view **BOBBIN LACE** (VVP). You'll be taught all the basics of bobbin lacemaking as you progress through five projects of graduated difficulty. These projects are an easy way to get started and can quickly and easily be adapted to produce other creative works.

Tatting is great fun and one of those things you can take with you wherever you go. You can become well acquainted with this fascinating lacemaking technique through **TATTING I: THE BASICS** (VVP). Besides learning the traditional shuttle tatting method, you will also learn the vocabulary and how to successfully read and diagram a pattern. It won't be long before you're ready to continue your study with **TATTING II: BEYOND THE BASICS** (VVP). The camera work in both these tapes is excellent, and each step can be followed with ease.

Another popular craft you may be interested in learning is **BASIC NEEDLEPOINT** (VVP). This is a comprehensive program that will teach the viewer everything needed to get started in this versatile craft. Be sure to go on to **NEEDLEPOINT: UNUSUAL-UNIQUE TECHNIQUES** (VVP). This video is full of creative inspiration and unique approaches to non-traditional needlepoint. Or perhaps your interest lies in **CROSS STITCH & FINISH-ING TECHNIQUES** (VVP). You'll learn all the basics of cross stitch as you complete a strawberry design that is included with the tape. All of these videos will give you loads of ideas for future projects.

If you've always wanted one of those beautiful Victorian-style lamp-shades, now you can create two of them by following the detailed instruc-tions in **VICTORIAN STYLE LAMPSHADES** (VVP). The Victorian oval and the classic flower tulip shades that you'll create will add a touch of romantic elegance to your home. And if you have the perfect spot for a one-of-its-kind stained-glass window, the video to view is **MAKING STAINED GLASS WINDOWS** (VTX). This is an outstanding program geared for the novice. You'll see the creation of a window especially designed for this video that touches on every aspect of the process. After viewing this comprehensive presentation, anyone with a soldering gun can tackle a stained-glass window project.

To make delicate silk roses and many other decorative projects, take a look at **THE ART OF RIBBON CRAFT** (VVP). Artist Susan Sirkis spent years researching out-of-print Victorian pattern books and adapting these trims to modern tools and materials. Take advantage of her knowledge and expertise through the detailed demonstrations in this excellent video. A brief explanation about ribbon embroidery is also included. Or learn to make dif-ferent types of bows as well as ribbon roses with **RIBBON MAGIC** (DIY). This video has dozens of projects and ideas for using ribbons in decorating the home, wrapping gifts, making baskets and decorating for the holidays.

Practices of the Victorian period were forerunners of many of the crafts we enjoy today. Ladies of this period collected beautiful greeting cards and illustrations and placed this scrap art in albums, hence the term "scrap book." **VICTORIAN PAPER SCRAP ART** (VVP) takes this scrap art even further as the viewer learns to create pictures, shadowboxes, bandboxes, decorative screens and wall hangings from beautiful collected images. You'll create lovely projects for yourself or for gifts. Another unique and fascinat-ing video reveals the secrets of **ORIGAMI: THE ART OF PAPER FOLD-ING** (VVP). By viewing this tape, your entire family can quickly learn the magic of this ancient art form. Step-by-step instructions are easy to follow for children as well as adults. You'll also learn about making origami paper, creating giant origami figures and a little history, too. A very enjoyable video.

Another unique and fun video that will give the viewer more hints and techniques for working with crafts is **STYROFOAM WIZARDRY** (DIY). This comprehensive presentation shows how to work with styrofoam, includ-ing cutting, preparing, pattern-making, painting and texturing. You'll learn to do dozens of projects, including display work, seasonal items, party themes and home decor. And the floral professionals and beginners alike will be amazed at the new techniques they will master when working with this tape.

SURFACE DESIGN TECHNIQUES

Fabric painting and dyeing is both fun and interesting. In the comprehensive, award-winning video course **FABRIC PAINTING WITH DYES** (VVP), the viewer will learn the skills needed to work with silk and cotton and produce some unique results. You'll be shown all the tips and techniques as you follow along to complete three projects. The creative innovations and variations you'll learn from this program will take you way beyond the basics and into creating designs of your own. Or perhaps you would be interested in the very specialized dyeing technique **JAPANESE TEXTILE DYEING** (VVP). This video is a good introduction to the paste-resit technique developed hundreds of years ago by the Japanese. This very informative instructional video guide is sure to arouse your interest in this fascinating art.

INTRODUCTION TO CREATIVE FABRIC PAINTING (VVP) presents the viewer with lots of ideas, tips and techniques in a fun, informal format. Learn the many styles of T-shirt painting with acrylic paints and let your free-hand flow as you learn a "batik" style of design. This excellent video is bound to lead you on to some great designs, as is another fine video, **BATIK AS FINE ART** (VTX). This program takes textile art into the realm of fine art and shows the viewer how to produce beautiful pictures by the alternate waxing and dyeing of cloth. It contains every step from making a pinning frame to framing your finished work to hang in your home or even at an art show.

A rather unique surface design technique for fabric, paper, clay, wood and even your shoes is marbling. Learn the methods as well as expert tips on this unusual craft by viewing **MARBLIN' MADE EASY** (VVP). The program also includes an insert of helpful hints that will make your marbling projects successful.

Another process you might want to try is **QUILTED PAINTING** (VVP). The presentation in this video is well organized and demonstrated with enthusiasm and enjoyment. As you follow along, you'll begin with a piece of fabric, transfer the design, paint it, pad it, stitch around and frame it. The end result is a beautiful decorative wall piece with a charming "quilted" look. The technique shown uses acrylic paints. You'll want to try it to create exciting works.

For techniques in decorating fabrics and walls, an excellent choice is **STENCILING FOR FABRICS, WALLS & FLOORCLOTHS** (VVP). The close-up videography in this program will teach you all about paint, tools and how to cut and mark a stencil using the three patterns enclosed with the tape. Tips, techniques and step-by-step instructions will guide you through the processes to achieve professional results.

WORKING WITH CLAY

One of the most satisfying craft experiences is working with clay, and one of the most popular videos to get you started is **CREATING YOUR OWN CERAMIC POTTERY** (EVN). This quick and complete course by a professional potter provides all the basics for working with clay in a lively presentation. Another excellent choice for the beginner to view is **HAND-BUILT POTTERY** (CEP). This introductory program demonstrates the various techniques of handbuilt pottery, including coil, hard slab, press molds and soft slab forming. Both tapes will get you off to a good start in this exciting craft.

If the mystic of the potter's wheel beckons, be sure to view **THROWING CLAY ON A POTTER'S WHEEL** (CEP). This informative program is a good introduction to clay throwing. Instructions are easy to follow with excellent overhead shots. And for a comprehensive course, you may wish to watch a three-tape ceramics series. **CERAMICS: THROWING ON THE WHEEL** (CEP), the first part of the program, thoroughly explains the equipment, tools and processes involved. Your education in clay will continue with **CERAMICS: THROWING FUNCTIONAL POTTERY, PART I & PART II** (CEP), where step-by-step instructions will enable you to obtain a high level of competency in creating useful and beautiful pieces of pottery.

Continue to increase your knowledge with **GLAZING AND FIRING** (CEP), which will give you all the basic information on the firing process and glaze chemistry. And to put your new skills to work, **ADVANCED THROWING: PROJECTS AND TECHNIQUES** (CEP) is a fast-paced, easy-to-use program packed with ideas and information. Finishing techniques for pottery are as varied as the types and styles of pieces themselves. A unique program that shows the viewers how to use a variety of decorating techniques is **POTTERY DECORATION: TRADITIONAL TECHNIQUES** (CEP). From marbled and mosaic patterns to incising and carving and much more, this video demonstrates the work of many different potters. You can also profit from the expertise of experienced potters with **FUNCTIONAL POTTERY AND CLAYWORKS** (CEP). This program includes examples of finished pottery that illustrates a variety of techniques, forms and functions. Demonstrations will introduce you to decorative finishes such as raku, china paints, lusters, decals and much more.

One of the oldest forms of clay artistry is sculpture, and an excellent, easily understood how-to video in this field is **ARLENE SIEGEL'S SCULPTURE CLASSROOM** (CEP). You'll be guided step by step through the sculpting process via graphic images. Additional helpful information presented at the end of the program covers any questions the viewer may have. To further explore the creative process of sculpturing, **SCULPTURE AND THE CREATIVE PROCESS** (CEP) lets the viewer see an artist in his studio as he converts his ideas into three-dimensional forms. This tape is a good overview of the sculpturing process, and tips from the artist are a strong motivation for any craftsman.

One of the most interesting forms of clay artistry is **RAKU CERAMICS** (VTX), which is rooted in sixteenth-century Japan. Assuming that you have done some basic pottery, the program will teach you all you need to know for making raku pieces. This form of clay work especially invites experimentation, and this program promotes the viewer's creativity. Another excellent candidate for your library is **SLIP CASTING** (CEP). This video illustrates the step-by-step process of preparing a plaster of paris slip-casting mold for producing multiple copies of an original. Explicit instructions are given on the various techniques, and the program is full of useful information.

****

The many different types of crafts you've mastered with the preceding videos can be put to good use in many different areas of your life. The techniques and creativity you've developed plus a video from the ART INSTRUCTION section of this chapter can further help you express yourself in an artistic endeavor. Other skills you've developed can be a beneficial supplement when you use the ideas presented in the PARTY TIME segment of the AROUND THE HOUSE chapter. And armed with a video from the DECORATE LIKE A PRO segment of that same chapter, you can put your own unique craft masterpieces to good use in making your home a showcase.

CREATING WITH PLANTS & FLOWERS

What more beautiful way to express your creativity than with plants and flowers. The ancient art of bonsai can be a fascinating and fulfilling hobby. Or try your hand at flower arranging. Many videos are available to aid you in learning to create masterpieces with both fresh and dried flowers. And for a real challenge, be sure to check out the videos on flower arranging for weddings.

FASCINATING BONSAI

BONSAI: THE ART OF TRAINING DWARF POTTED TREES (ACB) is a spectacular video guide to discovering the fascinating world of bonsai. This award-winning program was beautifully photographed in the Brooklyn Botanic Gardens. If you have an interest in this ancient art form, be sure to watch as an expert instructor demonstrates the techniques for shaping and maintaining bonsai, including container selection, wiring and general care.

For more information on this rewarding hobby, see **EXPLORING BONSAI** (ACB), another excellent video program photographed in the Brooklyn Botanic Gardens. The viewer will learn how to select a tree and how to design, shape and maintain the work. Bonsai is an art that can be indulged in and admired by everybody from city dweller to farmer.

FLORAL CRAFTS

You can begin your lessons on basic floral design with several outstanding and fun videos. **WORKING WITH FLOWERS** (DIY) shows all the helpful hints you need to know to make your flower arranging easy and quick, whether you plan on using silk or live flowers. This program begins with popular arrangements in line design, the mound, triangle and horizontal. In no time at all, you'll be creating perfect centerpieces. Continue your floral lessons with an easy and enjoyable program on simple color coordination. **WORKING WITH COLORS: THE ASYMMETRICAL "L" AND CRESCENT** (DIY) will teach you three popular styles often used in room decor. To explore the many and varied uses of the Hogarth "S" basic technique in floral design, **FOLLOWING THE SEASONS** (DIY) is the video to watch. You'll make an elegant tabletop arrangement and also learn to vary style for a myriad of door and wall decorations.

41

Other videos are available for learning basic flower arranging. In **SECRETS OF FLOWER ARRANGING** (ACB), a professional flower designer demonstrates the fun and enjoyment of creating your own flower arrangements. You'll learn about the tools and materials of the trade. If you're interested in enhancing your home decor with your own floral creation, be sure to view **FLOWER ARRANGING IS FOR EVERYONE** (ACB). A professional florist will introduce you to basic tools and techniques along with three arrangements demonstrated in detail. A booklet listing plant materials is also included with this excellent program.

The ancient Japanese art of flower arranging is rooted in the Ikebana school of techniques. **IKEBANA: THE OHARA SCHOOL** (ACB) is a beautiful program that presents six lessons in this most innovative design style. You'll receive step-by-step instructions for creating elegant flower arrangements with detailed closeups that are especially helpful for beginners. Designs in the Sogetsu school of techniques is presented in **IKEBANA: THE SOGETSU SCHOOL** (ACB). This program will introduce you to this ancient art form and show in detail how to create lovely yet simple arrangements. An additional tape well worth viewing in this particular discipline of flower arranging is **IKEBANA: TECHNIQUES FOR LONGER LASTING CUT FLOWERS** (ACB). Discover natural methods for preserving the vitality and freshness of your flower arrangements. These techniques have been developed over six hundred years and include the use of many common household items.

DRIED FLOWER FANTASY

Dried flowers are perfect for any decor. They are long lasting, easy to work with and lend themselves to creative arrangement. For extensive information on working and caring for dried materials, **DRIED FLOWER FANTASY** (DIY) is an excellent choice. Contemporary design is taught along with three styles of period arranging (Williamsburg, Victorian and Colonial). After viewing this tape you'll soon be creating wreaths, swags and garlands as well as topiary trees and baskets.

In the elegantly photographed **DRIED FLOWER DESIGN** (ACB), viewers receive an introduction to the techniques of drying and preserving a wide assortment of flowers and plants. This tape was filmed at the Brooklyn Botanic Gardens and not only shows some spectacular views but also imparts practical advice on decorative uses for dried flower arrangements.

SILK FLOWER ARTISTRY

To learn how to create breathtaking arrangements with realistic silk flowers, be sure to view **SILK PLANT SHOP** (EMG). True artistry is demonstrated before your eyes as you are taught the seven rules of design of this fascinating skill. You'll also be taught the secrets of the business along with the tools of this profession.

FLORAL DESIGN ESPECIALLY FOR WEDDINGS

If you're planning on doing your own or a friend's wedding flowers, there is a unique video series that will help make the experience both rewarding and enjoyable. Learn all the information you'll need to easily and professionally complete an entire wedding from beginning to end. **THE BEGINNING: BOUQUETS AND HEADPIECES FOR THE BRIDE** (DIY) will show you where to begin. This tape presents numerous selections for the bride's flowers and headpiece that will complement the chosen wedding style. An enjoyable bonus is the insight on the meaning of wedding flowers.

To aid you in selecting bouquet styles, flowers and colors for all the attendants, **ATTENDANTS FLOWERS: BRIDESMAIDS, FLOWER GIRL, RING BEARER AND HEADPIECES** (DIY) is an excellent watch. Step-by-step instructions are given for all arrangement styles with a special section on how to carry bouquets.

And do be sure to continue on to **THE FINISHING TOUCHES: CORSAGES, BOWS, DECORATING THE CHURCH AND RECEPTION** (DIY). This program is full of ideas and instructions for adding those final and lovely touches to the wedding plans. Viewers will learn how to create quick, easy and professional-looking corsages and boutonnieres as well as classical arrangements for the church reception. This series is exceptionally well presented and could also be helpful to anyone who is contemplating "wedding work" as a business.

****

If you've watched one or more of the above videos on working with flowers, you'll want to carry your newly learned skills over into other areas. So why not try taking these skills along as you watch a DECORATE LIKE A PRO video or a tape from the GREEN THUMB TECHNIQUES section, both from the AROUND THE HOUSE chapter. Or if you want to put your abilities to a practical use, a program from the business advice section of PRACTICAL, VOCATIONAL & UNUSUAL SKILLS could provide you with some excellent information.

FUN & GAMES

While a TV/VCR can be fun in itself, it can also be a good vehicle through which to learn about other engaging activities. Adults of all ages can learn the thrill of magic and juggling. Those with a little gambling in their blood can take a crash course in strategy to become an unexcelled card player or to up their luck at the casino. And for the youngsters, videos abound that will delight and entertain them as they put their own special creativity to work.

GAMES & SLEIGHT OF HAND

Two tapes are available to help kids of all ages become master jugglers. View **LET'S JUGGLE—THE VIDEO** (BNS), and within one hour you'll learn the basics, perform show-stopping tricks, fine tune your eye-hand coordination and gain confidence in mastering a new skill. **JUGGLING STEP-BY-STEP** (COF) presents the complex skill of juggling in a step-by-step manner. The lessons are broken down into units, with each lesson including a slow-motion recap and a skillful performance by an acknowledged expert. Both these tapes are a lot of fun to watch and follow.

If you've always been fascinated by magic, consider becoming a magician yourself. Video is available to help you master the skills you'll need. By watching **BE A MAGICIAN** (SMV), you can learn wonderful sleight-of-hand tricks to entertain family and friends. Practice step by step with a master until you're perfect. To become an instant magician, **QUICK TRICKS: FUN AND EASY MAGIC** (BBC) is the tape to view. Magician Peter London shows how to perform ten amazing magic tricks that will have you dazzling your friends in no time.

Children are especially fascinated with magic, and there is a video available geared specially for the six- to ten-year-olds. **RAINY DAY MAGIC SHOW (**COF) is a colorful tape with a professional magician as teacher. The instructions are clear and to the point, revealing secrets of the trade. These simple, yet magical tricks are bound to enthrall youngsters both as performers and observers. The kids will learn magical skill as easy as Abracadabra!

An exciting and unique video is **THE NEW GAMES VIDEOS** (COF). This tape is for kids of all ages, as it stresses attitude toward play. The cooperative games you'll learn involve people, not expensive equipment. Everyone is encouraged to play together and have fun, which is one of the best ways to break through barriers between people. A companion tape you may be interested in viewing is **NEW GAMES FROM AROUND THE WORLD** (SMV). Again, these games are excellent for people of almost any age, size and ability level. The setting for this unique tape is the Olympic Stadium ground in Munich. Both videos are worthwhile viewing.

A game you might not associate with video instruction is chess. **PLAY CHESS** (COF) will teach you all you need to know to start playing and enjoying this universal game. The viewer will get a clear explanation of the pieces, the board, basic moves and key terms. Winning tips from the experts will help you make the best opening moves, establish game control and avoid common mistakes. Or learn to **PLAY BRIDGE WITH OMAR SHARIF** (TWV). With Omar Sharif as your partner, you'll learn a variety of techniques to help improve your bidding and playing.

PLACE YOUR BETS

Lottery fever is undeniably on the rise around the country. If you've been afflicted, you may want to take a dose of **THE LOTTERY VIDEO** (JPV). This is a practical, no-nonsense guide to number selection and wheeling systems. This unique perspective on lotteries is based on extensive analysis of probabilities and historical patterns. A great video for all lottery players from the casual to the regular enthusiast.

One of the most popular card games ever devised by man is poker in all its variations. If this is your game or you would like it to be, several videos can help you improve your skills and impress your fellow players. **TABLE POKER** (JPV) shows actual playing simulations that illustrate the Big Six of poker: knowledge, tactics, deception, money management, psychology and guts. This tape also contains a practical exam of winning strategy in draw poker. In addition, there is help for becoming a master at **7-CARD STUD POKER** (JPV). Watching this tape will give you insight on the tactics and playing strategies that you need to become an expert player.

44

For insight into a popular new card game, try a look at **PAI GOW POKER** (JPV). All the aspects of the game are covered in detail, starting with the basic method of play. Tips and techniques you'll learn will help you master all the key strategic decisions you'll face in every hand. And for a twist on the basic poker game, **VIDEO POKER** (JPV) is an informative tape to watch whether you use the knowledge for fun at the local mall or profit in the casino. Demonstrations will help you learn to make the correct draw/discard decisions, and a handy, pocket-size strategy card is enclosed for casino use.

If the casino is where you're headed, take some time out first to arm yourself, via video, with some tips from the experts. Sam Micco, gambling instructor from the Las Vegas Hilton, is one of these experts. His **PLAY TO WIN: AN INSIDER'S GUIDE TO CASINO GAMBLING** (FSV) will teach you to play the games and win. Learn the secrets to gaining the winner's edge over the house advantage and the best bets for some of the most popular games. At the blackjack table, at a live craps game, at the roulette wheel, step-by-step instructions and concise reviews will help you master the game. From the baccarat pit to the slot machines, this comprehensive video is a sure bet to increase your odds.

For an excellent beginner's guide to blackjack, roulette and craps, **CASINO SURVIVAL KIT** (JPV) is one video you shouldn't miss viewing. The lively program covers rules, procedures, betting options and etiquette as well as simplified playing strategies for each game. To increase your chances of winning, a look at **CHARTING THE TABLES** (JPV) is a safe bet. Expert players will show you the techniques they use to isolate favorable betting situations and pave the way to successful casino gambling. Or for a condensed but exact overview of casino skills, **BEAT THE HOUSE!** (JPV) is worth a look. This tape summarizes key gambling ideas and money management philosophy.

Most people flock to the basic casino games of blackjack, craps and roulette, and there are specific videos available on each to teach you how to up the odds of winning. **BASIC BLACKJACK** (JPV) is a concise blueprint to basic strategy for the beginner blackjack player. The tape covers all key strategic decisions and explains how to manage your bankroll like a professional. And for the serious player who wants to learn the more sophisticated methods expert players use, **ADVANCED BLACKJACK** (JPV) will increase your chances of beating the house.

First-time craps players might feel intimidated by this fast-paced game. To learn the rules, procedures and betting options first, **CRAPS** (JPV) guides the viewer step by step through simplified playing strategies. And when you're ready to move on to more advanced techniques, **BASIC/INTERMEDIATE CRAPS** (JPV) is loaded with expert advice and theories of right and wrong betting. To top off your skills and techniques, **ADVANCED CRAPS** (JPV) is for the experienced player who is looking for professional tips to help reduce the house edge. Even veteran crap shooters can take advantage of video to improve their game with **STRONG CRAPS** (JPV), a tape for high-level players.

Roulette is one of the most popular casino games, and you can learn to master it via video before you lay down your money. **BASIC ROULETTE** (JPV) is a step-by-step primer on winning roulette for novices and intermediate players. The viewer will be introduced to the action number system and other tested strategies. And for a comprehensive overview for more experienced players, **ADVANCED ROULETTE** (JPV) delves deeper into technique. You'll be able to learn the strategies favored by the experts, including the "Z" system and the "31."

Another rather intimidating game the casino visitor will come across is baccarat. Gear up for the thrill of this game by watching **BACCARAT** (JPV), a program that graphically illustrates rules and procedures through actual playing sequences at the table. And of course the game most associated with casinos around the world is the one-armed bandit. The video **SLOTS** (JPV) is a fascinating, behind-the-scenes look at slot machines. You'll learn about the many different types of machines that are waiting to gobble up your coins and how to tilt the odds in your favor. This comprehensive video also teaches sensible money management programs to keep you in the game longer.

"Place Your Bets!" is not always heard just in the casino or at the neighborhood card game. It has a meaning all its own at the race track, and millions of people answer its call. If you're new to the "betting scene," maybe your best bet would be a look at the video **HARNESS RACING** (JPV). This tape is an indispensable guide to harness race handicapping for novices and intermediate players. You'll learn the theories expert players use to isolate winners at the track to make your betting pay off. And for occasional racegoers who want to make their visits to the track more profitable, a good pick is **THOROUGHBRED HORSE RACING** (JPV). The unique insights of Rick Lang, track analyst for the *New York Post*, will help you learn to interpret past performance charts to pick recent winners.

If you always throw into the office pool or make a friendly wager with your neighbor on the week's football game, there are two videos available that might be of interest to you. **PRO-FOOTBALL HANDICAPPING** (JPV) and **COLLEGE FOOTBALL HANDICAPPING** (JPV) are both comprehensive guides to successful handicapping methods. You'll learn basic fundamentals to advanced statistical theory and special techniques to apply to each game. After viewing these informative tapes, be sure the pool is a large one because you're likely to be the winner.

****

The above videos can provide you with hours of fun and entertainment and open up new interests. But don't stop now. Be sure to take a look at the chapter on THE GREAT OUTDOORS. There's sure to be a video that will capture your imagination as you learn about some exciting outdoor activities. Or if you're sports minded, you may want to pick something from the SPORTS, SPORTS & MORE SPORTS chapter. There are videos on sports geared to all ages and all levels of experience. Why not try something new or brush up on the skills you already have?

KIDS' CRAFTS & ACTIVITIES

One of the many areas in which videos abound is "Things for Kids To Do." When you hear that old refrain "But I don't know what to do," surprise and delight your youngsters with a video that will hold their attention and fire their imagination. Creative tapes will have your children learning artistic expression, producing creative crafts and, best of all, being occupied constructively. Let a video especially geared to kids' activities turn any dull day into a creative day.

ART FOR KIDS

Learning to draw has never been easier. **LET'S DRAW** (RHV) is a unique video guide that shows even the youngest artists how to find their own best way to draw. The program teaches basic principles using familiar shapes and figures in an interactive and easy-to-follow format. This video will provide hours of drawing fun while encouraging creativity and building self-confidence. You'd better have a lot of drawing materials handy if your kids watch **SQUIGGLES, DOTS & LINES** (BNS). Using computer graphics, this program teaches how easy it is to draw anything in the universe. Guaranteed to unlock the creativity in every youngster.

A child's imagination and creativity are something to behold, and many videos are geared to promoting these youthful gifts. Taught by an art teacher, **EASY ART PROJECTS FOR CHILDREN** (SMV) demonstrates three easy-to-follow art lessons. Children will learn to use the techniques of oil pastels as a medium for their imagination, and their creativity is also sure to show in their foil art and printmaking projects. Another program that will hold the budding artist's interest is **EASY WATERCOLOR TECHNIQUES FOR CHILDREN** (SMV). Step-by-step demonstrations show how easy it is to produce beautiful watercolors using simple, inexpensive materials.

Other videos for youngsters demonstrate rather unique techniques. **FUN WITH PAINTS** (DIY) teaches the art of stenciling. Kids can learn how to make their own stencils, including potato stamping, and personalize their work with markers. Best of all, water-based paints are used for easy cleanup. Or let the children **PAINT WITHOUT A BRUSH** (SMV). This tape will show them a whole new technique in painting with just some cotton swabs, tempera paint and construction paper. Add a ball of string and an old sponge to these supplies and the video **PAINT WITH STRINGS AND THINGS** (SMV) for another new way for kids to paint and have fun.

All children love cartoons, and what fun they can have creating their own. **BE A CARTOONIST** (SMV) shows children how to use their imagination and create cartoons from familiar shapes, letters and numbers. This excellent program teaches how to add motion, expressions and words to make comic strips, greeting cards, posters and other fun projects. This is a tape that is sure to be used over and over again.

LOTS OF ACTIVITY

Even the smallest tots can be enticed with an action-packed video designed specifically for them. Recommended for ages two and up, **CRAFTS AND ACTIVITIES FOR KIDS** (BBC) is an exceptional tape from the people at Good Housekeeping. This lively program teaches children basic learning concepts while providing loads of creative activities. Another delightful video you may wish to consider for children two years old and up is based on the world famous Montessori education principles.

47

MONTESSORI IN YOUR HOME (BBC) shows fun and easy activities using common household items. Again, this tape will help children to develop important early learning skills.

There are also videos available that have been produced for the five and up age group. **MY FIRST ACTIVITY VIDEO** (SMV) is another easy-to-follow, step-by-step instructional tape that your kids will want to view time and again. They'll learn how to make unique and clever items using everyday materials found around the home such as crazy paper puppets, animal masks, pasta jewelry and lots of other crafts. More creative projects are offered in **LOOK WHAT I MADE** (SMV) with the emphasis on paper playthings and gifts. This delightful program instructs children at their own pace through projects they can do on their own or with adult supervision.

One of the most enchanting videos your children can watch is **SHARI LEWIS' 101 THINGS FOR KIDS TO DO** (SMV). This program will provide hours of entertainment as they view Shari Lewis' delightful performance with her puppet friends. The tape is filled with magic tricks, riddles, quickie puppets, novel games, silly stunts and instant crafts. This is truly a worthwhile video to have and one your children will treasure. Another children's activity video that provides hours of fun is **RAINY DAY SUNDAY** (ACN). This tape was designed for interaction between children and the TV for hands-on fun. Young viewers have the opportunity to periodically stop the tape and create their own arts and crafts using common household items.

For family fun at Halloween, take a look at **HOW TO CARVE GREAT FACES FOR HALLOWEEN** (BBC). Just follow the directions of Gordy Falk, The Pumpkin Man, and you and your children will learn everything you need to know to carve the most spectacular pumpkin faces on the block. Follow the video trail from Halloween pumpkins to fairy tales. Another unique video for children is **SIGN ME A STORY** (RHV). Simple sign language that children can easily pick up is taught at the beginning of the tape and then used to act out two classic fairy tales. This tape is both entertaining and educational and is perfect for both hearing and hearing-impaired children.

POTPOURRI OF KIDS' CRAFTS

Let videos teach your children about basic American heritage crafts. **FUN WITH HERITAGE CRAFTS** (DIY) uses graphics to make everything simple and easy to do. Along with some history, your children will learn about American crafts such as pine cone crafting, lap weaving, handquilting and embroidery. It might be that Mom and Dad will enjoy watching this program also. And for an exciting program designed to help young children enjoy Christmas, take a look at **RAINY DAY CHRISTMAS CRAFTS** (SMV). This is an interactive video program that will help youngsters to feel part of the whole holiday season. Using construction paper, glue, paper cups and pipe cleaners, they'll learn to make six Christmas decorations that they will be proud to display for the whole family to see.

Seems like all children are enraptured by puppets. Why not a video that will teach them to make their very own? **BEAUREGARD'S BOTTLE BUDDIES** (SMV) shows the youngsters an easy way to make puppets from recyclable plastic bottles and other household items. Using simple techniques, they can make puppets in thirty minutes or less. Or if an ordinary paper bag is the material of choice, let them watch **MAKE A PUPPET, MAKE A FRIEND** (SMV). After only a few simple instructions, your children will be able to create playful characters they'll enjoy for years.

Other tapes available for children definitely have a hands-on approach. **FUN WITH CLAY** (SMV) is a good introduction to this creative medium. Children will learn the pinch, coil and slab methods to make such clay treasures as pots, animals, beads and much more. Or for a different type of hands-on feeling, try **E-Z BREAD DOUGH SCULPTURE** (SMV). The process of breadmaking is simply explained in this live-action video, and the fun begins when your child learns how to sculpture various shapes out of bread dough.

Printing sets always seem to amuse children, and two videos are available to show them how to create their very own unique printing set. Using items found around the home, **PRINTMAKING GADGETS** (SMV) will have your children creating their own pictures, greeting cards, pen holders and even wrapping paper. And for some very unusual printmaking tools, the **VEGETABLE PRINT SHOP** (SMV) is sure to delight children and encourage their creativity as they learn to print with sliced artichokes, apples, pears and other fruit. These are two great child-designed tapes.

****

There are large numbers of instructional videos that both teach and entertain youngsters. Be sure to check out the chapter on THE WORLD OF MUSIC, DANCE & THEATRE for more ways to fire up your children's imagination and let them creatively express themselves. Or you may want to take a look at some of the tapes in the ACADEMIA chapter. While these programs are essentially educational, they will provide hours of fun for your children as they learn new skills and important information about the world around them.

SEW LIKE A PRO

Videos are a great way to learn about sewing. Hands-on demonstrations that can be rewound and replayed over and over again are invaluable aids for the novice learning to sew as well as the more experienced. The wealth of how-to tapes available in this subject range from basic sewing to professional and industrial tips and techniques. So pick a program that interests you, start up the VCR and get ready, get set and sew.

BASIC COURSES IN SEWING

BEGINNING SEWING TECHNIQUES (CEP) is an excellent tape for the beginner. This step-by-step program starts with a trip to the fabric store and tips on determining pattern size. You'll learn construction techniques that are basic to sewing a variety of easy-to-make garments. Also designed for people who have never sewn before is **SEW EASY—SEW BEAUTIFUL** (VVP) from the American Home Sewing Association. This video will enable the viewer to sew confidently and comfortably at virtually any machine. Step-by-step instructions are easy to follow, and a companion guide that comes with the tape offers valuable information you'll refer to time and again.

To learn dozens of fundamental sewing techniques that are clearly demonstrated, consider viewing **SEWING ABC'S** (CEP). This comprehensive program covers sewing tools and supplies as well as hints for using information on the pattern envelope and inside guidesheet. If your machine's a little dusty at the moment, be sure to take a look at **SEW AGAIN—A REFRESHER COURSE** (NNL). This tape will not only help you update your sewing techniques but will teach new, easy shortcuts and tips on adding professional looks.

Another video that is perfect for the beginner as well as the seasoned sewer is **A GALAXY OF SEWING TECHNIQUES** (NNL). This program provides step-by-step instructions on sewing shortcuts and demonstrates how to achieve perfect sleeves in challenging fabrics, no-gap deep V necklines, plus much, much more. And you'll want to view **BEYOND THE PATTERN: GREAT SEWING TECHNIQUES** (TAU), which provides those of all skill levels with techniques to create beautiful clothing they'll be proud to wear.

For the viewer who wants to learn how to sew in a limited time, a must-see program is **10-20-30 MINUTES TO SEW** (NNL). This upbeat tape has crisp, clear instructions and a wealth of how-to tips. You'll learn how to organize in minutes, create fast fashion elements and modify pattern instructions. **THE BUSY WOMAN'S SEWING COMBO VIDEO** (NNL) is another fast-moving program demonstrating many contemporary sewing techniques. You'll learn all the secrets used in ready wear and many time-saving techniques. And for more shortcuts in time, but not in quality, an excellent video to watch is **INDUSTRIAL SHORTCUTS FOR HOME SEWING** (NNL). This program will teach you authentic sewing methods from the garment industry and have you creating great-looking garments in just half the normal time.

As many sewers may have found out the hard way, no matter how beautiful a garment you turn out, it isn't beautiful if it doesn't fit. To avoid this frustrating problem, plan on investing a little time in learning fitting techniques. Divided into a series of fitting challenges and solutions, **THE BUSY WOMAN'S FITTING TECHNIQUES VIDEO** (NNL) provides time-saving fitting procedures and explains how to finetune the fit. Another excellent program that goes a little further is **FITTING FOR STYLE** (NNL). In the privacy of your own home you can learn how to analyze your figure, determine your body silhouette and see what works best. Whether you have a triangular, full-figured, petite, top heavy or ultra-slim shape, this program will help you create the illusion of a perfect figure. This is a great video for all levels of sewers.

EASY AND FUN SEWING PROJECTS

Decorative sewing for the home can be fun as well as economical. To put your talents to use and save on your decorating budget, take a look at **DECORATING ON THE DOUBLE** (NNL). Learn to use double-width fabric and quick techniques to make valances, dust ruffles, chair coverings, window shades, shower curtains and lots more. Or to create unique home-decorating accents for holidays and special occasions, learn the techniques for producing **FABRIC WREATHS** (NNL). Starting with heart-shaped and circle wreath forms, you'll see how fabric, bows, ribbons, lace and flowers can be used to embellish and ensure truly remarkable wreaths that will enhance your home.

Sewing can also help trim your entertainment budget. For easy sewing ideas, menus and recipes for birthday and dinner parties, a worthwhile view is **SEW ENTERTAINING** (NNL). This excellent sewing aid is jammed with great things to create, including reversible table runners, favor bags, napkin rings, centerpieces and a puppet theatre. Continuing along the entertainment theme, be sure to take a look at **QUICK NAPKIN CREATIONS** (NNL). Eighteen complete napkin projects are detailed to help you create an oasis of color and piazzas on your table. Or learn to use napkins as pillow covers, gift wraps and home decorations. This fun program lets you learn to sew, serge and fold napkins with a flair.

For those on your gift list, maybe something "home-made" would be appreciated. **GIFTS FROM THE HEART** (NNL) shows the viewer how to create easy-to-sew gifts in minimal time. Among the many detailed projects, you'll find gifts for the traveler, gifts for the host or hostess and even gifts for sewing friends.

And let's not forget the kids. For sewing projects that are both quick to sew and fun for children to use, try viewing **KIDS' STAR ATTRACTIONS** (NNL). The many and varied projects on this tape include Splish Splash Towel Wraps, Activity and Quiet Books, Pillow Buddy, Circus and Space Ship Table Tents. And for a treat just for travelers, **TRAVEL GEAR AND GIFTS** (NNL) presents easy-sew time- and money-saving accessories for trips around the corner or the world, including luggage tags, shoe bags, drawstring bags and more.

POTPOURRI OF SEWING TAPES

If you hesitate about sewing suede fabric, **SUEDE—ULTRA FUN TO SEW** (NNL) is the video for you. This program takes a simple approach to teaching the basics of working with this lovely, luxurious fabric. Starting with several small gift projects, you'll soon be on your way to suede garment sewing. Or if plaids are your choice of design, **PLAID POINTERS** (NNL) will help you select appropriate patterns and determine how much fabric to buy. And to accommodate different waistlines, **ELASTICS UPDATE** (NNL) has great ideas on using button-up elastic and stitch 'n stretch elastic as well as other elastic tips.

Design and detail are extremely important in sewing, and tapes are available to make you an expert on these finishing touches. **POPULAR PATTERN POINTERS** (NNL) is a great way to learn simplified means of stitching pattern details. You'll learn to make perfectly shaped scallops, flawless princess seams, sharp crisp pleats, invisible zippers and finished neckline facing. And to reproduce that extra special design detail, **DESIGNER DUPLICATES** (NNL) demonstrates how to use "Pearls 'N Piping" and "Sequins 'N Ribbon" for the ultimate look.

The unique **SEW AN HEIRLOOM** (NNL) video will teach you to sew and serge beautiful keepsake garments. You'll be able to create some lovely creations using laces and trims, batiste, pintucks, stitching crossover tucks and puffing strips.

For a sewing video loaded with ideas, **THE SEWING WITH NANCY CHALLENGE** (NNL) is a good way to go. This tape combines winning garments and techniques from a contest that celebrated seamstress Nancy's tenth anniversary on TV. This tape will be used again and again to learn such techniques as applique on crinkled cloth, Brazilian machine embroidery, Seminole quilting, ballerina bunny appliques, 3-D flowers and more. A good addition to your sewing video library.

SPECIALIZED SEWING TECHNIQUES

Tailored sewing is in a class of its own, and videos can help you discover all the techniques needed to create elegant, custom-fitted garments that look like the best money can buy. **SHIRTMAKING TECHNIQUES** (TAU) is an excellent program for the home sewer who wants to sew shirts that really fit. By exploring the construction of garments from the world's finest shirtmakers, you learn to get professional results from casual to elegant. If you feel there's nothing new under the sun in sewing, try **SHIRTS, ETC.!** (NNL). You'll learn industrial techniques for innovative shirt construction methods that are equally applicable to other sewing projects.

An exciting new venture into sewing professional-looking jackets is also available. **JACKET TRIO** (NNL) will show the viewer how to achieve three different looks from one basic jacket pattern. Add to your wardrobe with a basic collarless jacket, a reversible jacket and a serged jacket. Or learn the techniques needed to whip up **QUICK JACKETS** (NNL). The speedy construction method taught in this tape is applicable to both serged and conventionally stitched jackets. And to get pants that really fit to complement your new jacket, learn to draft your own pants pattern with **PANTS, ETC.!** (NNL). Accuracy is essential in the skills you'll learn from this program, but the rewards are well worth it.

Two more specialized areas of sewing can be learned easily via video. **LUXURIOUS LINGERIE** (NNL) can be yours for the making. See how to use woven and knit fabrics, add laces, create picot edge trim and create antique lace. Recycle outdated or unworn garments to give them a fresh contemporary look as you learn how to use braids, trims, fabric scraps and scarves by viewing **STITCH-AGAIN WARDROBE** (NNL).

****

Whether you're a beginner or more experienced, the tapes in this section will help you sew up a splendid wardrobe for yourself or your children, uniquely decorate your home and make some sure-to-be treasured gifts for family and friends. Once that great new wardrobe is completed, use videos to make sure the body is in great shape to show off your creations. Take a look at the videos in the FEEL FIT/LOOK GOOD chapter for some help in getting and staying in shape.

COLLECTING

Collecting baseball cards is a hobby that appeals to kids of all ages. For an entertaining, fact-filled look at this favorite American hobby, be sure to view **BASEBALL CARD COLLECTOR** (COF). You'll learn all about the fascinating world of baseball card collecting from the early days of the black-and-white tobacco cards to the golden age of baseball. From the exciting era of the seventies and eighties to the superstars of today and tomorrow, this video is both entertaining and educational and can be enjoyed by the entire family.

One of the world's most popular hobbies is stamp collecting. If you've always wanted to enter this interesting arena or even if you're already there, you'll want to view **THE VIDEO GUIDE TO STAMP COLLECTING** (FSV). Host Gary Burghoff (Radar of "M.A.S.H.") explains to the viewer the different types of stamps and collections, plus where to get stamps, stamps as investments and much more. A great introduction to a great hobby.

For information on another interesting area of collecting, you may want to take a look at **COMIC BOOK COLLECTOR** (FSV). In this fun-filled video guide, you'll see the outrageous super heroes and notorious villains who made comic history. Host Frank Gorshin is sure to stir up interest in this fascinating collecting hobby.

****

*I*f being a collector appeals to you, why not branch out into a new area? With the help of this book you could soon have your own "instructional video" collection.*

SOURCES

(See Chapter 11 for a complete alphabetical listing of all sources with addresses and phone numbers.)

ACB	-	A.C. Burke & Co.
ACN	-	Acorn Media
ACV	-	Artist's Club
AVP	-	Artists' Video Productions
BBC	-	Better Books Co.
BNS	-	Brainstorms
BWV	-	Barb Watson Video
CEP	-	Cambridge Educational Products
COF	-	Champions on Film
DIY	-	Do-It-Yourself Inc.

EMG	-	Entrepreneur Magazine Group
EVN	-	Educational Video Network
FIN	-	Finley-Holiday Films
FSV	-	Fusion Video
JPV	-	John Patrick Productions
NNL	-	Nancy's Notions
RHV	-	Random House Inc.
SMV	-	Schoolmasters Videos
TAU	-	Taunton Press
TWV	-	Time Warner Home Video
VTX	-	Video Textbooks
VVP	-	Victorian Video Productions

CHAPTER 3:

THE WORLD OF MUSIC, DANCE & THEATRE

EXPLORE YOUR MUSICAL TALENTS - EXPRESS YOURSELF THROUGH DANCE - VISIT THE THEATRE - SOURCES

EXPLORE YOUR MUSICAL TALENTS

Music-making is good for the soul, and it's never too late to begin. Videos are great learning tools for musical instruction. You hear it, you see it and you can even rewind to hear it a thousand times more. Want to learn a new instrument or improve your technique? Want to learn to read music or maybe train your voice? There are excellent videos available to help you fulfill your musical aspiration.

THE BEAT OF THE DRUM

Do you have dreams of "jamming" with the greats? Do you visualize yourself pulling a Gene Krupa? Well, get started on those dreams via video. If you can count to four, you can play the drums. **DRUMMING MADE EASY** (CEP) is for beginners of all ages. You'll learn to play the drums right away with this easy-to-follow, hands-on video course. On-screen graphics will help to reinforce this complete drumming primer as you learn all the techniques and tools to develop your own groove. Or for a program that approaches the subject of drum playing at its more basic level, try viewing **DRUM COURSE FOR BEGINNERS** (CEP). Especially designed for those just starting their drumming career, this video covers everything you need to know, and sight-reading exercises will help you apply your newly gained music knowledge. This tape is a very effective approach to learning the drums thoroughly and easily right in your own home.

HOW TO PLAY DRUMS (CPP) is another video course designed to introduce the beginner to the drum set. Using the instructor's unique system of vocalizing each drum sound, you'll learn to play a drumbeat in the very first lesson. Included are nine play-along songs in different styles, such as rock, blues and funk. Or get off to the right start with your drum set with the two-tape **DRUM SET TECHNIQUES** (CEP). **VOLUME I—BEGINNING TECHNIQUES** explains basic set-up and techniques along with the concepts of time, style, sound and groove. Move along to **VOLUME II—**

55

INTERMEDIATE TECHNIQUES for further development of the skills and concepts you've learned. Excellent tapes for developing drummers no matter what type of music they enjoy playing.

Invite one of the most in-demand drummers in rock and roll, Kenny Aronoff, into your home. His video **BASICS OF ROCK DRUMMING - LAYING IT DOWN** (CPP) is ideal for beginning/intermediate drummers and also offers valuable tips for the advanced player. Learn to create a drum part, keep steady time, make the beat groove and develop your own beat creatively. Or take a look at a user-friendly video guide, **FINDING YOUR WAY WITH HAND DRUMS** (CPP). John Bergamo will take you on an exploration of the spiritual and musical essence of hand drumming. You'll learn all the technical aspects and variations of this drum style and learn to drum on non-conventional or "found" instruments.

If you're fascinated by the unique sounds of drum brushes, Clayton Cameron has an excellent video for you. **THE LIVING ART OF BRUSHES** (CPP) covers brush patterns, original and traditional specialty strokes, practical tips and much more—all from the musician who reinvented the brush technique in both the jazz context and funk and fusion fields. Or share the incredible technique of Joe Franco in **DOUBLE BASS DRUMMING** (CPP). This nicely produced tape is packed with vital information and features the first practical approach to playing double bass drums. This musician demonstrates fills, rolls, beats and exercises that will enable you to develop independence and control.

Another unique drum style with a wide range of sounds is conga drumming. In a most efficient and relaxed manner, Jerry Steinholtz's **THE ESSENCE OF PLAYING CONGAS** (CPP) makes learning and playing the conga a real joy. Steinholtz shows the viewer how to produce the widest range of sounds, tones and dynamics. For a valuable reference video on the snare drum, **SNARE DRUM RUDIMENTS** (CEP) is a perfect way to learn the basic techniques and apply them in a creative, innovative way to your drum set. And be sure to consider a lesson from a true rock legend. Levon Helm invites both beginners and professionals into his studio with his excellent tape **LEVON HELM ON DRUMS AND DRUMMING** (CEP). He teaches his unique drumming style as he demonstrates the Delta blues, country music, the Memphis sound, rockabilly and music of The Band. You'll master drumming in no time with this comprehensive video drum course.

Drum players of all levels can benefit from Peter Erskine's **EVERYTHING IS TIMEKEEPING** (CPP). This video provides a wealth of ideas and information plus incredible presentations. Erskine demonstrates and discusses the jazz ride pattern, cymbal technique, basic coordination, improvisation and much more. And **PUTTING IT ALL TOGETHER** (CPP) is another video you'll want to add to your musical reference library. Rod Morgenstein shows the viewer how to develop versatility and how to create a drum part. He demonstrates techniques for playing in odd time signatures and his approach to ghost strokes and double bass drumming. On-screen graphics are used to help viewers follow along and become more proficient in no time.

GUITAR PICKING TECHNIQUES

Here is your chance to learn **HOW TO PLAY THE GUITAR NOW** (CEP). Your video tutor will teach you the parts of the guitar, how to read music and how to hold and tune the instrument, finger picking, strumming and much more. By the time you complete these lessons, you'll have a handful of songs you can play plus a sturdy foundation for guitar playing. Or if you're really in a hurry, **PLAY GUITAR OVERNIGHT: BASICS** (CEP) will introduce you to the basics in a solid, straightforward and relaxed style. The instructor goes from selecting an instrument through tuning, tablature and accessories to teaching chord progression in country, folk and rock styles.

Another great way to get started on your guitar-playing journey is provided by Barney Kessel, a grand master of the guitar. In **ELEMENTARY GUITAR CLASS** (CEP), this noted guitar teacher shares his unique method of instruction in a course specially created for beginners. You'll attain the satisfaction of being able to immediately play songs on your own guitar. Or for a comprehensive video course, you may want to view **YOU CAN PLAY GUITAR 1, 2 & 3** (CEP). This three-tape series is taught by Happy Traum, one of America's best-known guitar teachers and authors. Starting with volume I and the basics, you'll continue through all three tapes as you gain a complete understanding of the instrument.

LEARNING TO FINGERPICK (CEP) will add interest and excitement to guitar playing. An elementary knowledge of guitar chords is all the viewer needs to get started with this lesson on fingerpicking blues and country style demonstrated in the first volume. For a variety of techniques and tips, be sure to go on to the intermediate level taught in volume II. And for an amazing lesson in the roots of American guitar music and beyond, **HOT GUITAR TECHNIQUES I & II** (CEP) is a progressive and lively way to go. Follow Bob Brozman through the two-tape lesson as you learn dynamic fingerpicking and acquire a deep understanding of traditional styles. This video course will help build instrumental skills and enhance understanding of the guitar.

One of the most gifted guitarists of our times is now available to give you a personal lesson on the **ACOUSTIC GUITAR** (CPP). Learn Phil Keaggy's approach to alternate tunings, harmonics and more. Or take advantage of his expertise in **ELECTRIC GUITAR STYLES** (CPP), which contains techniques and important tips. Keaggy takes you through solos and licks from sixteen songs spanning nine albums. Most are played twice, once regularly and once slowly as you gain valuable insights from a world-class guitarist.

For an excellent guide to the bass guitar, see Mark Egan's **BASS WORKSHOP** (CPP). Egan's overall approach to playing the bass provides practical advice and demonstrates amazing techniques. This is a popular and informative instructional video. And for another comprehensive tape you're sure to enjoy, take a look and listen to **ELECTRIC BASS: A DICTIONARY OF GROOVES AND TECHNIQUES** (CPP). Drummer John Patitucci guides the viewer through fifteen different styles, including funk, samba, jazz, shuffle, Latin and rock. He also provides excellent discussion of the variations and techniques of each style. This is another great addition to any instructional musical library.

The styles and techniques of guitar playing are numerous. If the blues is your thing, **PLAYIN' THE BLUES** (CPP) provides an excellent opportunity to enhance your skills in this classic style. You'll be able to learn Robben Ford's favorite blues scales and phrases along with his unique fingerings for string bending and vibrato. For the country sound, there's no better teacher than Jerry Donahue, one of the hottest new country pickers. In **COUNTRY TECH** (CPP), Donahue demonstrates his own special blend aided by great close-up visuals and on-screen music graphics. And to learn about the creative and exciting style of jazz, John Scofield offers the viewer a two-tape video course that will help you develop your own style and improvisations. **JAZZ-FUNK GUITAR I & II** (CPP) is an electrifying and in-depth study covering the compositional aspect of Scofield's multi-faceted style.

Guitar players at all levels will enjoy Scofield's fluid style in **ON IMPROVISATION** (CPP). This tape covers major modes and scales and various approaches to improvisation. Scofield's inventive and versatile approach will help you learn to express your own individual style. And Marty Friedman's **MELODIC CONTROL** (CPP) includes exciting demonstrations on how to gain control as a lead player and develop creative melodic solos. The exclusive close-up footage of Marty's blistering leads caps this must-have video.

ALL THOSE KEYBOARDS

LET'S PLAY THE PIANO AND ALL THOSE KEYBOARDS (CEP) is a unique video course crammed with information and instruction. The informative study method shows the viewer how to develop the techniques and skills to play the piano and all electronic keyboards. You'll be delighted with all the different forms of music included, such as classical, country, jazz, pop and rock. This is one video that you will refer to again and again as you learn at your own pace. For an approach that budding musicians find immediately rewarding, **TOM PARENTE PIANO VIDEO** (CEP) teaches even the "first timer" to play. The two-tape course uses familiar tunes to teach concepts and skills. And this easy-to-understand video method for learning to play piano has the added advantage that you are able to play along with the instructor and repeat any areas that were hard to pick up on the first try.

An innovative and successful method of teaching piano and keyboard can be seen in the three-tape series **HOW TO PLAY PIANO** (CPP). This easy-to-follow video will equip you with the skills necessary to play piano in no time. The first tape covers learning the keyboard, reading music, beginning ear training and more basics to help beginners learn to play at their own pace. In tapes 1 and 2, pianist Richard Bradley covers major and minor chords, notes and rests, blues and improvisation and much more. With practice and these excellent tapes, you'll soon be able to recognize and interpret chord patterns and play a wide range of music. Or you may wish to view another unique approach to learning piano playing in **PLAY THE PIANO OVERNIGHT** (BNS). This quick-learn video eliminates tedious exercises and teaches you how to "feel" the music. You'll learn to form chords and even create your own composition as you learn to play the piano in your very first lesson.

Another good musical tutor for those wishing to learn the basics of playing the piano or any other keyboard instrument is the two-tape series **VIDEANO—BEGINNING KEYBOARD** (CEP). Your own private tutor in this program is a nationally accredited piano instructor who has been teaching privately and at college level for more than twenty years. You'll learn to play the keyboard freely and easily while learning various techniques and selected pieces. Learning the keyboard has never been so easy.

KEYBOARDS TODAY! (CEP) is a unique three-tape video series whose pace and schedule you determine. Once you've completed these tapes at your own pace, you'll be able to read and understand most simple arrangements that can be purchased in any music store. This is an excellent way to avoid expensive lessons if you've always wanted to play the piano or electronic keyboard. And a good follow-up video after you've learned the basics is Chick Corea's **KEYBOARD WORKSHOP** (CPP). This influential keyboard player and composer provides insights into practicing, composing and improvising.

As with all musical instruments, styles and types of music vary greatly. If the "blues" strikes a cord with you, Richard Bradley's **HOW TO PLAY BLUES PIANO** (CPP) is a tape you'll want to view. Suitable for piano and portable keyboards, this program takes you through the basic blues progression by demonstrating chords, inversions, bass patterns, blue notes and more. It breaks down the blues scale into an easy formula, allowing both amateurs and professionals to play effortlessly in any key. For an introduction to playing piano or keyboard jazz, let Richard's **HOW TO PLAY JAZZ PIANO** (CPP) be your video guide. Recognizable musical patterns enable the player to hear what to play and provides a repertoire of chords and chord progressions in several forms. Jazz standards and ballads, ragtime and Dixieland, Latin jazz and new age music are all introduced via this video.

So you already know how to play the piano/keyboard but want to improve or branch out. Videos are available that will enable you to try out any field that looks interesting. **ROCK KEYBOARD AND BEYOND** (CPP) with T. Lavitz provides some great tips and tricks for soloing, comping and rhythm. **KEYBOARD/VOCAL ACCOMPANIMENT** (CPP) provides the benefit of George Duke's expertise as he shares his vast experience with various artists. And accompany George in the relaxed seminar setting on **KEYBOARD IMPROVISATION** (CPP). This well-produced video covers left-hand comping and phrasing, chord voicing and substitutions and the compositional basis for improvisation. Let your imagination soar and play along with these great artists.

MUSICAL POTPOURRI

The **VIDEO MUSIC LESSON SERIES** (CEP) is taught by experienced studio musicians, composers, arrangers and educators and offers a number of different instruments and styles. Hands-on instruction guides the viewer through the basics and teaches the special skills needed to master the instrument of choice. Take your pick of instruments from **BASIC BLUEGRASS BANJO, DOBRO** and **COUNTRY FIDDLE**. Learn to **PLAY THE ACCORDION** or the **BASIC JAZZ SAXOPHONE** or **LEARN THE HAMMERED DULCIMER**. Perhaps your taste runs to the **PEDAL STEEL GUITAR, THE ROCK AND ROLL GUITAR** or **THE COUNTRY PIANO**. Each video includes examples of chord and scale theory, numerous tips for technical improvement and several complete songs to

59

teach the principles of each instrument. Whatever your choice, these excellent videos will get you started on your way to musical accomplishment. Another video tool designed for the beginner is the **MAESTRO INSTRUCTIONAL SERIES** (CEP). These tapes include clear-cut examples and demonstrations for aspiring students and beginners. Again, take your pick of instruments and let experienced performers lend you their expertise in **FLUTE FOR BEGINNERS, CLARINET FOR BEGINNERS,** or **TROMBONE FOR BEGINNERS**. If one of these tapes doesn't fit the bill, perhaps **TUBA FOR BEGINNERS, TRUMPET FOR BEGINNERS** or **SNARE DRUM FOR BEGINNERS** is what you're looking for. Or if string instruments are your forte, you can chose from **VIOLIN FOR BEGINNERS, VIOLA FOR BEGINNERS** or **CELLO FOR BEGINNERS**. Add a little twist to your musical instruction and learn by video.

Ever dream of jamming with B.B. King or Jon Gindick? **THE NATURAL BLUES AND COUNTRY WESTERN HARMONICA** (AOF) lets the viewer do just that. You'll learn the basics of the harmonica with step-by-step instructions and slow-motion examples as you jam along with the greats. Another fun tape, **BLUES HARMONICA** (CEP) will teach you how to blow blues, rock and country tunes with the best of them. Popular harmonica player John Sebastian teaches all the basics you'll need and passes along helpful tips. This tape lays down a solid foundation for more advanced study.

Some very unusual musical instruction videos are available to be enjoyed in your home via your VCR. **TEACH YOURSELF TO PLAY THE CASTANETS** (AOF) teaches the techniques of playing this exciting Spanish tradition. The commentary on the tape is in Spanish, but you'll be able to follow along anyhow because of detailed, close-up, step-by-step visuals. Violin students are sure to be interested in the two-tape program **THE HEIFETZ MASTER CLASSES** (KUL). Violin genius Jascha Heifetz is shown guiding promising students in a rare seminar taken from his legendary workshops at USC, Los Angeles. Anyone who studies and/or loves the violin will find these master classes with the century's greatest violinist essential viewing.

Other videos available for your education and enjoyment include **PLAY SAX: FROM DAY ONE** (CPP), a complete introduction to the saxophone for the beginner. Starting with an overview of each type of sax, the program offers pointers in all areas of saxophone playing. The clear and easy-to-follow manner makes this tape an invaluable tool for beginners and intermediate musicians. And for intermediate and advanced sax players, **MODERN SAX** (CPP) offers a broad range of tips and techniques. Eric Marienthal offers technical exercises and a detailed overview of improvisation and jazz harmony. For an introduction to the trumpet plus a dose of music theory, **TRUMPET COURSE: BEGINNER-INTERMEDIATE** (CPP) is a well-produced how-to video. Teacher Clark Terry has played trumpet with such legends as Duke Ellington and Dizzy Gillespie, and this tape makes him available as your own private tutor.

Strike up the band! There really are videos available to help you do just that. Whether you're a band director or simply a participant, the **MARCHING BAND SERIES** is a useful, informative and extremely educational series of tapes covering all aspects of the marching band. **CONTEMPORARY DANCE AND FLAG TECHNIQUES** (CPP) is a two-tape program that incorporates the elements of modern dance into the band auxiliary unit. And for complete equipment fundamentals for a flag corps, **FLAG FUN-DAMENTALS** (CPP) is designed for the beginning corps, and **ADVANCED FLAG FUNDAMENTALS** (CPP) continues with more advanced techniques. Step-by-step instruction in the basic skills of handling a rifle in guard situations can be found in **RIFLE FUNDAMENTALS** (CPP), and to view all the standard marching commands and positions be sure to watch **MARCHING FUNDAMENTALS** (CPP). The remaining tapes in this comprehensive video course deal with percussion marching. Begin with **FUNDAMENTAL TECHNIQUES FOR MARCHING PERCUSSION** (CPP), and follow through for more advanced knowledge in the two-volume program **MARCHING PERCUSSION SERIES** (CPP). These tapes are well worth adding to your library if there's a marching band in your life.

For anyone who loves to sing or would like to learn, **ENTER THE VOCAL ZONE** (CEP) is a comprehensive introduction to vocalizing. Buddy Mix, award-winning singer/songwriter, explains in detail how to strengthen your voice and make the most of it. Extensive explanations, diagrams and exercises are provided for both the male and female voice, and the section on performance tips is sure to be of interest to any aspiring singer. Another video that will be of interest to all singers is **VOICE: THE UNIVERSAL INSTRUMENT** (CEP). Starting with the premise that everyone can sing, this live program follows several students who learn both how to develop their singing voices and how to achieve their own styles. All the aspects of voice training are covered and are related to the underlying theme that learning to sing can provide enduring enjoyment.

A wonderfully easy way to learn how to read and understand music is available through the delightful video **HOW TO READ MUSIC** (CEP). This program is perfect for anyone interested in music, either singing or playing. The clear and logical presentations will help build a solid foundation of musical knowledge for all age groups. Or you may wish to try a view of **READ MUSIC TODAY** (CEP). With the aid of detailed computer graphics, this easy-to-understand lesson explains what you need to know to learn beginning through advanced topics. You'll learn to understand the piece you would like to play or sing immediately, without memorizing it by ear. These two videos are both excellent educational aids.

For an entertaining and informative introduction to the symphony orchestra, join Dudley Moore in **AN INTRODUCTION TO THE ORCHESTRA** (BBC). Featuring maestro Sir Georg Solit and the musical talent and humor of Dudley Moore, this three-tape series traces the development of the orchestra from the time of Bach and Handel to the present day. A most valuable reference for player or listener.

****

*W*hether you're a skilled musician or an amateur music lover, you'll probably also enjoy one of the many videos detailed in the following section, EXPRESS YOURSELF THROUGH DANCE. There's sure to *be one or more excellent programs that appeal to your particular musical interest. And if your musical talents and aspirations take you into the realm of theatre, be sure to take a look at the great programs available in the VISIT THE THEATRE section.*

EXPRESS YOURSELF THROUGH DANCE

Whether you want to learn how to dance or learn a fun social way to keep fit, videos are an ideal method of instruction. The powerful combination of video demonstration and music will enable you to learn quickly in the privacy of your own home—for far less cost than dance lessons. Videos abound in this area, and you have your pick of a variety of different dance types. From ballroom dancing to tap to country music dances, with many other styles along the way, videos will have you dancing up a storm in no time.

BEAUTIFUL BALLET

Ballet is a very expressive and beautiful dance form enjoyed by both participants and spectators. If your desire is to be a participant, begin the journey to your dream by viewing **BRYONY BRIND'S BALLET: THE FIRST STEPS** (KUL). No previous ballet training is needed, as this revolutionary new ballet video teaches the basic principles and movements of ballet. The viewer will be taken step by step through primary ballet movements and will learn to use them to increase muscle strength and flexibility. This is a rare chance to share a master class with one of the world's great ballet teachers.

Another unique lecture-demo video that guides the dancer's first tentative steps is **POINTE BY POINTE** (KUL). This program provides the technique and guidelines necessary to develop safe habits and muscle strength necessary for pointe work. The dancer will develop an excellent foundation needed to progress to higher levels of training.

One of the greatest assets of video is accessibility, and this is especially true in the field of ballet instruction. It's possible to bring a famous ballet school from Manhattan's Upper West Side right into your home via video. **BALLET CLASS FOR BEGINNERS** (KUL) does just that. In the privacy of your own home and at your own pace, you can use David Howard's ballet instructions to introduce you to the techniques of the dance. You'll learn all the basic positions and arm and leg movements and gain an excellent overview of ballet vocabulary. Continue practicing and learning with **BALLET CLASS: INTERMEDIATE-ADVANCED** (KUL). Your skills, as well as your classical ballet vocabulary, will increase.

Another famous ballet artist is also available as your own private tutor. In **BUJONES IN CLASS** (KUL), Fernando Bujones demonstrates his personal ballet technique that has made him world famous. This unique video instructional program is an excellent learning tool. Custom-designed by Bujones, the emphasis is on posture, placement and classical ballet movements. Or invite Ilona Vera into your home. **ILONA VERA'S BALLET CLASS** (KUL) is especially for dancers who have already reached the intermediate level. Vera will enable you to develop your own personal style as you reach a greater degree of professionalism in your dance.

For dancers of all levels, an invaluable reference work can be found in the **VIDEO DICTIONARY OF CLASSICAL BALLET** (KUL). This is a comprehensive program of classical ballet movements performed by principal dancers of leading ballet companies. In two tapes, you'll be introduced to the complete language of ballet. And for easy reference, each tape contains a complete numbered index of all the movements and variations presented. This is the only video reference work the ballet student will ever need. A truly worthwhile addition to your video library.

MORE DANCE STYLES

For a truly creative and expressive dance style, you'll want to watch **DISCOVERING YOUR EXPRESSIVE BODY** (PBC). This program is a comprehensive demonstration of the basic concepts in modern dance training. Exercises in total body connectedness, full range mobility and weight transference will encourage your own individual style and creativity. And to blend your own spontaneity and interpretation into a free-flowing dance style, be sure to view **DANCE FREESTYLE** (COL). This beginner's tape shows the core moves used in all non-touch dancing. Lend your own expression to rock, Latin, fusion, jazz and disco.

If jazz is your music of choice as well as your dance, videos are available to increase your skill and knowledge of this most enjoyable dance style. **JAZZ DANCE WITH CHRISTY LANE** (PBC) is a four-tape series that teaches jazz dance techniques and combinations in easy-to-follow demonstrations. The charismatic Christy Lane covers all the techniques and moves from beginner and intermediate to high intermediate and advanced. Each tape also includes a syllabus of the instructional material covered. A great way to jazz it up.

Another famous choreographer has turned his talents to jazz for your benefit. **JAZZ DANCE WITH GUS GIORDANO** (PBC) covers the basics from jazz stance to more advanced center movements in a progressive presentation. Or get fit and get jazzy with **JAZZ WORKOUT WITH ANN COOMBES** (PBC). This program incorporates flexing and firming your body to upbeat music with an introduction to the basics of jazz dancing. First you'll warm up. Then you'll learn a variety of jazz steps and combinations that are later incorporated into a complete jazz dance routine.

Maybe tap is your game. All the basics of tap you need to know are taught in **TAP DANCING FOR BEGINNERS** (KUL). Instructor Henry LeTang has taught Billie Holiday, Eleanor Powell and Bette Midler, and now he's available to teach you via video. Or join actress Bonnie Franklin in **I HATE TO EXERCISE—I LOVE TO TAP** (PBC). Ms. Franklin will teach you all the basic steps as well as a great fitness workout. You'll learn how to build combinations and dance such popular routines as the waltz clog, the soft shoe and the time step, all at your own pace tap by tap.

Aerobics are not only for fitness. They can be expanded into unique dance situations. **SOCIAL DANCE AEROBICS** (SDA) is the original social dance for fitness video. For fun and health, you'll learn combinations in East Coast swing, chacha, samba, polka and the Viennese waltz. A great fun, fitness and dance video. Or dance along internationally with **FOLK DANCE AEROBICS** (SDA). Learn such international folk dance favorites as the Miserlou, the Alunelul, the Hora, the Savila Se Bela Loza and the Harmonica as you shape up your body and your dancing skills.

Want to know what's happening at the nightclubs today? Bring the night life into your home with **LET'S DANCE AMERICA** (COL). Even experienced dancers will love this video as they learn new combinations and the latest contemporary dancing styles. This tape teaches nineteen different moves that can be combined in countless variations and ends with a very impressive hip-hop dance demonstration. A great way to keep up with the dancing times.

To learn a rather unusual dance from Spain that is currently spreading around the world, try **SEVILLANAS** (AOF), the national dance of Spain. This unique dance is the refined result of Spanish folk song and historical dances. The video will help you master the four main verses and learn all the variances through detailed close-ups and excellent visuals. Or turn to the Middle East and set your sights on **BELLYDANCE! MAGICAL MOTION** (COL). Beautiful, fun and healthy for mind, body and spirit, this ancient dance form is easy to learn via video. A master bellydancer will show you how to create alluring routines that both soothe and invigorate. The program features warm-up exercises, isolated bellydance movement, finger cymbals, veil dancing and costumes. What a fun way to stay in shape and express yourself through dance.

BALLROOM DANCING AT ITS BEST

The magical world of ballroom dancing can be yours via video as you learn in the privacy of your own home, even if you've never danced before. **INTRODUCTION TO BALLROOM DANCING** (KUL) is the tape for those who have always wanted to feel confident on the dance floor. Via this video anyone can learn the swing, rumba, chacha, waltz and fox trot right at home. Another great video for those with little or no previous dance experience is **BALLROOM DANCING FOR BEGINNERS** (KUL). No need for expensive dance lessons at a studio. Bring the studio to you via video as you master the basic techniques of ballroom dancing.

Dance lessons are a natural for videography, and many excellent series are available. Lessons by one of the world's most known and loved dance instructors can be yours via your VCR. The **ARTHUR MURRAY'S DANCE MAGIC SERIES** (PBC) combines superb musical quality, costumes and instruction, which carry you into the wonderful world of ballroom dancing. Work your way through one, several or all of the following instructional videos available from this world-famous dancer. Learn to do the old favorites like the **CHACHA, FOX TROT** or **WALTZ**. Get into the Latin rhythm with the **MAMBO, MERENGUE, RUMBA, SALSA, SAMBA** and the **TANGO**. Or to really get into the swing of things, try a tape on **SWING, DANCING DIRTY** or **NIGHTCLUB**. These excellent videos can open up a whole world of delightful ballroom dancing.

Or you might want to discover the joy of dancing by bringing the Kathy Blake Dance Studios right into your home. Kathy and her partner are champion, award-winning professional ballroom dancers, and the **LET'S LEARN HOW TO DANCE FOR ADULTS SERIES** (BFV) contains tapes you'll want to use again and again. If you go to parties, nightclubs or office parties that play rock music, you might want to consider **NIGHTCLUB I** (Freestyle Rock and Slow Dancing) or **NIGHTCLUB II** if you're over forty-five and weren't exposed to rock music in your teens. Planning a cruise? Go for the Latin dance tapes and learn to **SAMBA, TANGO, MAMBO, RUMBA, MERENGUE, BOSSA NOVA, CHACHA, PASO DOBLE, SALSA** and **BOLERO.** If you're a big band fan, you're sure to enjoy learning the **FOXTROT** and **JITTERBUG.** And in many parts of the country, **POLKA** is a must for just about every partying occasion. You'll learn in minutes dance steps that you will use for years.

LEARN TO DANCE WITH THE CHAMPIONS (DVU) is the slogan for a comprehensive series of instructional dance videos that offer the viewer three different areas of dance. In the American dance style, champion ballroom dancer Ron Montez teaches the novice **BEGINNING RUMBA & CHACHA, BEGINNING WEST COAST SWING & EASTERN SWING** and **BEGINNING MAMBO & BOLERO.** And choreographer Chuck Bannister is available to show you the **BEGINNING WALTZ & FOXTROT** and **BEGINNING TANGO & VIENNESE WALTZ.** You'll master these tapes in no time at all and be ready to go on to Montez's **INTERMEDIATE RUMBA, INTERMEDIATE CHACHA, INTERMEDIATE WEST COAST SWING, INTERMEDIATE EASTERN SWING, INTERMEDIATE MAMBO** and **INTERMEDIATE BOLERO.** Or maybe you'll decide to take advantage of Bannister's expertise in **INTERMEDIATE WALTZ, INTERMEDIATE FOXTROT, INTERMEDIATE TANGO** or **INTERMEDIATE VIENNESE WALTZ.**

If you've always wanted to try the international dance style, you'll want to join champion instructors Victor Veyrasset and Kathryn Schaffer. They'll soon have you gliding across that dance floor with their **BEGINNING WALTZ & FOXTROT** and **BEGINNING TANGO & QUICKSTEP.** Be sure to improve your new-found skills even further with their **INTERMEDIATE WALTZ, INTERMEDIATE FOXTROT, INTERMEDIATE TANGO and INTERMEDIATE QUICKSTEP.** And to really round out your dancing repertoire, don't miss a view of **ADVANCE WEST COAST SWING,** which is taught by Buddy Schwimmer, honored in the Dancer's Hall of Fame as the "King of Swing." This series is certain to contain one or more dances you can't wait to learn.

To spice up your dance life with some fancy footwork, be sure to take a look at **JITTERBUG: BEGINNERS** (PBC). You'll learn twenty-one different moves from the basic first steps to the East Coast swing and the sultry West Coast swing. Improve on your newly learned dance skills with **JITTERBUG: INTERMEDIATE** (PBC) with even more stylish moves like the snap turns and sugar push. And if swing has captured your fancy, **WEST COAST SWING** (SDA) will teach you the dance that's always popular. Learn turns, whips, loops, the butterfly, roll-out, sugar push, hook and freeze and more. Or let video teach you turns, the cradle, tuck and catch for the **EAST COAST SWING** (SDA). These videos contain a variety of patterns, slow motion and closeups and clear, step-by-step instructions that will have you dancing along for fun, practice and fitness as well as make you look good on the dance floor.

COUNTRY/WESTERN'S LATEST

Put extra life and variety in your dancing by learning the country dances that are sweeping the country. And to learn from the best, **THE COUNTRY DANCE SERIES** (SDA) is the way to go. The clear, step-by-step instruction in these programs is available to you anytime you wish with a push of the VCR button. You will be treated to instruction by national award-winning professional Phil Martin and many fun patterns/dances, all for less than the price of a private lesson. Starting off with **COUNTRY LINE DANCING I** (SDA), you'll learn country line dance favorites, including black velvet, Elvira, slappin' leather, tumbleweed, boot scoot boogie and tush push. Dance on to **COUNTRY TWO-STEP** (SDA) to learn the basic rhythm pattern, basic step, underarm turning left, underarm turning right, cradle and more. This fast-paced video will also teach the techniques of leading, following, movement, partnership and timing and provide plenty of insights to help you get the most out of your learning time.

Be sure to dance on over to the **COUNTRY WALTZ** (SDA). You'll continue to use your new-found dancing feet as you learn the waltz versions of patterns taught in previous videos. Step-by-step instruction characterized by high technical quality and a beautiful set will help you polish up your new dancing skills with lots of close-ups of important points. To ensure you look good on the dance floor, view **BOOT SCOOT DANCE-OUT** (SDA). Enjoy dancing along to original country music as you keep fit practicing today's popular line dances. This excellent tape also includes a section on aerobic guidelines and a warm-up to keep you in top country line dancing form.

Another series of easy-to-understand lessons is the **TEXAS DANCE PRODUCTION** series. These programs introduce beginner and intermediate steps and continue with more advanced techniques. Dust off your boots, grab a partner and begin with the **TWO-STEP BASIC/INTERMEDIATE** (CEP), the **POLKA BASIC/INTERMEDIATE** (CEP) or the **WALTZ BASIC/ INTERMEDIATE** (CEP). And be sure to move on to **WALTZ ADVANCED** (CEP) and **ADVANCED TWO-STEP** (CEP) to really shine Texas style.

Achy breaky is everywhere, and line dancing is sweeping the country. You can be part of the fun with **CHRISTY LANE'S LINE DANCING** (PBC). Volume 1 will have you dancing the tush push, the boot scoot, the electric slide, slappin' leather, the freeze and the alley cat. In addition to the achy breaky, Volume 2 will show you all the moves you need to enjoy the cowboy boogie, cowboy chacha, Elvira dance and the walkin wazie.

For more fun, take a look at **WILEY HICKS' COUNTRY LINE DANCING** (COL). This national line dance champion shows you more than just steps. You'll learn what to do with your body and how to really get into the music and have fun. Or consider a look at **LINE DANCING IS IT** (CEP) for adults of all ages who love line dancing. This live-action program includes an overview of basic line dance steps of five popular dances. The basic steps can also be used to create your own dances, and this video will meet the needs of any age group and provide hours of fun.

ESPECIALLY FOR KIDS

Music and dance appeal to all children, and what a great way for them to express their individuality and creativity. Even the youngest child can appreciate dance by watching **CREATIVE DANCE FOR PRESCHOOLERS** (COF). This program is a series of dance-related activities that acquaint the small child with different rhythms and dance movements. For children of all ages, **CREATIVE MOVEMENT: A STEP TOWARD INTELLIGENCE** (PBC) is a unique and fun-filled video. The program encourages children to have fun as they clap, sing and move to music. Through the dance-related games and improvisation, children will develop self-awareness and come to appreciate their expressive potential. Improved body awareness, self-confidence and coordination are only a few of the benefits they'll derive from this video that promotes music readiness as much as dance.

A unique video ballet class created especially for the preschooler is **A FANTASY GARDEN BALLET CLASS** (PBC). This enlightening program will delight children as it associates basic ballet steps with flowers and animals. Beautiful melodies and memorable lyrics introduce them easily to ballet terminology. For the six to eleven age group, **I CAN DANCE** (PCB) is a perfect introduction to ballet. The program presents the five basic positions plus bar work, center work and reverence. French terms are also introduced and explained in easy-to-understand kids' language. And another worthwhile tape for this age group is **BALLET FOR KIDS** (COF). The future prima donna will learn a series of dance movements in ballet that are then combined to make up a complete dance routine.

Jazz music isn't just for listening. It lends itself to very creative dance movements that children can easily execute. **JAZZ FOR KIDS** (PBC) is a three-volume series for beginner, intermediate and advanced. The series teaches the techniques of jazz dance plus a short routine for each level using children of different ages as models. The many variations demonstrated are designed to enhance a young dancer's technical level and ensure lots of fun.

All the latest moves kids love and want to know can be found in **CATHY'S CLASS STREET JAMMIN'** (COF). This upbeat and lively program was designed especially for kids by an award-winning choreographer. All the dances are broken down and demonstrated so kids learn easily and experience success. The three different dance routines will interest, motivate and excite the eight- to fourteen-year-old age group.

****

Dancing can be a lot of fun but also a lot of stressful movement. To make sure you're in top shape to really enjoy learning these new dances, be sure to take a look at the videos in the FEEL FIT/LOOK GOOD chapter. There are even some great fitness videos for the kids to help them get in shape and then stay there through dancing.

VISIT THE THEATRE

Is acting "in your blood?" Whether your visions are set in a community theatre or a Broadway stage, there are videos available to help you pursue your dream. From performing to directing, from speaking to makeup, use videos to learn the inside techniques and secrets in this fascinating world.

PERFORMANCE THEATRE

An excellent series of videos is specifically designed to help viewers learn how to successfully act in, direct and manage a stage production. **THE DIRECTING PROCESS** (CEP) is extremely informative for would-be directors. This program addresses the entire process of directing a theatrical production. Starting with the history of directing, it moves on to selecting a play and text analysis. This is a great educational tool for any aspiring director.

The main focus of any production is the character or characters around which the plot evolves. **BUILDING A CHARACTER** (CEP) guides the viewer through all the elements of character building. Character analysis, vocal work, emotional work, rehearsal tips and more make this an enlightening video to view. And for an indepth reference guide to the fundamentals of mime, **MIME OVER MATTER** (CEP) takes the viewer through easy-to-follow mime exercises. Exaggerated action, isolations, body sections and plenty more make this an invaluable guide to enhance your acting skills.

Another worthwhile watch for the budding actor is **CREATIVE DRAMA & IMPROVISATION** (CEP). This program will enthusiastically unleash your imagination as you are encouraged to participate in creative exercises, dramatic plays and improvisational exercises. And to add further to your repertoire of skills, **COMBAT FOR THE STAGE** (CEP) teaches the fundamentals of stage combat through well-planned choreography. Learn the correct way to execute stage falls, unarmed and armed combat choreography, swordfighting and many more expert techniques that will help you prepare for a stage career.

For the novice and experienced alike, auditions can be a frightening experience. To prepare yourself for successful auditions in high school, community or university theatre as well as professional theatre and theme parks, **AUDITION TECHNIQUES** (CEP) is an excellent video to view. You'll learn how to analyze and rehearse monologue, prepare for auditions, warm up, prepare a resume and photographs and much more. Calm your pre-audition jitters by watching this video first.

TECHNICAL THEATRE TECHNIQUES

Just as important as the actors on stage are the behind-the-scenes preparation and ongoing activity. If scenery is your responsibility, you might be asking, **WHERE DO I START?** (CEP). This video is the place to start to learn about economical and effective set construction techniques. And you'll certainly want to go on to expand your knowledge with **HOW DO I PAINT IT?** (CEP). The illustrated, step-by-step scene-painting techniques you'll learn through this program will help you to dramatically improve your sets.

A very important technical aspect of a production is, of course, the lighting effects. For a live-action view of what is involved in stage lighting, **SHEDDING SOME LIGHT** (CEP) does just what the title implies. This video provides a tour of a typical theatre, introducing tools of the trade, lighting instruments and accessories and lighting safety information. The techniques and expert tips presented here will enable you to design creative and effective lighting for any production.

Another technical effect that is paramount in many productions is costumes. Like scenery, costumes lend authenticity and aura to a production. **THE BASIC COSTUMER** (CEP) highlights three major time periods frequently used in theatre: the Elizabethan era, the Victorian era and the jazz era. The entire costuming process is demonstrated with helpful tips on how to costume a production efficiently and cost-effectively. You'll be able to adapt the skills you'll learn watching this tape to any production.

THEATRICAL MAKE-UP TIPS

MAKE-UP FOR THEATRE—AND FOR FUN (VTX) is an informative and entertaining program to view. The charismatic and knowledgeable teacher discusses and demonstrates all that is important in make-up and in the use of hair pieces. Split-screen inserts are used to clarify the process by showing the make-up chart at the same time that the paint is applied. You'll be both educated and entertained with demonstrations on glamour and period make-up, old-age make-up, hair piece construction and many more tips and techniques that you'll use time and time again.

You may wish to follow several actors through an actual make-up workshop. **THE MAKE-UP WORKSHOP** (CEP) shows each actor being consulted individually about the specific character's design and application. You'll be fascinated watching a step-by-step creation of the old-age look and other special-effect techniques in this excellent video.

Another ideal instructional video is **FACE TO FACE: AN AMATEUR'S VIDEO GUIDE TO PERFORMANCE MAKEUP** (CEP). This program explains in great visual detail the vast gamut of make-up techniques—from applying the base to taking off the make-up. This is a three-video package that addresses in-depth basic makeup techniques as well as solutions for specific make-up challenges.

MORE ON THEATRE

Three exciting how-to videos have been designed to offer an introduction to the lucrative field of voice-overs. Learn the fundamentals of voice-over acting by watching **THERE'S MONEY WHERE YOUR MOUTH IS!** (CEP). Continue on to an in-depth analysis of radio and television commercial scripts and industrial narration with **INVEST IN YOUR VOICE** (CEP). This video "workout" comes with a fifty-plus-page workbook for timeless reference. And as a final step to getting voice-over work, prepare yourself by viewing **MARKETING YOUR VOICE** (CEP). This educational tape provides instruction on preparation of demo tapes, mailings to agents and advertising agencies, promotional ideas and etiquette on the job or audition. These tapes are a worthwhile series to view.

69

An excellent training resource for actors is **EXPRESSIVELY SPEAK-ING** (CEP). Hollywood speech coach Steve Whiteford offers his experience in how to obtain a well-trained, communicative and persuasive speaking voice. Step-by-step training for better diction, tone, volume and general vocal image is combined with expert techniques to ensure confidence, expression and control over all presentations. This is a video you'll want to refer to often.

WHAT'S THE SCORE?—TEXT ANALYSIS FOR THE ACTOR (CEP) provides the performer with a valuable video workshop. The program is divided into three parts: text analysis, transactional analysis and introduction to script analysis. Another video guide that offers the viewer a leading edge in getting the part is **COLD READING MADE EASY** (CEP). The step-by-step approach demonstrated by a professional acting coach gives the viewer expert techniques needed to perform a successful cold reading.

No one is born a star. Everyone must start somewhere, and a good place to start if acting is your aspiration is **BECOMING A SUCCESSFUL ACTOR** (CEP). This video is all about what it takes besides talent to become successful. You'll be introduced to the types of training needed, information and facts on the agent's role, how the audition and casting processes work and many more facts important in the life of an actor.

****

For anyone with theatrical aspirations, a look through the available videos in the SELF-HELP VIDEO GUIDES chapter will turn up one or more beneficial tapes. The tapes in the motivational and personal growth sections could be valuable aids in building self-confidence and motivation for a theatrical career.

SOURCES

(See Chapter 11 for a complete alphabetical listing of all sources with addresses and phone numbers.)

AOF	-	Audio Forum
BBC	-	Better Books Co.
BFV	-	Butterfly Videos
BNS	-	Brainstorms
CEP	-	Cambridge Educational Products
COF	-	Champions on Film
COL	-	Collage Video
CPP	-	CPP Media Group
DVU	-	Dance Vision USA
KUL	-	Kultur Videos
PBC	-	Princeton Book Company
SDA	-	Sodanceabit
VTX	-	Video Textbooks

CHAPTER 4:

SPORTS, SPORTS & MORE SPORTS!!

BATTER UP! - HOOPS & DUNKS - TRADITIONAL FOOTBALL - SOCCER FOR EVERYONE - EXCEL AT GOLF - SERVING UP TENNIS - KEEP YOUR EYE ON THE BALL! - RACK 'EM UP! - TRACK & FIELD EVENTS - A MEDLEY OF SPORTS - SPORTS FOR KIDS - SOURCES

BATTER UP!

As American as apple pie, the game of baseball is one of our nation's favorite pastimes. From the empty neighborhood lot to the professional stadium, millions of people enjoy both watching and playing baseball. Whether you play for fun or are in serious competition, why not invite your own personal trainer into your home via video to help you sharpen your skills?

BASEBALL CLINICS

Many baseball greats, from players to managers, are available via video to teach you all the ins and outs of this great game. In **SPORTS CLINIC BASEBALL** (COF), Dick Williams, Seattle Mariners manager, gives you expert advice on pitching, batting, fielding and base running. This information-packed video is sure to give you the winning edge in any competition. Or get some more high-quality instruction by viewing **DO IT BETTER BASEBALL** (ESP). California Angels pitching coach Marcel Lacheman and Cleveland Indians field scout Vincent Cappelli team up in this lively program to offer expert advice on the mechanics of throwing and the special techniques involved in hitting. This video will help you play better ball.

More baseball greats are yours with just the push of a VCR button. In **BASEBALL FOR ALL AGES** (COF), former big-league star and White Sox manager Don Kessinger takes you through the basics of an all-round game, with inside secrets on pitching, hitting, fielding and base running. To further expand your know-how, join some of baseball's best, including the legendary Reggie Jackson, as they come together to show you how to **PLAY BALL** (COF). Reggie and his all-star lineup show you the proper skills, techniques and drills you need to improve your game. Or let well-known sportscaster Tom Kelly and Dodger manager Tommy Lasorda entertain and educate you with **BASEBALL OUR WAY** (COF). This top-notch video is full of instruction, insight and professional secrets from six great major-league stars.

71

Compliments of the National Collegiate Athletic Association, there are videos available that will introduce you to some of the finest coaches in the game. The **NCAA BASEBALL VIDEOS** (CEP) is a series of instructional tapes that will teach you the skills and drills used to create consistently top-ranked teams. Ben Hines teaches you all about **HITTING**, Joe Russo demonstrates **BASERUNNING** and Bill Permakoff shows you the skills of **CATCHING**. For **PITCHING ESSENTIALS** and **PITCHING DRILLS**, your personal trainer is Howie Gershberg. And to become an accomplished all-around player, continue on with Jerry Kindall for **INFIELD PLAY** and Jerry Stitt for **OUTFIELD PLAY**. A very impressive series to improve your skills.

Another excellent instruction series is presented by the Los Angeles Dodgers coach, **THE MARK CRESSE SCHOOL OF BASEBALL** (CEP). This two-volume course offers helpful hints, strategies and different techniques for players at every level. You'll see great visuals demonstrating techniques that any novice baseball player can understand and put into practical use on the playing field. Or get some expert advice from a National League batting champ by taking a view of **TONY GWYNN'S BASEBALL** (CEP). In this two-tape series, Gwynn provides insights into key areas of offense and defense that most instructional programs cover only briefly. And to learn how to play like the pros, you won't want to miss viewing another worthwhile series, **PLAY BALL THE MAJOR LEAGUE WAY** (COF). This three-tape program covers all the fundamentals of **HITTING & BASERUNNING, PITCHING & CATCHING** and **FIELDING**. These are outstanding videos for your sports library.

You can also use videos to increase your knowledge and gain a better understanding of the game. In **BATTER UP: HOW TO BECOME A BIG LEAGUE BALLPLAYER** (COF), former Cincinnati Reds baseball scout Ed Howsam has gathered some of baseball's top players and managers to offer their personal advice on how to become a major-league baseball player. Interviews with the greats provide an in-depth insight as you learn all the ins and outs of this popular sport. And for even more baseball know-how, **THE PINKSIDE OF SPORTS: BASEBALL** (COF) is an excellent video to watch. Jay Johnstone, a former major-league baseball player, explains the basic rules, equipment, field layout and advanced strategies of baseball. Actual footage from past baseball games makes this tape both educational and entertaining.

If you're involved in serious coaching or just in charge of a friendly game, be sure to take a look at **A COACHING CLINIC** (CEP). You'll learn how to structure an enlightening practice as you build a winning team. This training video includes drills for all levels of players from beginners to accomplished as well as specific drills for infielders, outfielders and pitchers. A great video for coaches and players alike.

Or try one of the more comprehensive coaching programs available. **BASEBALL SKILLS AND DRILLS** (CEP) is an excellent six-tape series of proven fundamental skill exercises that improve baseball talent. **DEFENSIVE SKILLS** and **FIELDING** discuss all fielding responsibilities, while **HITTING** and **PITCHING** give the viewer a comprehensive action course in these areas. **BASERUNNING**, a surefire video to enhance your baseball skills, concentrates on moving across the bases, a subject often overlooked in baseball instruction. Designed especially for coaches is **COACHING PSYCHOLOGY.** This invaluable instructional tool presents the methods for maximizing a player's potential and defining and meeting goals.

SPECIAL SKILLS & DRILLS

From one of the most respected names in baseball comes a live-action video for coaches and players of all levels. **HOW TO TEACH AND LEARN THE ART OF HITTING WITH HARVEY KRUPNICK** (CEP) will visually teach you the art of wrist hitting. This fast-paced instructional video provides the viewer with all the tools necessary to hit better and score more runs. Or let batting coach Vada Pinson make it easy for you to hit. By watching **THE ART OF HITTING** (COF), you'll learn everything from power hitting to bunting, and the slow motion enables you to study key points like wrist action and hip movement.

Continue to improve your batting average with **THE ART OF HITTING .300** (COF). With the help of players Carlton Fisk and Greg Luzinski, professional coach Charlie Lau explains and demonstrates his "Ten Absolutes of Hitting." You'll improve your stance, shift your weight, adjust your swing and raise your batting average to hit like the pros. And Rod Carew, American League batting champion, is also available as your personal video trainer in **BASEBALL WITH ROD CAREW** (COF). Carew's teaching methods and a series of repeated movements combine to make this a sure bet to improve your batting average.

If pitching is your forte, be sure to view the milestone video **NOLAN RYAN'S FASTBALL** (CEP). Pitching legend Nolan Ryan reveals his pitching secrets for the first time ever in this exciting video. This video is more than the standard instructional tape, as the viewer is also treated to motivational tips, anecdotes and philosophical insights from the legend himself. To further enhance your pitching arm, take a look at **TECHNIQUES OF PITCHING** (COF) with Roger Craig. You'll learn all phases of pitching as well as the different pitches, such as the fast ball, curve, slider and Roger's most successful split-finger fast ball. And for some more basics and also some practice drills and common mistakes to avoid, **THE SCIENCE OF PITCHING** (COF) is a worthwhile watch. Great close-ups and slow-motion visuals will enable you to study all the key points you need to pitch the perfect game.

More specialty tapes are available for your education and entertainment. Join a former American League all-star in **BUCKY DENT'S SHORTSTOP SKILLS** (CEP), as Dent demonstrates the techniques that made him one of the best shortstops in the majors. His informative instruction and excellent tips are reinforced with noteworthy graphics and actual major-league baseball footage. And good running techniques can be yours by watching **RUNNING BASES** (COF). You'll also pick up some great tips on stealing, sliding, leading off, hit and run and more.

WINNING SOFTBALL

If softball is your game, you'll want to view The Amateur Softball Association's seven-tape **VIP SOFTBALL SERIES** (CEP). This comprehensive course teaches every phase of the game and clearly explains all the

73

fundamentals. You'll learn from game footage, expert instruction and the leaders in softball. The series consists of **BEGINNING FAST PITCH PITCHING** and **ADVANCED FAST PITCH PITCHING, DEFENSIVE FUNDAMENTALS DRILLS, FAST PITCH STRATEGY, TEAM DEFENSE & SLIDING** and **SLOW PITCH STRATEGY, TEAM DEFENSE & SLIDING**. Two very important tapes designed especially for coaches, **COACHING FAST PITCH SOFTBALL** and **COACHING SLOW PITCH SOFTBALL**, complete this excellent series.

Another good series to view is the two-tape program **CHAMPIONSHIP SOFTBALL PITCHING** (COF). Designed to provide one-on-one instruction, this series is hosted by two of the nation's finest pitchers, Kathy Van Wyk and Don Sarno. These sports greats will give you private video lessons in all phases of softball pitching as well as basic drills to develop the pitches you'll learn. Or use another noted instructor to improve your hitting. In **HITTING SECRETS FOR WINNING** (COF), Bobby Simpson covers everything from the dugout to the plate and bat selection to a solid line drive. Bobby's tips, tests and drills will help every hitter improve, from beginner to advanced player.

One of the most comprehensive single videos on this entire game is **SOFTBALL: PUTTING IT TOGETHER** (COF). The viewer will be presented all the skills and strategies necessary for successful softball mastery with topics including skill analysis, position play and practice drills. You can also learn from the experience of manager/pitcher Rob Whittleton in **DO IT BETTER: SLO-PITCH SOFTBALL** (ESP). This USA Hall-of-Famer will come into your home via video and teach you everything you need to improve your game. Or use the excellent program **WINNING SOFTBALL** (CEP) to help you and your team bring home a trophy. Every player—from beginner to advanced—can learn something from this video.

Another video you may wish to view to become a better and more efficient hitter is **SLO PITCH SOFTBALL** (CEP). The program will show you hitting tips and mental imaging methods to raise your batting average and increase hitting productivity. This tape is filled with simple, solid advice. Or go "downtown" with the best power hitters in slow-pitch softball and learn their secret hitting tips. **POWER HITTING IN SOFTBALL** (CEP) features five power hitters who will provide you with practical tips for consistent power hitting. You'll learn the critical "power swing" to blast the ball out of the park. And a special pitcher's perspective is added to let the batter into the pitcher's psyche. A great tape that can improve your game.

****

*B*aseball is a great game for kids of all ages, so be sure to check out the videos in the SPORTS FOR KIDS section of this chapter. You'll find some excellent instructional videos geared especially for the younger baseball players.

HOOPS & DUNKS

Basketball is another great sport that is enjoyed by men and women alike as well as kids of all ages. Whether you're shooting a few through the garage basketball hoop or involved with serious team playing, videos are available to help improve your skills. Both beginners and experienced players can benefit, via video, from the expertise of many star players and managers of this popular sport.

BASKETBALL CLINICS

If basketball is your game, you can now train with the pros. In **SPORTS CLINIC BASKETBALL** (COF), NBA all-stars will how you how to improve your game with the same drills and training exercises used by the top pro teams. Via video, you can have private lessons with the best in the game. You can also have a look at **DO IT BETTER: BASKETBALL** (ESP) and learn to do just that. You'll be shown all the skills you need for footwork, ball handling and shooting. And for the special skills and strategies of the ladies' game, be sure to view **DO IT BETTER: WOMEN'S BASKETBALL** (COF).

Whether your goal is just making the team or making the Hall of Fame, the four-tape series **PISTOL PETE'S HOMEWORK BASKETBALL** (COF) will show you all the basic fundamentals as well as the advanced tips for game-breaking strategies. View along and learn with Pistol Pete Maravich in **PISTOL PETE'S SHOOTING** and **PISTOL PETE'S PASSING** videos. Continue on as he offers instruction, motivation and one-of-a-kind drills in **PISTOL PETE'S BALLHANDLING** and **PISTOL PETE'S DRIBBLING**. If you master his approach, you should have the edge over any opponent.

From the National Collegiate Athletic Association come some very high-quality instructional videos presented by some of the finest coaches in the game. **NCAA BASKETBALL VIDEOS** (CEP) is a seven-tape course to teach you everything you need to know to master this popular game. In the offensive-based tapes, Ray Meyer will teach you **BALL HANDLING & DRIBBLING**, Tom Davis shows his **PASSING TECHNIQUES**, Jim Valvano teaches **SHOOTING** and **OFFENSIVE POST PLAY** is presented by Jim Dutcher. On the defense side, learn **INDIVIDUAL DEFENSE** from Larry Farmer, **REBOUNDING** from Denny Crum, and let Lou Carnesecca teach you all about **DEFENSING THE PIVOT MAN**. Here's a great chance to learn from some of the best coaches in the business.

Video is also the perfect medium for UCLA coach Jim Harrick as he opens his playbook and team practices with a great instructional series. **THE JIM HARRICK APPROACH TO WINNING BASKETBALL** (COF) is a comprehensive, seven-tape course that is sure to leave the viewer with a greater understanding of basketball and the skills and techniques involved. Take advantage of Harrick's winning approach in **THE FAST BREAK, PLAYING BASIC DEFENSE** and **BEATING THE ZONE AND MATCHUP**. Learn his philosophy and strategy for **PREPARING FOR SPECIAL SITUATIONS** and **THE BALANCE COURT HIGH POST OFFENSE**. See the little parts of the game that help win the close ones in **THE WINNING DIFFERENCE**, and use the how-to guide for **PRACTICE**

PLANNING for simple and effective practices. A worthwhile addition to your sports video library.

Professional coach Rick Pitino is also ready to share his expertise with you and the other players on your team in his four-volume instructional series. Viewing **RICK PITINO: OFFENSE I & II** (CEP) will show you everything you need to know to improve your offensive playing, while **RICK PITINO: DEFENSE I & II** (CEP) is sure to do the same for your defense skills. Each program presents a one-on-one clinic with one of the best minds in the game of basketball. And from a leading coach of women's basketball comes a series of high-quality instructional videos designed to get you performing at peak level. Coach Tara VanDerveer's **BUILDING A CHAMPIONSHIP OFFENSE** (CEP) and **BUILDING A CHAMPIONSHIP DEFENSE** (CEP) are designed especially to help the female player do just that.

From the **BASKETBALL OF THE '90s** series, an excellent two-tape program is available from coach Jerry Tarkanian. **THE SHARK ON OFFENSE** (COF) and **THE SHARK ON DEFENSE** (COF) are live-action tapes that you'll want to review again and again. And if you're involved in high school basketball, you'll want to view two tapes from America's number one high school basketball coach, Bob Hurley. In his series **BOB HURLEY BAS-KETBALL** (CEP), this popular coach is all yours as he teaches you his techniques and tips for winning **OFFENSE** and **DEFENSE** skills.

DEVELOPING THE BIG MAN (COF) is another excellent video guide that teaches the procedure, psychology and physical and skill development for the big man in today's basketball game. For playing the back court, **DEVELOPING THE PERIMETER PLAYER** (COF) presents a complete range of ball-handling drills and shooting skills. And to put some championship experience on your team, be sure to take a look at **FAST BREAK I & II** (COF). No matter what your skill level, a session with these tapes will help you perfect the pick and roll, blocking out, passing to and from the low post and shooting that three-point shot.

There are also some very complete one-tape programs that will give the viewer the edge in honing basketball skills. **BASKETBALL SKILLS** (COF) teaches all the basic techniques of ball handling, dribbling and shooting. To improve your foul shooting by up to ten percent or more, be sure to watch **FOUL SHOOTING** (COF). You'll be treated to dozens of motivational concepts and ideas along with step-by-step, easy-to-follow instructions on the proper mechanics of foul shooting. And for an in-depth look at the proper techniques and mechanics of free-throw shooting, **COACH DOUG NOLL'S FREE-THROW SHOOTING** (CEP) is the tape to view. With practice, you can learn the skill and gain the confidence to step to the line and sink the shot that sends your team home victorious.

Especially designed to give coaches of all levels a guide to the important **BASKETBALL SKILLS AND DRILLS** (COF), this video workshop series is an invaluable tool for coaches and players alike. Each tape breaks down a specific skill and relates its value to team and individual play. Learn from coach Don Meyer all about **FIELD GOAL SHOOTING I & II, FREE THROW** and **PASS & CATCH**. Improve your **FOOTWORK, DRIB-BLING** and **REBOUNDING**. Take advantage of the expert advice in **GET OPEN TO SCORE, PERIMETER PLAY, POST PLAY** and **SETTING**

USING SCREENS. And of special value to coaches is **TEAM ATTITUDE** and **TEACHING TIPS**. An excellent, comprehensive course in basketball.

PLAY WITH THE STARS

Rev up your VCR and bring some of basketball's stars into your home via video. Curly Neal, former Harlem Globetrotter, is available for a visit with his **BASKETBALL CAMP** (COF). He'll show you the strategies and tricks that made him famous with easy-to-follow graphics and instructions. Or you may want to invite a former ABA and NBA scoring leader. In **RICK BARRY: SHOOTING AND OFFENSIVE MOVES** (COF), Barry breaks down the five key elements of shooting and covers one-on-one tips.

You can learn **DALE BROWN'S TRANSITION OFFENSE** (COF) and **DALE BROWN'S FREAK DEFENSE** (COF) as you view one of college basketball's master coaches. Brown utilizes the video chalkboard as he combines diagramming game action and playbook strategy. Or view along with **BOEHEIM ON BASKETBALL** (COF). Syracuse University basketball coach, Jim Boeheim, will show you all the techniques that make his team a perennial winner.

For 100 percent Michael Jordan, you won't want to miss viewing **MICHAEL JORDAN: COME FLY WITH ME** (COF). This program features rare footage from college and spectacular highlights from his NBA career and all-star games. You'll be inspired to great heights in your own game as you watch Michael's slam dunks and gravity-defying shots. Or **PUT MAGIC IN YOUR GAME** (COF). Magic Johnson will show you his tricks of the trade, including dribbling, passing, rebounding, defense and shooting. After viewing this excellent program, you'll be on your way to playing better basketball and having more fun every time you do.

You can learn some very special techniques from a very special coach. **MORGAN WOOTEN: TEACHING BASKETBALL** (COF) provides insight into Wooten's approach to life, the game and his players. His teams are known as the benchmark by which to judge excellence in scholastic athletics, and now you can take advantage of that excellence as you learn from one of the best. Another one of the greats is also awaiting an invitation to come into your home via video. Carol Menken-Schaudt, a three-year veteran of the U.S. National Team, is ready to share her expertise in step-by-step, easy-to-understand demonstrations and explanations. **GOLD MEDAL BASKETBALL FOR WOMEN** (COF), a two-volume program, is a worthwhile view.

MORE ON BASKETBALL

Now you can turn your TV-watching time into a primetime workout program that is sure to improve your game. **BASKETBALL WORKOUT: WORKOUT PROGRAMS** (COF) will show you techniques to increase your vertical jump by eight inches or more. This easy-to-follow workout shows dozens of basketball drills, ideas and concepts to help tune up your skills. A perfect off-season training program for guards, forwards and centers is **BASKETBALL WORKOUT: FOR CENTERS/POWER FORWARDS** (COF). Let your VCR guide you through an advanced workout program that will help you improve offensive moves and build confidence in your play. And **BASKETBALL WORKOUT: FOR GUARDS/SMALL FORWARDS** (COF) is sure to do the same for guards and small forwards.

Another three-tape series to help basketball players of all levels strengthen their game through specific drills is the **DRILL FOR SKILL** (CEP) series. From **BEGINNER** to **INTERMEDIATE** and on to **ADVANCED**, each of these videos focuses on various drills designed to improve speed, quickness, dribbling, passing and shooting skills while simulating basic game situations. Each program features more than forty drills that are specific to various age and ability levels. An excellent reference program to add to your sports video library.

Two veteran university coaches are ready to come into your home via video with their programs designed especially for women's basketball. Gloria Soluk, formerly of the University of Michigan, teaches the jump shot in a very unique way, using a chair, in **WOMEN'S BASKETBALL: JUMP SHOT** (COF). You'll progress from there into various techniques for the layup shot. And be sure to continue on with her excellent program **WOMEN'S BASKETBALL: OFFENSIVE MOVES BEFORE THE DRIBBLE** (COF). Soluk will show you many offensive moves that are used prior to the dribble and are sure to increase your success rate on the court. For **WOMEN'S BASKETBALL: OFFENSE** (COF), join Cathy Benedetto, New Mexico University, as she illustrates everything from shooting to offensive strategy. And her **WOMEN'S BASKETBALL: DEFENSE** (COF) will show you individual and team defense that will enable you to play effective defensive basketball.

Another excellent video instructional guide to women's basketball is **SUCCESSFUL COACHING** (COF). This documentary-style, instructional video shows the day-by-day organization of one of the most successful high school girl's basketball teams. Coach Jan Lahodny of the Victoria Stingarettes of Victoria, Texas offers her unique and innovative coaching tips and techniques. This tape is a must for both coaches and players.

****

Once you've used some of the above tapes to become a top-notch basketball player, be sure to take a look at the videos geared to other popular sports. The sections on SERVING UP TENNIS and EXCEL AT GOLF might just hold something of interest for you.

TRADITIONAL FOOTBALL

Whether it's played in a vacant lot, a high school field or the NFL, everyone seems to get excited about football. Many of the sport's greatest players and managers have produced some excellent videos to help you learn the game, improve your skills and become a proficient player. Do your learning at home in front of your VCR and then go on out there and put those skills to good use.

LET'S PLAY FOOTBALL

One of best ways to get started in your football career is to enlist the aid of the NFL. Seven NFL all-stars will come into your home via video in **LEARNING FOOTBALL THE NFL WAY: DEFENSE** (COF) and offer tips on what makes them the best defenders in their respective positions. This program offers easy-to-follow, step-by-step instructions, training tips and practice techniques. Be sure to extend the same invitation to the five NFL all-stars in **LEARNING FOOTBALL THE NFL WAY: OFFENSE** (COF). Color-coded segments in this program make it easy for the viewer to locate information on each position. A great way to learn all the fundamentals of football.

Another high-quality instructional video series has been produced by the National Collegiate Athletic Association, making use of some of the finest coaches in the game. This eight-tape **NCAA FOOTBALL VIDEOS** (CEP) course is divided into offensive and defensive segments. On the offensive side you'll learn **RUNNING BACK TECHNIQUES** from Earle Bruce and all about **PASS RECEIVING** from Bobby Bowden. Doug Scovil shares his expertise in **THE QUARTERBACK**, while Mervin Johnson introduces **OFFENSIVE LINE TECHNIQUES**. Defensively, you'll be taught **DEFENSIVE LINE TECHNIQUES** by Paul Wiggen and **DEFENSIVE BACK DRILLS** by Bobby Proctor. **PUNTING AND KICKING** techniques are covered by Lou Holtz, and the ins and outs of **LINEBACKER PLAY** are presented by Foge Fazio. An excellent chance to learn from the best in the business.

For more tips from the experts, you'll want to view Coach Tom Landry, another football great, as he teams up with various football stars to bring his knowledge and expertise to you via video. You'll get the benefit of decades of experience in line play from Landry and Pete Brock in **OFFENSIVE LINE** (COF), and then join Landry and Mike McCoy to learn all about the **DEFENSIVE LINE** (COF). Archie Griffin and Steve Largent team up with Landry to teach you the proper techniques for the tailback and fullback in **RUNNING BACK & WIDE RECEIVER** (COF), and linebacker strategies are explicitly detailed by Bob Bruening and Mike Haynes along with Landry in **LINEBACKERS & DEFENSIVE BACKS** (COF). Complete this excellent educational video course with Landry and Jim Zorn as you learn everything you need to know about the **QUARTERBACK** (COF).

For some comprehensive one-tape programs that provide a good basic foundation, you may want to take a look at **FOOTBALL FOR ALL AGES** (COF). In this program, techniques and skills are taught with intelligence and precision by pro teammates Jeff Kemp and Mike Barber. Or try a view of **FOOTBALL TECHNIQUES** (COF) for a good basic working knowledge of all the different positions of the game. To learn the same techniques and training exercises used by top pro teams, **SPORTS CLINIC FOOTBALL** (COF) is a worthwhile view. All-star coach George Allen and his staff are excellent instructors, plus you'll get an inside look at "The Pros Playbook" featuring top plays and formations.

For a comprehensive course in the game of football, you'll want to consider the eleven-tape program **CHAMPIONSHIP FOOTBALL COACHING SERIES** (CEP). These videos are endorsed by the National

79

Federation of Interscholastic Coaches Association and are taught by some of the best coaches in the business representing many of the well-known pro teams. Start your learning experience with **DEFENSIVE MIDDLE GUARD, QUARTERBACKS** and **LINEBACKERS**. Build on your skills with **DEFENSIVE SECONDARY** and **RECEIVERS**. Continue on with **DEFENSIVE ENDS, DEFENSIVE LINE, OFFENSIVE BACKS** and **OFFENSIVE LINE**. And to complete this thorough and extensive course, **KICKING GAME** and **PUNTING** will round out your education.

POSITIONAL TECHNIQUES

No matter what position you take on the field, via video you can now learn the specific techniques and fundamentals you need to excel. In **ALL-PRO PUNTING TECHNIQUES** (CEP), professional kicking coach Steve Hoffman will walk you through the warm-up exercises and drills that have been fashioned from years of experience. This is a high-quality instructional punting tape. Or learn about the techniques and philosophy of Michigan's tenacious defense in **ANGLE DEFENSE** (COF). The front seven positions are discussed individually, starting with stance and alignment. All the key points you'll learn are illustrated in slow motion and reinforced with game examples.

From the coaching staff of Brigham Young University, **THE PROTECTORS: PREPARING OFFENSIVE LINEMEN** (COF) is a live-action video that will teach you and your team mates all the skills necessary for improving your team's passing attack. Let these proven methods become a part of your winning tradition. Or if defensive back is your position, you'll want to view **BUMP AND RUN: DEFENSIVE BACK** (CEP). Developed by Greg Brown, defensive back coach at the University of Colorado, this is the most comprehensive video ever on the bump-and-run style coverage of receivers. Every phase is demonstrated in detail with techniques, fundamentals and drills presented in a close-up clinic format. This high-quality program is excellent for all players and coaches from junior high to the pros.

For the quarterbacks in the video viewing audience, there are programs available dedicated strictly to your unique skills. **QUARTERBACK FUNDAMENTALS AND TECHNIQUES** (COF) is an excellent instructional video featuring Joe Krivak, head coach at the University of Maryland. Joe and three of his former players do a great job of explaining and demonstrating all the fundamentals and techniques necessary to produce a good quarterback. To take advantage of the firsthand knowledge of well-known quarterback Fran Tarkenton, you'll want to view **QUARTERBACK TECHNIQUES** (COF). By utilizing these drills, you'll improve your skills and gain confidence in your passing.

Penn State University's legendary Joe Paterno is also available for your viewing entertainment and education. In **DEFENSING WISHBONE 'T'** (COF), Paterno illustrates the three defenses he employed in stopping the Wishbone 'T'. Diagrams, freeze frames and slow-motion footage clearly detail all the techniques in this program. And for a view of the Wishbone 'T' from the other side, **WISHBONE 'T'** (COF) was developed by former University of Texas coach Darrell Royal. Freeze-framing and game films aid Coach Royal in explaining the triple option offense, which Texas ran to perfection and which revolutionized football.

MORE ON FOOTBALL

The complete introduction to football—the rules, procedures, terminology and philosophy—is now yours for the viewing via video. Bob Schembechler's **VIDEO RULES OF FOOTBALL: UNDERSTAND THE GAME** (COF) is a must-watch for players, coaches and football fans alike. A complete course on understanding the game from A to Z, the program also compares the rules of high school, college and pro football. A must-have addition to your sports video library.

The rigors of football training are legendary, and now video can aid you in developing the body you need for this rough and strenuous game. **BASIC WEIGHT TRAINING** (COF) is specifically designed to teach football players and other athletes the basic techniques of weight training, with tips for the more advanced. To develop speed and strength on the playing field, see the unique video **INCREASING SPEED AND STRENGTH** (COF). Detailed documentation on stretching drills, warm-ups and lengthening the stride plus methods for preventing muscle pulls and much, much more will soon have you in top performing shape. And for advanced strength training techniques developed by coach Dana LeDuc, **STRENGTH TRAINING FOR FOOT-BALL** (CEP) includes all the drills and workout techniques used by the pros. This tape should be an indispensable part of every player's library.

TOM TUTKO'S COACHING CLINIC (COF) is designed especially for football coaches. This excellent tape discusses many of the most common personality and competitive situations that you, as a coach, will face both on the field and off in dealing with your athletes. This program can make your job as a coach easier and much more rewarding. The tape is divided into eight areas of interest to all coaches: The Coach, The Athlete, Motivation, Communication/Discipline, Coaching Challenges, The Parents, Building Character and the Athlete's Bill of Rights. Designed to be used as a reference dictionary and for easy location of topics, the video is packaged with a card that lists topics covered and time location.

****

Football is a very rough-and-tumble, strenuous game, so be sure to take a look at some of the excellent videos available in the FEEL FIT/LOOK GOOD chapter. Or help keep your body in excellent condition by partaking of other popular activities you can learn via videos from THE GREAT OUTDOORS chapter.

SOCCER FOR EVERYONE

Soccer can be a very rough, fast-paced game but also challenging and fun. It is one of the fastest growing sports in America, and videos can teach the basics to the novice as well as help the more experienced players perfect their skills. From tapes that teach the fundamentals to specific programs from the sports stars, there is sure to be one or more videos that you'll want to view on this great sport.

LEARN THE FUNDAMENTALS

A great way to start your soccer career is with **SOCCER FOR EVERY-ONE** (CEP). This instructional program begins by establishing the basic soccer rules with easy-to-follow examples. Players of all ages demonstrate the fundamentals and tactics involved as well as exercises to improve strength, endurance and playing skills. To further lay a good solid foundation for the game, you'll want to view **SOCCER FUNDAMENTALS** (COL). Bob Guelker of Southern Illinois University will teach you all you need to know to participate in this fast-paced sport.

Technical skills are essential on the soccer playing field, and an excellent way to master all the fundamentals and more is with **SOCCER FUNDA-MENTALS WITH WIEL COERVER I, II & III** (CEP). Coerver is known as the soccer guru for coaches and players of all levels. His three-tape video series is a way for you to have your own soccer guru in your home. These well-produced videos demonstrate Coach Coerver's extraordinary ability to make practice enjoyable. You'll become eager to learn and soon develop remarkable skills to take with you onto the soccer field. An essential learning tool you'll enjoy viewing.

Another chance to take a lesson from a pro is **SOCCER FOR ALL AGES** (COF) with Steve Long, an experienced soccer teacher. Long provides valuable inside tips on all phases of soccer playing. **DO IT BETTER: SOC-CER** (ESP) will help you do just that. Coach John Boyle and players Gregg Murphy, John Benbow and Peter Farrel join forces to help you reinforce the fundamentals and then take your game to a higher level. **SOCCER IS FUN** (COF), a two-tape series, teaches everything you need to know about the game while also stressing the importance of enjoying your playing time.

SOCCER WORKSHOPS

The National Collegiate Athletic Association has drawn on the expertise of some of the finest coaches in the game in its exceptional, high-quality instructional series **NCAA SOCCER** (CEP). This three-tape course can teach you the skills and drills used by the pros to create consistently top-ranked teams. You'll learn **JUGGLING, DRIBBLING & PASSING** and **GOAL KEEPING** from Joe Morrone, and Bill Muse will show you all the techniques of **SHOOTING**. This is a good learning series that you'll want to refer to again and again.

Another excellent and comprehensive workshop series is **HUBERT VOGELSINGER'S SOCCER SERIES** (COF). The five volumes in this program cover all areas of soccer playing, and Coach Vogelsinger is an expert not only at coaching but at teaching the viewer all the ins and outs of the game. Each tape is carefully designed to enable the viewer to grasp easily and clearly all the techniques and sensitive details that are often overlooked. **KICKING** and **BALL CONTROL** will teach the necessary skills in these areas, as will **DRIBBLING & FEINTING. SOCCEROBICS** is an ingeniously designed system of exercises with the ball that incorporates soccer skills with aerobic conditioning and physical development. **SUPER SKILLS AND HEADING** is a two-part program with slow-motion replays and world game-action footage to help illustrate proper skills. Another excellent video training series for your sports library.

MORE ON SOCCER

A beneficial video for all players from beginner to advanced is **SOCCER SET PLAYS** (COF). The program lets you see the advantages of attacking from set plays, and you'll learn how to bring about more skillful passing. The close-up visuals in this program are excellent, and stop action will assist you in learning the techniques and tips offered.

Then, be sure to view the informative and enjoyable video **PELE THE MASTER** (COF), from one of soccer's greats. Pele teaches the viewer the most comprehensive system for soccer ever presented. The program encompasses each aspect of soccer, including ball control, trapping, goal-keeping, penalties and free kicks. A special section on physical conditioning will help you tone your skills and your body.

You'll want to view a rather unique video that will enable you to learn **NEW SOCCER FOR FUN & SKILLS** (COF). This program not only demonstrates the basic skills of soccer but also presents games to enjoy that will further develop these skills along with team building. The games can be played on a grassy area or soft surface and require only a ball and cones or other kinds of markers. You're sure to have fun with this enjoyable video.

****

While soccer is one of the most popular field sports, other games might also be of interest. Take a look at some of the excellent videos in the TRACK & FIELD EVENTS section of this chapter, along with some special and unique programs you'll find in the segment A MEDLEY OF SPORTS.

EXCEL AT GOLF

Millions of people every day of every year hit the "greens" and "tee off!" If you're one of these dedicated golfers or just play an occasional game for fun, there is a video available to improve your techniques as well as your score. Take advantage of "bad-weather" time by popping one of the excellent tapes detailed below in your VCR and, in the privacy of your own home, learn from the pros. Next time you hit the greens, you'll be pleasantly surprised at how much you've improved your game.

TEE OFF

An excellent beginner's guide to the game of golf is **GOLF FOR ALL AGES** (COF). You'll learn the fundamentals along with techniques that will have you out on the green in no time. A full range of graphics heighten the learning experience as you receive lessons from pro-golfer Kermit Zarley.

83

Another great tape for beginners at all levels is **GOLF THE EASY WAY** (COF) with Wally Armstrong. Highlights in this enjoyable and informative program include segments on swings, putting, pitch shots, sand shots and short and long games. You'll learn how to add distance to your drive and take strokes off your game.

For more instruction in golf fundamentals, the world-famous Ben Sutton School instructors will come into your home via video and demonstrate how to apply the successful Sutton swing mechanics to every shot. **GOLF FUN-DAMENTALS** (ESP) and **GOLF FUNDAMENTALS: WOMEN** (ESP) detail the differences between men's power game and the finesse game of women. Without abandoning your natural swing, you can dramatically improve your play by mastering these two tapes.

Other tapes designed especially for the woman player are available. **BEGINNING GOLF FOR WOMEN** (COF) is an instructional tape specifically for those women who have never played or are just beginning. Donna White, LPGA tour veteran, shows the viewer how simple learning golf can be. She makes learning the basic techniques of golf fun and easy to understand through her creative and simple teaching style. Top British professional Diane Barnard provides easy-to-follow instructions in **GOLF FOR WOMEN** (COF). Starting with building the swing, you'll travel through all the fundamentals you need to get started.

MASTERING THE BASICS: A GUIDE FOR THE WOMAN GOLFER (CEP) is taught by professional LPGA instructor Annette Thompson. She demonstrates all the fundamentals necessary for developing a good golf swing. You'll also learn about the problems most often encountered by both beginning and accomplished golfers and the solutions to overcome them. This video contains excellent pre-swing thoughts that you can use to become a more complete player. To improve on these fundamental skills, you'll want to view **NANCY LOPEZ: GOLF MADE EASY** (COF). One of the top putters on the circuit, Lopez gives you time-proven tips and step-by-step demonstrations of techniques and innovative methods for becoming an excellent golfer.

Another excellent, comprehensive series on the game of golf is the **GOLF DIGEST SCHOOL LEARNING LIBRARY** (COF), a five-volume program taught by Bob Toski, Jim Flick and John Elliott. Start your course with **A SWING FOR A LIFETIME** and **FIND YOUR OWN FUNDAMENTALS**, two tapes that cover all aspects of your swing, stance and grip. For a proven way to add length and consistency to tee shots, continue your viewing with **DRIVING FOR DISTANCE**. Keep watching and learning with **SHARPEN YOUR SHORT IRONS** to see proven methods of hitting your nine to five irons crisply and straight. And wrap up the course by learning the main elements that affect successful bunker play in **SAVING PAR FROM THE SAND**. A truly valuable reference program you'll want to refer to time and again.

For a good one-tape program on all the factors that make up a great golf score, you'll want to consider viewing **AL GEIBERGER: GOLF** (COF). This pro-tour golfer, whose score of fifty-nine for eighteen holes is the lowest ever recorded, is available on home viewing to teach you the techniques of the perfect drive, the fairway wood, the two iron, five iron, nine iron, pitch chip and putt. Or learn the correct position of the body and club at critical stages of each stoke with **GOLF** (COF), demonstrated by Michigan State University's Bruce Fossum. Succinct captions aid you in learning the skills involved in grips, stance and address, clubs and swings, pitching and chipping, putting and trouble shots.

LEARN GOLF WITH THE PROS

What better way to learn golf than with the pros. And the many available instructional videos let you do just that. Engage all-time great Lee Trevino and let him instruct you in **LEE TREVINO'S PRICELESS GOLF TIPS** (CEP). This three-tape series is Trevino at his best, and he'll soon have you at your best, too. All the mechanics of **CHIPPING AND PUTTING** (CEP) are discussed and demonstrated in volume one. Volume two, **GETTING OUT OF TROUBLE** (CEP), covers a wide variety of troublesome shots and shows techniques for using various clubs from different and demanding lies. You'll also learn to put consistency and predictability into your golf game with all the techniques and tips you'll learn in volume three, **SWING FUNDAMENTALS PLUS DISTANCE AND CONTROL**. A worthwhile viewing experience.

To learn the dynamics of golf from another one of the game's greatest players, be sure to see **JACK NICKLAUS: GOLF MY WAY I** (COF). This exceptionally high-quality instructional program discusses every aspect of the game. Each crucial point is highlighted in slow motion so you can study every detail. Stay with Jack into **GOLF MY WAY II: PLAYING THE GAME** (COF). He begins with a thorough review of the fundamentals of shotmaking and a couple of tips on properly preparing yourself before play. Moving on, he covers all the techniques, approaches and strategies that you'll need to conquer this challenging game. The final segment covers in detail perhaps the most neglected subject in the game, which is how to practice productively. The perfect package of videos for any golfer.

More pros are available for your educational golf viewing. Tom Kite is a great teacher who will help you reach full potential. In **DEVELOPING MAXIMUM CONSISTENCY** (COF), Tom and friends show you all the golfing essentials from tee to green. And to join Tom in an actual round of golf and be part of a private lesson golfers dream of, be sure to view **STRATEGIES AND TECHNIQUES** (COF). Or perhaps a private lesson with senior golf pro Billy Casper interests you. Casper's **GOLF LIKE A PRO** (COF) covers all aspects of the game and is perfect for either the beginner or the seasoned pro. **GOLF THE MILLER WAY** (COF) brings yet another golf pro into your home via video as Johnny Miller demonstrates the skills that have helped him capture many prestigious tournament titles. You'll also learn the famous "C" position and how to improve your swing. To improve your putting, view Ben Crenshaw's **THE ART OF PUTTING** (COF) and benefit from the master's expertise.

Here are some more pros to pick from. As golf's biggest hitter, John Daly shows you some of his secrets in **GRIP IT & RIP IT** (COF). You'll also be entertained and informed by Daly's theories on the game and a dose of philosophy. And you may want to take a look at Fred Couples and top instructor John Redman in **ON TEMPO** (COF) as they explain why tempo is the most important element in the game. You'll receive an excellent education on the three wood, the three, five and seven irons, and the wedge in addition to tips on keeping your tempo consistent with all clubs.

MORE ON GOLF

Geared to seniors' golf, **50 PLUS SENIORS GOLD** (COF) offers excellent video instruction on achieving greater distance and developing more accuracy as well as proper posture and grip and much more. Whether you're experienced or just starting out, you can significantly improve your game with this program. To improve your "short game," be sure to benefit from the expertise of Steve Ballesteros via his video **THE SHORT GAME** (COF). Easy-to-follow instructions are designed specifically to help you improve your game from 100 yards and in. And to improve your driving distance and accuracy, take a view of Mike Dunaway's **POWER DRIVING** (COF). Dunaway's unique neuromuscular training systems that are detailed in this first-rate video will make you a winner in golfing circles.

Another interesting way to lower your score and your chances of golf injuries is to follow along via video with Bob Anderson in his unique tape **STRETCHING FOR BETTER GOLF** (COF). Anderson has been the stretching consultant to college, professional and Olympic teams, and his expertise and knowledge are now available for your viewing education. This video is helpful for both the beginner and the advanced golfer.

Golf instructors, players and fans alike will want to view the excellent and comprehensive video program **THE RULES ON GOLF** (COF). This informative tape looks at more than thirty different rules in the game of golf. The running counter visible throughout the video allows the viewer to find the rule in question by using the handy reference guide that is time-coded. You might also be interested in a companion reference video, **THE RULES OF GOLF** (COF), the official video of the U.S. Golf Association. This unique video lets you watch as the world's joint rules-making organizations review most recent changes in the rules as well as fundamental principles and the philosophy governing the game. Two very worthwhile reference productions.

For a hilarious tongue-in-cheek look at golf, you're sure to thoroughly enjoy watching **LESLIE NIELSEN: BAD GOLF MADE EASIER** (FSV). According to Nielsen, bad golf can always be made easier. Once you apply his entertaining rules, you can lower your scores immediately even if you remain a "bad golfer." With that in mind, Nielsen teaches you how a golf ball is never lost, just missing, and that there should be no penalty stroke because someone will eventually find it. He'll also help you find creative ways to mark your ball on the green to make short putts shorter! Be sure to watch this one.

****

The game of golf is a sport that can be enjoyed well into your mature years. And to make sure your senior years are golden ones, be sure to check out the excellent tapes in the HEALTHY LIVING chapter. These videos, combined with a selection from the FEEL FIT/LOOK GOOD chapter, will help you enjoy many years of golf.

SERVING UP TENNIS

Another popular sport that lends itself to video instruction is the game of tennis. You can practice with the tennis greats in the privacy of your own home as you learn from their expert tips and advice. And when it comes time to hit the courts, you'll dazzle your friends with your new-found skill.

YOUR SERVE!

If you're interested in learning to play tennis but private lessons are inconvenient and expensive, consider learning the video way. **TENNIS FOR ALL AGES** (COF) is a one-on-one video lesson, just you and your coach in the privacy of your own home. You'll gain perspective and be able to prepare yourself through mental imaging with expert guidance and instruction on the basic tennis strokes. For more fundamentals to get you started, a view of **TENNIS** (COF) is worthwhile. This program carefully analyzes all the essential strokes of the game. You'll learn easily through close-up photography, slow-motion sequences, freezes and captions.

Also available as your private tutor is one of the world's most renowned tennis coaches, Vic Braden. Via his series of videos, he offers the viewer scientifically proven techniques that will help you develop a very reliable game. Start with **TENNIS BY BRADEN** (COF) for a comprehensive introduction and then view **PRACTICE WITH THE PROS** (COF) as the next step in developing your abilities. Using slow-motion and professional players, these information-packed videos provide excellent examples of correct form, footwork and body placement. Continue on with **PLAYING DOUBLES** (COF) to learn the team concept of the game, and let **VIC BRADEN'S COURT ETIQUETTE** (COF) provide you with humorous guidance on winning, losing and playing graciously. Be sure to round out your tennis education with **VIC BRADEN'S QUICK CURES FOR COMMON TENNIS PROBLEMS** (COF). This video is worth its weight in gold. If your tennis game suffers from a specific weakness, simply tune in to Vic's concise solution.

Another world-famous teaching professional, Dennis VanDerMeer, is also ready to come to you via video with his three-volume instructional course **THE TENNIS TEACHING METHODS OF DENNIS VANDERMEER** (CEP). This program comprehensively covers every aspect of the game. Each of the three tapes, **ESSENTIAL STROKES, THE TACTICAL GAME** and **THE ATTACKING GAME**, is divided into chapters in which the pro explains, demonstrates and gives explicit close-up shots to illustrate his points. These programs contain tips and playing tactics designed for players of all ages and abilities. A worthwhile reference course.

And from the National Collegiate Athletic Association comes a four-volume series, **NCAA TENNIS VIDEOS** (CEP), which is guaranteed to help the viewer learn all the essentials of tennis that will result in improved performance on the court. Coach Dennis Ralston is on hand to teach you **SERVE & RETURN OF SERVE**, and **THE VOLLEY** is fully and concisely explained by Coach Allan Fox. To learn control and strength of **THE**

FOREHAND, the viewer is treated to the expertise of Coach Bob McKinley. And Coach Brian Esner is an excellent instructor on powerfully developing **THE BACKHAND**. These are superb instructional tapes you'll want to refer to time and again as your game continues to improve.

LEARNING FROM THE STARS

Arthur Ashe, Stan Smith and Vic Braden join forces to bring the video viewer a great comprehensive guide to tennis. **TENNIS OUR WAY** (ESP) teaches the forehand, backhand, the serve, the volley, the overhead, the lob, doubles and much more. You'll not only be training with the stars of the tennis world but also getting lots of priceless expert advice. And for **MAXIMIZING YOUR TENNIS POTENTIAL** (COF), take advantage of the innovative techniques and enjoyable personal style of Vic Braden in this informative and entertaining tennis lesson. The slow-motion photography and graphic demonstrations of this tape will help you apply Braden's techniques to your game and really shine on the courts.

In **VISUAL TENNIS** (COF), John Yandell will show you how to unlock your natural visual ability to develop a powerful style. A series of still-frame progressions will help you develop classical models for all the basic strokes, and you'll also learn to do muscle memory correction. Or learn tennis secrets and tips from the world's best—John McEnroe and Ivan Lendl. In **THE WINNING EDGE** (COF), they will take you step by step through basic tennis maneuvers and all the way up to advanced strategies.

To see a real pro at work and learn from his expertise, be sure to consider two excellent instructional videos from the legendary Jimmy Connors. Viewing his **WINNING FUNDAMENTALS** (COF) will enable you to learn all the essential elements for a strong and consistent all-around game. Footage of other top tennis players is also certain to help you gain a better understanding of proper techniques, and in **MATCH STRATEGY** (COF) Jimmy shows the viewer what players must know to improve their game. Winning techniques and proven strategies from this great player will help to sharpen your skills for both singles and doubles play. An exciting way to improve your tennis game.

To learn tennis the champions' way, try the two-tape series **TENNIS TO WIN I & II** (COF), starring John Newcombe and Bjorn Borg. In the first volume, you'll join Newcombe, Ken Rosewall, Evonne Goolagong Cawley, Sue Barker and other top pros as you learn all the stages from basic to intermediate to advanced techniques. An added bonus is exciting highlights of Bjorn Borg's great Wimbledon matches, providing motivation to improve your skills. Volume two of this program is a unique tape concentrating on preparing for the game. Bjorn Borg and Virginia Wade demonstrate how to stretch and loosen up before a match, an especially enjoyable segment of this excellent series.

MORE ON TENNIS

All top-flight tennis players hit nearly every shot with some type of intentional spin. In **TENNIS, SPIN AND YOU** (CEP), teaching pro John

Smallfield shows you how to master this difficult skill and add the dimension of spin to your game. Utilizing slow-motion filming and full-range graphics, this tape is a virtual mini-clinic on the shots the pros hit for control and accuracy. If you're serious about raising your level of competition, this is definitely the video to view.

BODY PREP FOR TENNIS (COF) is an action-packed video containing the most effective tennis-related exercises. Pro tennis player Tim Mayotte and other outstanding players will show you how to get in shape for tennis. The dozens of exercises you'll learn to do with this excellent tape will directly benefit your tennis skills as well as help keep your body in tip-top shape for participation in this active game.

Another exciting way to get into shape and improve your tennis game at the same time is to follow along via video with **TENNISCISE** (COF). Tenniscise is a revolutionary new method of exercise designed to develop and increase tennis skills while simultaneously providing an invigorating aerobic workout. The routines are easy to follow and give maximum results in minimal time. So get started now and tenniscise your way to a better game.

****

Tennis is not only a very enjoyable, competitive game but also a great way to keep in shape. Other fun ways to keep fit and healthy can be found through video. Take a look at some of the excellent tapes in THE GREAT OUTDOORS chapter. These tapes can take you from skiing down a snowy slope to skiing behind a powerboat on a beautiful mountain lake.

KEEP YOUR EYE ON THE BALL!

Two different balls; two different games! Both are lots of fun. If your eye is on the bowling ball, there's a video below to help you rack up the strikes. Or if a volleyball is in your line of vision, pick a video in this field and you're sure to shine on the court or the beach.

LET'S GO BOWLING

If you want to join the 60 million people who have discovered the challenge of bowling, a good place to start is with a view of **LET'S BOWL** (COF). Hall-of-Famer Dick Weber will show you all the basics. As you practice the techniques, you'll learn and take advantage of his expert tips as your bowling game shows a marked improvement. For more fundamentals about this exciting game, you'll want to watch **BOWLING** (COF) with Bo Burton, Jr. He'll explain and demonstrate all the essentials of bowling as you learn the skills that made Burton a celebrated professional bowler. Watch these excellent tapes and then head for the nearest bowling alley to practice your newly acquired skills.

89

More bowling advice is yours for the viewing from the vice president of the Life-Time Sports Association. In his video **LYNDON LEE: BOWLING** (COF), you'll learn everything you need to know to get started in this challenging sport. And if you're already a fairly skilled bowler, you can improve your technique by learning perfect body positioning and balance as you view **BOWLING** (COF) with Marshall Holman and Johnny Petraglia. Perfect bowling form for both left- and right-handers will be imprinted in your mind by these two pro bowlers.

You might also want to try another world-class bowling professional who's available via video to teach you all about strikes. In **STRIKE: THE GUIDE TO CONSISTENT BOWLING** (COF), Joe Berardi shows you the techniques to help end frustrations and get more from your game. This is a tape you'll want to watch again and again as you continue to add up those spares and strikes. Or join professional bowler Marshall Holman as he demonstrates an easy five-point program for improved performance in **MAXIMUM BOWLING** (COF). Each step is clearly defined and illustrated and is sure to enhance performance and increase the average bowler's score by ten to twenty pins.

For more bowling greats, take advantage of Earl Anthony's excellent advice for beginning as well as advanced bowlers. **BOWL TO WIN** (COF) not only covers all the basics, including selecting equipment, but gives expert tips to take along to the bowling alley. **GOING FOR 300** (COF) shows you how to handle difficult lane conditions. Anthony's winning techniques shown in this program will help you maintain a high average even against keen competition. Practice at home with this bowling master and really impress your friends at the bowling alley.

Another great competitive bowler, Don Johnson, is an expert instructor you'll want to invite into your home via video. His two-tape program, **A PRO'S GUIDE TO BETTER BOWLING** (COF), can help you become top scorer in your league. In the first volume, Johnson explains and clearly and expertly demonstrates stance, timing, arm swing, footwork, follow-through and grip. You'll go on to learn proper release in volume two, with each point and step clearly illustrated. Johnson's instructions are as superb as his bowling. If you want to continue your private lessons with Don Johnson, be sure to go on to view **DON JOHNSON'S GUIDE TO MAKING SPARES** (COF). This comprehensive program was designed by Johnson with charts and graphs to guide bowlers in making the single-pin spares, clusters and baby splits.

Whether you're a novice or an experienced bowler, you can round out your video education with **RULES ON BOWLING** (COF). This informative program looks at the various rules and guidelines of the game. The running counter visible throughout the tape allows the viewer to find any rule by using the time-coded reference guide. A perfect program for all bowlers.

VOLLEYBALL FUN

Another ball you might be keeping your eye on is the volleyball. Volleyball is played by many just for fun, but others enjoy it as a keenly competitive sport. **DO IT BETTER: VOLLEYBALL** (ESP) teaches the basic techniques and provides valuable tips to make your game more successful and more enjoyable. Coaches Dave Shoji and Alan Rosenthal show you all the skills that were responsible for turning the University of Hawaii into a perennial volleyball powerhouse. For more expert advice to get you started in this fast-moving game, take a look at **VOLLEYBALL** (COF). You'll learn all about serves, forearm passes, overhand sets, spikes, dives and rolls and much more. Practice at home with your VCR and then go out and dazzle them on the court.

For a high-quality instructional series, you may want to take a look at **NCAA VOLLEYBALL VIDEOS** (CEP). This two-tape program from the National Collegiate Athletic Association uses some of the finest coaches in the game to teach the viewer the skills and drills of volleyball. You'll learn all about **SERVING, BLOCKING & INDIVIDUAL DEFENSE** (CEP) in volume one. And the live-action videography continues in volume two as the pros show you the techniques of **PASSING, SETTING & SPIKING** (CEP). If volleyball is your game, this is an excellent addition to your sports video library.

All levels of volleyball players can benefit from **U.S.A. VOLLEYBALL** (COF) with Olympic head coach Doug Beale. You'll see how the world's number one team serves, passes, digs, blocks and spikes. For **VOLLEY-BALL DRILLS** (COF) that are certain to improve your game, this video is excellent viewing. Fifty different volleyball drills are shown in a step-by-step manner by former U.O.P. players. Both you and your team can benefit from the training techniques and tips in this program. An excellent program featuring Coach Cecile Reynaud and the Lady Seminoles of Florida State University will introduce you to **WOMEN'S POWER VOLLEYBALL** (COF). The various skills of offense are closely examined, as are the techniques needed for good defensive play.

For a variation of the regular volleyball game, be sure to take a look at **DO IT BETTER: BEACH VOLLEYBALL** (ESP). The video will show you all the important strategies of this rigorous game. You'll learn the techniques of both the men's and women's game that you must master to play on sand. Again, practice at home with the masters and then go out and impress your friends on the beach.

****

The preceding videos deal with just two sports balls you may have your eye on. Don't forget the excellent instruction you can get in previous parts of this chapter if your game involves a basketball, football or baseball. You might also want to take a look at the instructional videos in the following section, RACK 'EM UP!

RACK 'EM UP!

You may have watched a pool or billiards pro match on TV and been impressed with the players' skills and expertise. Or maybe you've marvelled at the dedication and competitiveness of players of badminton, racquetball or ping pong. Now you can watch the masters on your VCR and develop your own skills in these fun and sometimes very serious games.

POOL & BILLIARDS

If you're ready to rack 'em up but need some help on just how to start, an excellent video that will acquaint you with a worldwide popular pastime is **BILLIARD BASICS** (COF). You'll learn all the fundamentals and techniques you'll need to participate in this fascinating game. For more strategy and valuable tips, you'll also want to view **BILLIARDS FOR ALL** (COF). Willie Mosconi, renowned billiard pro, will teach you proper hand position, placement of the cue ball and much more. This tape is perfect for both beginners and advanced players.

For eight private lessons with the Professor of Poolology, be sure to take a look at **POCKET BILLIARDS** (COF). Pro player Jack White shares excellent tips and advice on how to improve your game and win at billiards. Or view six of the world's top players at work in **TRICK SHOTS** (COF). In this superb video, the pros not only show you the trick shots they made famous but also help you learn how to make them yourself.

If both pool and billiards capture your interest, there is a comprehensive program on both for your education and enjoyment. **POOL & BILLIARDS** (COF) is a two-tape program hosted by pro Robert Byrne. In volume one, Byrne gives the viewer clear and complete explanations of the cue, the tip, the stance, the grips, break shots and more. The program continues in volume two with advanced techniques for expert play. This series is a top-quality production and is greatly enhanced with computer graphics to make learning both easy and fun.

If the lure of the pool table is strong, the first step is viewing **POOL SCHOOL: FUNDAMENTAL TECHNIQUES** (COF). Pro Jim Rempe and Loree Jon Jones guide the viewer step by step from beginner to intermediate techniques, including selection of the proper equipment. **POWER POOL** (COF) picks up where **POOL SCHOOL** leaves off. Rempe and Jones continue your education as they explain and illustrate more advanced techniques that are certain to increase your wins as you rack 'em up and impress the pool-table spectators.

POTPOURRI

Badminton is a fun game to play and easily learned via video. Beginning with the basics, **BADMINTON** (CEP) provides the viewer with an in-depth discussion of the game's requirements, rules, equipment and techniques. You'll also receive expert advice on singles and doubles competition, match play and even fitness training. To improve on these skills, take a look at **BADMINTON: WINNING FUNDAMENTALS** (CEP). Nationally ranked players Dean Schoppe and Tariq Wadood will show you all the strategies and tactics necessary to become a winning player. Players of every ability can benefit from **HOW TO PLAY BADMINTON** (COF), a program made by The Badminton Association of England. This video clearly demonstrates all the essential stroke techniques and strategies needed to make your game more successful and enjoyable.

RACQUETBALL FOR ALL AGES (COF) is an excellent introduction to this popular indoor sport. Pro Al Chassard shares his insider's expertise as he instructs you in the basics of a strong all-around game. For even more insight into this growing sport, be sure to take a look at **RACQUETBALL** (COF). The world's top professional racquetball player, Dave Peck, will teach you the perfect serve, cross-court kill, the "Z" ball and much more. These tapes are excellent tools to help you learn the game of racquetball for fun or competition.

Want to play better table tennis? **PLAY LIKE A PRO: PING PONG** (CEP) makes it easy. You'll view all the basic and advanced instructions covering footwork, strokes, timing, serves and more. Spectacular world-class competition footage is nicely interspersed to reinforce the key strokes as they are presented. Computerized graphics greatly enhance this enjoyable instruction tape.

****

The preceding videos are excellent for indoor sports. But don't spend all your hours indoors. Take just enough time to view some of the great tapes in THE GREAT OUTDOORS chapter and then head on outside for some more great recreation.

TRACK & FIELD EVENTS

Track and field events are very popular competitive sports, especially in schools and Olympic situations. Excellent tapes are available to help you train and succeed in one or more of the areas of your choice. And you'll also want to view a program especially geared to conditioning your body for participation in these strenuous events.

TRACK & FIELD TECHNIQUES

For those viewers who have an interest in track and field, there are videos available for every major event. **BEGINNING TRACK & FIELD INSTRUCTION VIDEOS** (COF) is an excellent twelve-tape series that will introduce the viewer to many areas in this widely practiced sport. Each of the videos is narrated and demonstrated by champions and world record-holders. You can pick from **MIDDLE DISTANCE RUNNING** with Sebastian Coe, **HIGH JUMP** with Dwight Stones, **RELAY RUNNING** with David Hemery or **SHOT PUT** with Parry O'Brien. Take advantage of the expertise of Miklos Nemeth in **JAVELIN**, Al Oerter in **DISCUS**, Tommie Smith in **SPRINTING** or David Hemery in **HURDLES**. Or perhaps your interest lies in the **POLE VAULT** with Jan Johnson, **LONG JUMP** with Lynn Davis, **ROAD RUNNING** with Joan Benolt-Samuelson or **HAMMER THROW** with Hal Connolly. All the tapes are exceptionally well-produced and will show you warm-up exercises and techniques for the particular event or events that you've decided to tackle.

Videos are also available to help both women and men improve their performance in their chosen field. Designed with women in mind, **WOMEN'S TRACK & FIELD** (COF) is hosted by coaches Nell Jackson and Elaine

93

Steiner. This tape will help the female viewer master sprints, hurdles, middle distance, the mile relay, the sprint relay and the long jump. Techniques are also shown to help you become proficient at shot put, the discus, the javelin and the high jump. Coaches Verne Wolf and Dixon Farmer have produced **MEN'S TRACK & FIELD** (COF) especially for male athletes. All the aspects of sprints, high and intermediate hurdles, middle distance, the steeplechase, pole vaulting and the high jump are covered. You'll also receive expert tips on improving your performance in the long jump, the shot put, the discus and the triple jump.

Both male and female athletes can benefit from **TRACK & FIELD TRAINING TECHNIQUES** (COF). Coach James Henry covers all the aspects of sprints, hurdles, the long jump and the high jump in detail, including basic form techniques and useful weight-training exercises. A specialized tape from Coach Tom Shaw may interest you. **TOM SHAW'S LONG & TRIPLE JUMP ENHANCEMENT** (COF) is the most efficient training program on the market in these events. Coach Shaw illustrates all the essential components in a step-by-step format, and his detailed drills are certain to help you improve your jumping ability. For an easy-to-follow program for the vaulter, view **TOM SHAW'S POLE VAULT ENHANCEMENT** (COF). This training tape delivers the best "learning by doing" format to increase your pole vaulting skills.

RUNNING FASTER

If running is your specialty, before you hit the track join Alberto Salazar as he shares his personal training and racing methods with you via video. In **RUNNING FASTER** (COF), this top runner of all time covers setting goals, running style, technique and injury prevention, along with his own brand of mental preparation for the race. And **DO IT BETTER: RUNNING** (ESP) will help you do just that. Distance runners Ingrid Kristiansen and Steve Scott will show you how to reach your running goals and have fun doing it.

For runners of all levels, be sure to view **RUNNING GREAT** (COF) with Grete Waitz. This program is ideal for both men and women, and Waitz reveals her own four-part training program and strategies to help you achieve your personal best. This excellent instructional video is certain to help make you a better runner. Another superbly produced tape you may want to view is **SPRINTING** (COF) with Carl Lewis. You'll learn the techniques, principles and training system that developed Lewis into such a consistent and efficient sprinter.

In **BILL RODGERS' RUNNING FOR FUN AND FITNESS** (CEP), the marathon champion sets the pace for safe and effective running standards. Whether you run for health and fitness or competition, his helpful tips make this a most informative and enjoyable video to view. And for a unique training program for the aspiring beginner or the seasoned professional, **TRIATHALON** (COF) is a must-watch program. One of the finest triathletes in the world, Dave Scott, gives precise instruction on techniques and general training guidelines. Dave's tips and excellent video footage are certain to excite and motivate any runner.

CONDITIONING

Over the years, off-season training has become an integral part of developing athletic performance in every sport. The A.I.T.P. system was designed as a series of training drills and exercises that provide a dynamic sport movement system to enhance natural athletic ability and improve agility. **ATHLETIC INTERVAL TRAINING PROGRAM** (CEP) is an excellent view for athletes at any level of competition. Utilizing the advice in this program is sure to improve movement skills and enhance performance. You also may want to take a look at **NIKE'S TOTAL BODY CONDITIONING** (COL). Featuring the use of weights, this tape ensures total cardiovascular conditioning.

For more video help in getting yourself into top shape, be sure to take a look at **NUTRITION IN SPORTS: FUELING A WINNER** (CEP). This informative video provides an entertaining look at how body composition, the right diet and weight control play a major role in the athlete's optimal performance. For a well-rounded strength training route that targets all of the major muscle groups of your body, **ONE ON ONE** (COF) is the tape you'll want to view. This video is an excellent conditioning program to get you in shape and also allows additional variety and challenges for the already fit individual.

MEN'S CONDITIONING (COF) was developed by Glenn Swengros, a member of the President's Council on Physical Fitness. The exercises and workouts were all designed especially for conditioning the male body. For the female athlete, **WOMEN'S CONDITIONING** (COF) was produced by Dr. Fay Biles of Kent State University. Cardiovascular endurance, figure control, balance and coordination are all covered by effective exercises and fun-to-do workouts. These tapes are a great way for any athlete to get in shape and stay there.

****

For more fitness programs to help you keep up with the rigors of various sports, pick a tape from the FEEL FIT/LOOK GOOD section. Practice at home with the experts will give you the winning edge in competition. And don't forget to exercise your mind as well. Some excellent videos in the SELF-HELP chapter will help you with mental preparation.

A MEDLEY OF SPORTS

Whether for fun or serious competition, sports are popular with millions of people. Some athletes even make a very good living at the sport of their choice. While we all can't afford the time or expense of personal trainers, we can take advantage of these same great instructors via video in the privacy of our own homes.

FIELD HOCKEY

To get the lowdown on field hockey basics, why not invite the pros into your home via your VCR? **FIELD HOCKEY: THE BASICS** (COF) is hosted by Australian champions Margaret Pierce, Greg Pearl and Stephen Pratt. These field hockey greats will show you all the skills needed to become a complete field hockey player. Learn to dribble, push and flick, trap, hit and tackle as well as goal-keeping as you get a close-up look at the action and watch important maneuvers in slow motion. This video is a sure way to become the best you can be in the sport of field hockey.

Go on to improve on the basic skills you've learned by watching U.S. coach Vonnie Gros. **FIELD HOCKEY: VONNIE GROS** (COF) covers everything from dribbling to advanced techniques. This tape is certain to help you improve your field hockey skills as you head out onto the playing field.

LACROSSE

Lacrosse is another field-playing sport that is gaining popularity, and a series of videos is available to help you learn and improve at this fast-paced game. Starting with **DEFENSE: THE LONG STICKS** (COF), the viewer will learn about equipment, stance and body position, passing and catching, playing the pick, basic clearing and penalties. This is an excellent way to learn the fundamentals of Lacrosse defense. To help you aggressively take the offense on the field, **ON THE ATTACK** (COF) teaches you everything you need to know. Highlights in this program include offensive penalties, stickwork and protection, scooping and dodging and attack offense. Be sure to continue your education with **THE MIDDLE** (COF) to learn faceoffs, checking, stand-offs, cutting, shooting and all the skills needed to perfect the middle position. Wind up the course with **GOALIE: THE LAST DEFENSE** (COF). In addition to learning all the necessary skills for this important position, you'll be given expert tips and advice as the last defense to stopping the shot.

For added reinforcement of your lacrosse skills, you'll want to add the **NCAA LACROSSE VIDEO** (CEP) series to your sports instructional library. This program was specially designed and produced by the National Collegiate Athletic Association to train, instruct and inspire athletes in the sport of lacrosse. The four-tape course starts with teaching **BASIC SKILLS**. It continues with instructions in **INDIVIDUAL OFFENSE** and **INDIVIDUAL DEFENSE** that are sure to raise your playing skills to a higher level. The last tape in the series, **GOALKEEPER PLAY**, will teach you the crucial techniques needed for this important position.

WRESTLING

For the athlete interested in wrestling, an excellent video to watch is **DO IT BETTER: WRESTLING** (ESP). Wrestling coach Bob Douglas has developed a unique understanding of what it takes to become a winner, and this video will enable you to take advantage of his expertise. His tips on fundamental and advanced moves, training techniques and drills mix step-by-step demonstrations with actual match footage. This is an excellent instructional video to get you started in wrestling for fun or serious competition.

A more comprehensive knowledge of wrestling can be gained by viewing a series produced by the National Collegiate Athletic Association. **NCAA WRESTLING VIDEOS** (CEP) is a three-tape program that features top-flight college coaches who present and demonstrate many valuable tips and techniques. You'll learn everything you need to know about **TAKEDOWNS** and **ESCAPES & REVERSES**. And you can complete your education in this sport by viewing **RIDING & PINNING**. This series is certain to provide the viewer with a good basic foundation in the sport of wrestling.

Another inspiring and informative instructional series for any aspiring wrestler is **FRASER'S EDGE INSTRUCTION VIDEOS** (COF). In this three-volume program, Olympic champion Steve Fraser will show you effective methods of **HEADLOCKS** and **ARM THROWS**. The slow-motion replay will allow you to effectively learn these moves. And to further improve your performance, **FRONT HEADLOCK & COUNTERS/DEFENSE TO LEG ATTACKS** is loaded with techniques and strategies that will enable you to become a successful and winning wrestler.

From Coach Tom Evans of the University of Oklahoma comes a unique two-tape program that will prepare you for competitive wrestling. In **WRESTLING I & II** (COF), you'll begin with the basics and continue through all the techniques and skills you'll need to become effective at this sport. Each basic move is shown three times, first at normal speed and then in slow motion with frames and captions to bring out key points. A final slow-motion review allows the instructor to provide his own commentary. A worthwhile program for all levels of wrestlers.

GYMNASTICS

The National Collegiate Athletic Association makes use of some of the finest coaches in the field to teach you the skills and drills needed to become proficient at gymnastics. **NCAA GYMNASTIC VIDEOS** (CEP) is a high-quality four-tape instructional video program that covers all aspects of this demanding sport. Coach Abe Grossfeld teaches the viewer basic skills and perfecting techniques on the **POMMEL HORSE** and the **HORIZONTAL BARS**. For expert lessons on the **RINGS** and **THE PARALLEL BARS**, Coach Francis Allen teaches important tactics and strategies to improve your performance.

To learn the Mulvhill System, which is used by many elite gymnasts, just power up the VCR. The four-tape **FOUNDATIONS OF GYMNASTIC EXCELLENCE** (COF) series is an easy-to-follow program highly recommended by gymnasts and their coaches. **PAD DRILLS** will introduce you to the terminology, body positions and fundamental skills, and **BEGINNING TUMBLING** focuses on pace, body awareness and increasing strength and flexibility. To further advance your gymnastic ability, you'll also want to view **INTERMEDIATE TUMBLING** and **ADVANCED TUMBLING**. This program is an excellent aid for achieving the highest levels of success in all gymnastic events.

The **MEN'S GYMNASTICS** (COF) series was specifically designed for the male gymnast. This three-tape program covers all the aspects of tumbling, the side horse, the horizontal and parallel bars, the horse, rings and even the trampoline. This is a comprehensive course for both beginning and more advanced male athletes. For the aspiring or advanced female gymnast, the two-tape **WOMEN'S GYMNASTICS** (COF) series also covers all the different areas of gymnastics. Both of these video instructional guides are worthwhile additions to your sports library.

97

More superb instructional tapes for both men and women gymnasts are available. For some one-tape programs on gymnastics, you may want to take a look at **GYMNASTIC EXERCISES FOR MEN** (CEP) and **GYMNASTIC EXERCISES FOR WOMEN** (CEP). You'll learn the basics of the sport along with individual skills and exercises to improve your strength, grace and flexibility. Or join energetic coach Bela Karolyi in **GYMNASTICS FUN** (CEP). This tape takes you from the fundamentals through the advanced Olympic-style routines that have left audiences breathless. Color-coded sections will help you focus on the area of your choice. As the title suggests, have fun!

MORE SPORTS

What does it take to become an auto racing winner? **RACING TOUGH WITH BENNY PARSONS AND BRETT BODINE** (ESP) will give you the answer. Benny and Brett take the viewer on auto racing's toughest driving test in this exciting interactive video. You'll learn what drivers and crews do to make their machines faster than the competition. For the inside story on stock racing, be sure to view **SECRETS OF SPEED: THE STREET FIGHTERS** (ESP). A successful team will explain how to get the most speed from the production street auto. **SECRETS OF SPEED: THE RIDING STYLE OF FREDDIE SPENCER** (ESP) will take you on a high-speed ride through the development of the techniques that led to Spencer's unique riding style. Slow-motion footage demonstrates to the viewer the secrets of dirt track riding, and there are tips on street riding and race strategy.

If you have an interest in learning to fence but no instruction is readily available, try viewing **FENCING** (CEP) from the National Collegiate Athletic Association. This high-quality program will train, instruct and inspire you in the art of fencing. You'll be treated to lessons and demonstrations from some of the top fencers in the field. This is still another unique program that allows you to learn via video.

Perhaps you never thought of jumping rope as a sport, but **ROPICS: ROPE JUMPING REDEFINED** (CEP) is certain to change your mind. This video includes step-by-step instruction on fifteen basic and intermediate-level techniques of ropics. It provides the viewer with challenging goals obtainable through the mastery of exciting techniques. Experienced jumpers will benefit from **ROPICS: LEVEL 2** (CEP). This exceptional program presents more advanced step-by-step instruction on more than twenty basic to advanced-level techniques. As an added bonus, you'll enjoy an exciting demonstration by The National Ropics Precision Team.

There are also two rather unique videos you may want to view. **WINNING DARTS** (COF) will take you step by step through the game in three in-depth chapters. The Novice Player will introduce you to the fundamentals, The Competitive Player will help you improve your performance, and The Tournament Player will enable you to play against the best and win. To learn everything you always wanted to know about frisbee throwing, be sure to watch **THE FRISBEE DISC** (COF). This instructional video covers throws and catches as well as entertaining frisbee games. The program takes the viewer through the many basic and advanced techniques as well as specialized frisbee exercises. These are two very enjoyable videos.

While cheerleading might not technically be a sport, it certainly enhances sporting events. If a cheerleading camp is out of your reach, you can get the same expert instruction and advice via video. **CHEERLEADING ROUTINES** (COF) guides the viewer through all the fundamental exercises and movements, and **CHEERLEADING TRYOUT SECRETS** (COF) gives the inside tips and advice that it takes to be a winning cheerleader. For special routines, be sure to take a look at **CHEERLEADING AND DANCE** (COF). You'll learn how to choreograph a championship routine, create your own material, develop climbing and safety techniques and gain some great new material for tryouts and games.

****

The MEDLEY OF SPORTS segment is just the tip of the iceberg in the world of sports. Be sure to review all the excellent sports instructional videos available in the previous sections. And don't forget the kids. The SPORTS FOR KIDS segment is next, and the videos you'll find there are sure to give you and your children hours of education and entertainment.

SPORTS FOR KIDS

You can turn your child's play into a lifetime of enjoyment. Through video, you can help your children build confidence, enthusiasm and solid skills in the sport of their choice. Videos are a unique teaching tool for parents to enjoy with their children.

BASEBALL FOR KIDS

Coach Jerry Kindall's dedication to fundamentals, effort and teamwork have made champions of his University of Arizona Wildcats, and in **TEACHING KIDS BASEBALL WITH JERRY KINDALL** (ESP) he shares his winning techniques with your child. This is an excellent tape to build solid skills in youngsters just starting out in the game. And you can also follow Jerry along to **BASEBALL TIPS FOR KIDS** (COF), where he demonstrates proper techniques of the game and stresses teamwork and hard work as the ultimate secrets of success.

To teach kids eight and up, you'll want to take a look with them at the **LITTLE LEAGUE BASEBALL SERIES** (COF). **HOW TO PITCH & FIELD** teaches the five phases of pitch delivery and the five basic fielding drills, covering every movement. For mastery of the winning skills of offensive baseball, be sure you and your children view **HOW TO HIT & RUN**. These programs will help to develop talented young players as well as beginners.

For more educational and informative viewing, you and your children can enjoy some exceptional instructional videos together. The demonstrations and expert advice in **HITTING FOR KIDS** (COF) and **FIELDING FOR**

99

KIDS (COF) will show them all the techniques of hitting and fielding from pro instructors. And for the future Hall-of-Fame pitcher, **PITCHING FOR KIDS** (COF) is a must-view tape.

BASKETBALL FOR KIDS

BEGINNING BASKETBALL (COF) is an excellent start for teaching beginning players the basic basketball skills. The fundamentals of dribbling, passing, shooting and defensive play are all expertly covered. To help your children achieve their own personal best, be sure to view **TEACHING KIDS BASKETBALL WITH JOHN WOODEN** (ESP). Coach Wooden will show you how to teach your kids the right techniques and attitude to make basketball more rewarding and fun. For more insight into the game, your children will also want to view coach Wooden in **BASKETBALL TIPS** (COF). They'll not only learn all the proper skills but will be well on their way to developing a winning attitude. Both kids and their parents can now go one on one with Dr. J via video. **DR. J'S BASKETBALL STUFF** (COF) is both an instructional program and an enjoyable viewing experience.

FOOTBALL FOR KIDS

To help your kids develop a good basic knowledge of the game of football, you'll want to view with them **TEACHING KIDS FOOTBALL WITH BO SCHLEMBECHLER** (ESP). Besides teaching all the fundamentals of offensive and defensive football, Coach Bo stresses that safety and proper mental attitude are as important as technique to the young player. And the youngsters will be delighted with his tape **FOOTBALL TIPS** (COF) as he continues to build on their knowledge of the game.

For a unique video that is certain to appeal to both kids and their parents, be sure to view **NFL KIDS: A FIELD OF DREAMS** (COF). You'll join four NFL all-pros as they transport a quartet of young football fans to a mythical "field of dreams." The youngsters meet their heroes of the football world, Boomer Esiason, Michael Irvin, Christian Okoye and Ronnie Lott. And along the way they gain some valuable lessons on playing the game. This is a well-produced video providing a delightful viewing.

SOCCER FOR KIDS

Help kids find their soccer balance early with the teaching video **TEACHING KIDS SOCCER WITH BOB GANSLER** (COF). Coach Gansler teaches the magic of ball control, passing, heading, dribbling, shooting and shield and simple drills to help sharpen your kids' skills. In his tape **SOCCER SPORT TIPS FOR KIDS** (COF), he shares his experiences and techniques to help young players learn to build confidence and a solid soccer foundation.

For a complete junior development program, you'll want to view **SPORTS CLINIC SOCCER** (COF). This excellent program includes games and exercises to improve skills, and the unique frame-by-frame demonstrations make for easier and faster learning. The training sessions are led by pros and can be watched over and over. For a video soccer lesson with the emphasis on fun, fundamentals and fitness, **HEAD TO TOE** (COF) is the program to watch. Athlete Wayne Jentas teaches the youngsters how to be successful at the game and also have great fun.

TENNIS, GOLF & BOWLING FOR KIDS

In **TEACHING KIDS TENNIS WITH NICK BOLLETTIERI** (ESP), Coach Bollettieri teaches his methods that make tennis fun and rewarding for the child just starting out in the game. His program also teaches parents how to give a child relaxed confidence and solid skills for a foundation of life-time tennis pleasure. This is a superb tape for any aspiring young player.

Instructors from the famous Ben Sutton School are also available via video to give your youngsters private lessons. **TEACHING KIDS GOLF WITH BEN SUTTON GOLF SCHOOL** (COF) uses bright computer graphics, props and fun drills to demonstrate all the basics from tee to green, including etiquette. The program is presented in a way that's easy for kids to understand and remember.

Another excellent tape you and your children will enjoy viewing is **GOLF FOR KIDS OF ALL AGES** (COF). This fun, instruction-packed golf video features PGA tour veteran Wally Armstrong, who demonstrates golf fundamentals with his son Scott. Gabby Gator, a lovable animated character, also adds fun to this delightful program. For tips from one of golf's greatest players, your youngster will especially enjoy viewing **TREVINO'S TIPS FOR YOUNGSTERS** (CEP). Trevino's mastery of golf techniques and warm, fun-loving guidance make this tape a priceless tool for young beginners.

An expert youth bowling coach and Team USA member is available via video as the host in **TEACHING KIDS BOWLING WITH GORDON VADAKIN** (ESP). Coach Vadakin will show the youngsters specific bowling techniques. In addition to a solid foundation of the basics, they'll also learn how to successfully put together all these skills as they become bowling experts. Just as important, they'll learn the proper attitudes that will help them bowl better and have lots of fun, too.

****

*C*hildren of all ages seem to enjoy sports, and the preceding videos will help intensify their interest. But don't forget to treat your children to some of the other excellent videos designed especially for them. Tapes from the chapter on HOBBIES, CRAFTS & MORE, THE GREAT OUTDOORS chapter and even the chapter on ACADEMIA will also hold their interest and provide hours of fun.

SOURCES

(See Chapter 11 for a complete alphabetical listing of all sources with addresses and phone numbers.)

CEP	-	Cambridge Educational Products
COF	-	Champions on Film
COL	-	Collage Video
ESP	-	ESPN Home Videos
FSV	-	Fusion Video

CHAPTER 5:

THE GREAT OUTDOORS

HUNTING TECHNIQUES - LET'S GO FISHING - BOATING - WATER SPORTS - OTHER OUTDOOR RECREATION - SOURCES

HUNTING TECHNIQUES

Whether your hunting interest is strictly small game or you dream of bagging the big "trophy," there is a video available to help make you an expert before you even leave home. So take advantage of the time before hunting season begins to prepare yourself via video. An added bonus of these excellent hunting videos is the great videography. You'll not only gain expert advice in your viewing, but you'll also witness some spectacular scenes of nature.

HUNTING SMALL GAME

Before the season even begins, you can learn the art of duck hunting right at home via video. Join experienced hunter John Fox and his team of experts in **DUCK HUNTING MADE EASY** (COF). Their excellent tape takes the viewer through a step-by-step program on all the ins and outs of hunting for ducks. You'll learn the best way of locating and identifying your prey, using a blind, selecting and setting decoys and calling, and there is a segment on shooting and equipment that the viewer will find extremely helpful. This informative video will let you in on the secrets of getting more ducks. You might want to join "Cowboy Jim" Fernandez, who is the manufacturer of Yentzen Duck Calls, and Cam Signer in another outstanding tape. In **SUCCESSFUL DUCK HUNTING** (COF), they take the viewer step by step through the basics and offer their expert tips gained through years of experience. You'll also see and hear what works best in various types of ponds and marshes. Be sure to round out your education with a view of **HOW TO CALL DUCKS** (COF). Experts Mike and Roger Morton will show you how to secure an area for call and exactly how to create the several different calls you'll want to use. In addition to the excellent instruction, the viewer is sure to enjoy the actual footage demonstrating how birds react to different calls.

If turkey is on your hunting menu, a good way to learn the techniques of a turkey hunt is to join the experts in **HOW TO HUNT WILD TURKEY** (COF). Noted experts Jerry Antley, Mike Morton and Rob Hazelwood show the viewer all about turkey behavior and biology, choosing and reading habitat as well

103

as call selection and techniques. Their advice on the right time to hunt and how to choose camouflage is certain to be beneficial. And for the secrets and tactics necessary to hunt this elusive bird with bow and arrow, **GOBBLER** (PSE) is a choice view. You'll learn all the necessary techniques from expert gobbler hunter Pete Shepley and also see splendid videography of Alabama and Florida.

Another video small game hunters are sure to be interested in is **HOW TO HUNT PHEASANT & QUAIL** (COF). From experts Gary Holmes, Tom Fox and Brad Bowdino, the viewer will learn types of shotguns and loads required, habits of pheasants and quail and how to successfully locate the birds. There is also an informative segment on hunting with and without dogs, and much more, in this first-rate program. Or perhaps you'd enjoy a view of **HOW TO HUNT RABBITS AND SQUIRRELS** (COF). Join hunting experts Melvin Stewart and Bob Porter as they teach you about the best time of day to hunt, location of habitat, use of dogs, field care and preparation. This program will teach you all the tactics necessary to consistently outsmart and harvest small game.

HUNTING THE BIG ONES

Before you take to the woods this hunting season, you may want to select several videos to make your hunting experience more enjoyable and successful. If deer hunting is in your plans, you'll want to watch **DEER HUNTING MADE EASY** (COF). Hunting expert John Fox will show you the basic skills and strategy every deer hunter should know. Topics cover locating and tracking, clothing, equipment and shooting. You'll also find the segment on conservation very informative. If you've always dreamed of taking that trophy, be sure to view **HUNTING TROPHY WHITETAIL DEER** (COF). You'll learn exactly how to read the whitetail habitat as you join three of America's leading hunters, Gene Wensel, Dick Idol and Rob Hazelwood. They'll take you into the field as they demonstrate how to find productive areas, how to stalk properly, arrow and bullet placement and much more.

To learn about bowhunting one of America's favorite big game animals, a view of **WHITETAIL FEVER** (PSE) is a must. Join the experts in Nebraska's cornfields and the brush country of South Texas as you learn ratting tips and stalking techniques in detail. Or you can journey to Utah and Nevada with Pete and Laura Shepley for bowhunting the Rocky Mountain mule deer via **BUCKS ON THE FRINGE** (PSE). This expert team will show the viewer the use of treestand and ground blind techniques to take advantage of mule deer feeding and watering movements. And a great program you're sure to enjoy is **ARCHERY TIPS FOR HUNTING DEER** (COF). Professional veteran hunter Paul Brunner demonstrates all the archery tactics you need for a successful deer hunt, including field practice, target practice, scouting and stalking, wind patterns and much more.

To share in the excitement of elk hunting in the mountains of Montana, the viewer is invited to accompany two top calling experts, Larry Jones and Rob Hazelwood, in **HOW TO HUNT TROPHY ELK** (COF). The viewer will learn the art of bugling, how to call in bull elk, stalking techniques, bullet placement and more. You'll also enjoy the spectacular scenery in this well-produced video. If bowhunting is your sport, you can experience elk hunting at its best in the Rocky Mountains. In **SUCCESSFUL ELK HUNTING TECHNIQUES** (PSE), bowhunters Pete Shepley and Jerry Morrison teach all the necessary skills, including diaphragm and grunt tube calling. You'll also be treated to great visuals and spectacular scenery.

More excellent videos on bowhunting may be of interest. **THE DOUBLE CHALLENGE FOR RAMS** (PSE) is an instructional adventure that you're sure to enjoy viewing. Hunter Pete Shepley takes you stone sheep bowhunting in British Columbia and desert bighorn hunting in Arizona's Grand Canyon. For excitement at its best, you'll want to view **GRIZZLY** (PSE). The viewer will travel with expert Pete Shepley as he follows the grizzly and black bear in Alaska and the Canadian Yukon. You'll learn the techniques of bowhunting these awesome animals as well as enjoy a scenic trip through the northern wilderness.

MORE ON HUNTING

Through the use of actual field demonstrations by professional hunters, you can learn via video **HOW TO FIELD DRESS BIG GAME** (COF). This program will show the viewer all the proper steps necessary to successfully prepare game and preserve it, including how long to hang the meat to age, what temperatures must be maintained, the importance of cooling and more. For dressing deer, two excellent videos are available. **DEER SKINNING & FLESHING** (RHI) and **DEER MEAT PROCESSING** (RHI) will teach you the secrets of quality and efficiency so you'll be well prepared when you've had a successful hunt.

Many hunters spend hours of their time preparing themselves for the actual hunt, and videos are available that can help you in your pre-season warm-up. **DOVES AND SPORTING CLAYS** (COF) is an introduction to this popular shotgun range challenge. Shooting expert Ted Dewey will help you develop your wingshooting skills to their utmost, and field advisor Ray Eng explains sure-fire dove hunting patterns. For important information on **TARGET AND SKEET SHOOTING** (COF), join national champion father and son team, Gene and Bill Clawson. You'll learn all about gun and ammo selection, proper leads and gun hold points, the mental approach to breaking targets and much more. It's like having your own personal shooting instructors right in your own home.

If you do your hunting with the aid of hunting dogs, be sure to take a look at **GUN DOGS** (COF). You'll see championship hunting dogs in action and learn how to teach your prized dog how to hunt and search. Many different breeds of dogs are shown in action over all types of terrain in this informative video. A must-see program for hunters of all types and levels is **FIREARM SAFETY: RIFLES AND SHOTGUNS** (COF). Safety instructor Jeff Peterson will take you into actual field situations to teach you firearm safety as you learn the accepted NRA safety and training requirements for rifles and shotguns.

Two videos designed especially for bow hunters may be of interest to you. **CRITTER CALLIN'** (PSE) offers the bowhunter and sportsman year-round shooting opportunities. You'll learn the sport of predator calling as Dr. Ed

105

Sceery, a pro hunter and call designer, exhibits the techniques to "bring 'em in." Another excellent how-to guide you'll want to view is **BOW HUNTING MADE EASY** (COF). Expert John Fox will give you valuable information on equipment selection, basic supplies and more. His important tips will make your bow hunting more enjoyable and successful every time.

****

Since hunters tend to be outdoor people, be sure to take a look at the other videos detailed in this chapter. There's plenty there for you to do—from the mountains to the sea.

LET'S GO FISHING

Whether you relax at the "old fishing hole" or ride the waves of the ocean in search of a catch, there is a video available you're sure to enjoy. Both the novice and the more experienced can benefit from the excellent and informative fishing guides available. So before you gather up your gear, take a look at one or more of the great programs that just might help you catch "the big one" before it gets away.

FISHING TIPS

If you're hungry for information on fishing, the video for you is **TOP 100 FISHING TIPS** (BMV). The program shows the viewer all the specifics of rods, baits, boats, casting, patterns, electronics and much more. No matter what you fish for or where, these tips will help you do one thing—catch more fish. A fun and informative video for your first time out is **INTRODUCTION TO FAMILY FISHING** (COF). Fishing professional Hank Barker has filled this program with many helpful fishing tips and insight on what it takes to be successful. This fast-paced, entertaining video is sure to make your first fishing trip enjoyable and productive.

EVERYTHING YOU ALWAYS WANTED TO KNOW ABOUT FISHING BUT WERE AFRAID TO ASK (BMV) teaches you just that. This is a perfect tape to answer all your questions about equipment and techniques. From waders to knots, from reels to fish formulas, you'll learn everything you need to know to become successful at fishing. For more information to improve your catch and enjoyment, be sure to view **BEST SECRETS FOR CATCHING MORE FISH** (BMV). You'll learn about backlashing, how to dehook your hand, how to rescue a lost lure and how to outsmart the fish. The experts in this tape have a wealth of information and expert tips that can be yours just for the viewing.

DOWNRIGGING TECHNIQUES FOR ALL FISHERMEN (COF) is another excellent program, designed to teach successful techniques of the experts. You'll learn about the equipment and tactics necessary to increase both your catch and your enjoyment. For a dream come true, you'll want to view **WHY FISH STRIKE! WHY THEY DON'T!** (BMV). See what types of action, lures, baits and scents actually motivate fish to strike. The dramatic underwater footage of actual strikes will give you the advantage in your fishing trips as well as enjoyable viewing.

FLY FISHING

An excellent tape to get you started in flyfishing is **FLY FISHING FOR BEGINNERS** (COF). Ross Jackson and Gary Kemsley offer their specialized knowledge in a very simple and straightforward manner. The step-by-step tactics of fly casting are dealt with in great detail, accompanied by a complete section on tackle. This program is a must view for the beginner. To learn how to nymph fish more effectively, join fly-rod world-record-holder Jim Teeny in **BASIC NYMPH FISHING** (COF). Jim shares his knowledge of fly fishing basics, stressing subsurface techniques that will help you catch more and bigger fish. Or you may want to take a view of **FLY FISHING MADE EASY** (TSV). You'll learn how to fly cast after a few hours' practice with this outstanding program. It's the fastest, easiest way to discover the magic of fly fishing.

For more information on the basics, you may want to take a look at **BASIC FLY CASTING** (TSV). You'll find that the easy-to-learn approach in this program will have you mastering the basic casting stroke and more in no time at all. Or try another excellent instructional program on flycasting. The two-tape series **THE ESSENCE OF FLYCASTING I & II** (VTX) with Mel Krieger makes what could be dry instruction top-drawer entertainment. Krieger is a master teacher who cajoles, kids and draws you through everything from basic casting to advanced specialty presentations for problem wind and water currents. In **TOP OF THE WATER FLYFISHING TECHNIQUES** (BMV), British champion Chris Ogborne takes you through a comprehensive program containing a wealth of information for successful still-water fishing from both boat and bank.

After the basics, be sure to go on to learn more techniques you can take with you to the water. **ADVANCED FLY CASTING** (TSV) will help you improve on the basics and further enhance your fishing skills. **ADVANCED FLYFISHING TECHNIQUES: THE MAYFLY** (VTX) is possibly the ultimate instructional fishing video, showing the most advanced techniques available. You'll see astounding close-up photography of the mayfly in its underwater environment as you learn the various techniques needed to enhance your catch and your enjoyment.

For a comprehensive video course on fly fishing, you may want to take a look at **JOE HUMPHREY'S FLY FISHING SUCCESS** (COF) series. This three-tape program encompasses Joe's fifty years of fishing experience. He shares his secrets and strategies with you in **NYMPHING STRATEGY** and **DRY FLY STRATEGY**. And you'll learn his time-tested techniques in **THE FUNDAMENTALS WITH JOE HUMPHREYS**. Each video will show you various problems in a specific topic area and then offer solutions. This is a perfect program for both the novice and the more experienced.

There are many more outstanding fishing videos available for your viewing. Hal Janssen, renowned author and award-winning designer of fly patterns, shares his thirty years of experience and knowledge with you in two excellent tapes. You can learn all about dry flycasting techniques by viewing his program **THE DRY FLY** (VTX). You'll see exciting fishing sequences that will teach you about tackle basics, dry flies, how to read a stream and more. Be sure to go on to view **THE WET FLY AND NYMPH** (VTX). You'll learn this expert's theories and methods for the most rewarding and productive fly fishing you'll ever experience. There is exciting action as well as great instruction in these two first-rate videos.

FRESHWATER FISHING

In the outstanding video **AN INSIDER'S GUIDE TO TROUT FISHING** (COF), Martin Gibbs introduces the viewer to the four basic elements of trout fishing: preparation, locating the fish, rigging and presentation of bait and hooking and landing the fish. This is an excellent guide to help you catch more trout. To enjoy an on-the-stream course in successful trout fishing, be sure to watch **FLY FISHING FOR TROUT** (TSV). Gary Borger, your private tutor, demonstrates proven techniques for fishing dry flies, nymphs and streamers.

Another expert trout fisherman, Doug Swisher, is also available to teach you the ins and outs of successful trout fishing. In his **STRATEGIES FOR SELECTIVE TROUT** (TSV), the viewer will learn how to read the water and identify feeding, sheltering and prime lies plus much more. This well-produced program will give you productive and exciting strategies for catching more and bigger trout. And be sure to go on to Doug's **ADVANCED STRATEGIES FOR SELECTIVE TROUT** (TSV). You'll discover even more techniques and formulas for confidently handling difficult fishing situations.

If it's bass you're interested in, **AN INSIDER'S GUIDE TO BASS FISHING** (COF) is a must view. Fisherman Martin Gibbs guides the viewer through the skills necessary to catch trophy bass like a pro. You'll learn to rig a weight, fish with roe and more tricks to nail that big bass. For a seasonal approach to bass fishing, be sure to view **CATCHING MORE BASS WITH RENAUD PELLETIER** (COF). Take advantage of this pro's expertise as he shows you where and how to fish year-round by adjusting to changes in seasonal water temperatures and the bass's habits. These are two excellent video guides.

If you're interested in spinnerbait fishing for the big bass, you may want to take a look at **BASS MAGIC: SUPER SPINNERBAIT TACTICS** (COF). Professional fisherman Babe Winkelman shows everything you'll need to master this technique of fishing. Be sure to take advantage of this expert's experience by also viewing **LARGEMOUTH SOLUTIONS** (COF). You'll learn what big bass do when the weather gets wild and just what it takes to catch them. The techniques you'll learn in this program will have you catching bass when the other fishermen are heading for home.

Walleye is a popular fish to catch, and **WALLEYE STRIKE ZONE** (COF) explains the variety of methods for putting your bait in front of these high-hanging fish. You're certain to learn many tactics to help you catch more walleye. If you fish for crappie, you'll want to view **UNDERSTANDING CRAPPIE MAGIC** (COF). Pro fisherman Babe Winkelman will teach you how to find and catch crappie. This is an in-depth how-to guide on catching this popular fish. Known as the "King of the Freshwater Gamefish," the musky has earned a reputation as a furious fighter. If you plan to engage this fighter in a fishing war, be sure to first view **GAMEPLAN FOR SUM-MER MUSKIES** (BMV). You'll learn all the tricks of the trade that will give you the edge against this worthy competitor. And for bluegill and catfish strategies, you'll want to take a look at **CATCHING PAN FISH** (BMV). You'll learn all the necessary strategies along with tips on choosing the right bait, reading a bobber and other techniques for landing freshwater panfish.

SALTWATER FISHING

LET'S GO SALTWATER FISHING (BMV) is a great first tape for the beginning saltwater fisherman. In easy-to-learn sections, the viewer will see how to pick tackle, where to fish, how to rig the best lures, baits and hooks and how to land your catch. The program covers the most popular sportfish, such as cobia, mackerel, amberjack, snapper and tuna. This is the perfect video way to get you started on this exciting sport. If you plan to saltwater fish in the surf, you'll want to view **SURF FISHING** (BMV). This video takes you to the beaches of North Carolina as you learn to select tackle, artificial lures and the many bottom rigs that catch fish. This instructional video is enjoyable viewing.

To understand the different challenges encountered in big game fishing, an outstanding program to view is **BASICS OF BIG GAME FISHING** (BMV). You'll see, hear and experience valuable techniques on the use of a fighting chair, on using high-speed lures, on tackle selection and much more. For another invaluable guide to aid you in this popular sport, be sure to view **HOW TO CATCH BAIT FISH** (BMV). Any professional sport fisherman will tell you, "The fresher the bait, the better the catch." This video demonstrates the best methods for casting shrimp nets and other methods to ensure bait for an abundant catch. This is a great video reference to add to your fishing library.

A must-view video guide for all saltwater fishermen is the **ENCYCLO-PEDIA OF SALTWATER SPORTFISH** (BMV). This excellent production will answer your questions regarding fish identification, locations, patterns, bait, tactics and best conditions. You'll also learn how to catch forty-eight of the most popular sportfish from all around the country. For more knowledge of saltwater fish, you may also want to view **GUIDE TO INSHORE SALT-WATER FISHING** (BMV). Through a combination of on-camera instruction and action footage, you'll learn different species of fish and where, when and how to catch them. Another great how-to video guide.

Tuna is a popular fish to eat and to catch. **TUNA TACTICS** (BMV) shows albacore, yellowfin, bluefin and skipjack tuna at their fighting best. You'll learn how to get the most from your bait and tackle and how to get down for the big ones. This video will help you increase your tuna catch and fill your freezer with delicious filets. If bluefish is more to your taste, be sure to view **BLUE FISH ON LIGHT TACKLE** (BMV). You'll learn proven techniques for finding and catching these delectable fish on spinning, plug casting and flyfishing gear. Regardless of the conditions or the season, this video will enhance your fishing success.

BIG GAME FISHING TECHNIQUES (BMV) is certain to be of interest to those whose designated catch is the marlin. This program covers the life cycle of the blue marlin and gives you expert tips on best sea temperatures, bottom contours, currents and seasonal migration. This entertaining video is a sure way to learn how to hook this king of the sportfishing world. Or if you dream of hooking one of the most sought-after fish in the sea, be sure to watch **THE KING MACKEREL VIDEO** (BMV). This program shows how to get the most out of your kingfishing along with lots of fast action and great tips.

If you've ever thought about fishing for amberjack, you'll want to view **HOW TO CATCH AMERJACK** (BMV) hosted by Dr. Jim Wright, an award-winning fisherman. In this excellent video, Wright shares all the secrets you need to catch more amberjack. And he also reminds you that you don't have to kill them to enjoy catching them. If your fishing dream includes the great shark, the video to view is **SHARK FISHING MADE EASY** (BMV). You'll learn all about special tackle, bait and equipment needed and receive expert advice on catching one of these fascinating fish.

Other excellent fishing tapes are also available that are dedicated to a specific class of fish. If you're contemplating a fishing excursion on the Pacific, you're sure to enjoy watching **PACIFIC OCEAN SALMON FISHING** (BMV). Spectacular underwater footage in this video will show you all the techniques you need to be an expert salmon fisherman. Or maybe your interest lies in **ROCK COD FISHING** (BMV). This is a superb video by noted author and angler Charlie Davis. You'll learn the tactics of this popular wintertime saltwater species that will work anywhere there are deepwater bottom fish. And for detailed tips on catching one of the tastiest prizes you can get from the sea, take a look at **HOW TO CATCH SNAPPER** (BMV). You'll learn detailed information on the most popular species of snapper including red, white, grey, lane and vermillion.

MORE ON FISHING

Hosted by Homer Circle, angling editor for *Sports Afield* magazine, **TIPS ON TACKLE** (BMV) can clear up any confusion the viewer might have on fishing tackle. You'll find out about the best buys in lures, hooks and lines, along with casting techniques and when to use artificial lures. If you use any type of light tackle in your fishing experiences, you'll want to watch **LIGHT TACKLE TIPS** (BMV), which contains invaluable hints and expert advice on this particular type of fishing tackle. These are two very good tapes to add to your fishing video library.

If you're **IN SEARCH OF THE ULTIMATE LURE** (BMV), you'll certainly want to view this excellent tape. In this detailed presentation, expert Charlie White shows you the best lures in the world, both above and below the water, for all types of fish. As all fishermen know, the knots you tie can make the difference between losing and landing your fish. **FISHING KNOTS** (BMV) is a first-rate how-to video. It teaches the basics that will ensure your knots deliver their full potential in holding power. The clearly visible close-up photography makes it simple for you to learn with this video guide.

If you're going saltwater boat fishing, you won't catch many fish unless your boat is rigged correctly. In **HOW TO RIG YOUR BOAT FOR FISH-ING** (BMV), expert Gary Ross shows the viewer how he rigs his boats with fighting chairs, outriggers, downriggers and rod holders. Everything you need to know is here in this informative video. To become an expert boat handler and a better fisherman, be sure to view **BOAT HANDLING TECH-NIQUES FOR FISHERMEN** (BMV). This tape is perfect for all kinds of boats and will show you everything you need to know to handle your boat for the best fishing results.

****

*A*ll fishermen have a special affinity for the water. So be sure to take a look at the available videos in the next section, BOATING. From boating basics to water recreation, there's sure to be a program that will interest you and perhaps open up new horizons.

BOATING

No matter what type of boating craft you own, be it a rowboat, power-boat, sailboat or a yacht you're dreaming of owning, you'll want to take a look at the excellent instructional videos available in this section. Besides boat handling videos, you'll also find some first-rate guides on boat mainte-nance and safety.

BOATING BASICS

For first-time boaters, **THE BOATING BASICS** (COF) video boating guide is an excellent introductory tape. The viewer will learn all about choos-ing the right boats, boating laws, navigation rules and aids, getting underway and much more, including how to come back to dock safely. The informa-tion in this video encyclopedia of boating is the same used in state boating courses in many states. Another excellent introduction to the exciting world of boating is **THE BOATER'S VIDEO** (BMV). Created for both powerboats and sailboats, this program covers such topics as small boat handling, dock-ing and safety. This is also a great refresher course for the seasonal boater. Remember, the more you know about boating, the more fun you'll have on the water.

If you already have a powerboat or intend to buy one, the video to watch is **LET'S GO POWER BOATING** (BMV). This comprehensive video covers all the major principles of boating, including terminology, safety gear and nav-igation. The viewer will learn all the information needed to ensure years of safe and pleasurable boating. Another top-rated tape you may want to take a look at is **HIGH-PERFORMANCE BOAT HANDLING** (BMV). You'll learn how to handle your high-powered boat and pick up expert tips on docking, undocking, planing, high-speed turns and safety.

To learn more about boat handling skills, you'll also want to watch **HANDLING AND ANCHORING YOUR BOAT** (BMV). For both powerboats and sailboats, this great tape shows you exactly how to put your boat where you want it and keep it there. The viewer will learn all about docking and the required maneuvers. The anchoring section will demystify the whole subject and make you an expert on anchoring. If you have to haul your boat to the water, be sure to view **TRAILER BOAT HANDLING** (BMV). The information in this tape is presented clearly and concisely and covers everything you'll need. As an extra bonus, the viewer will also receive a reusable checklist that covers safety equipment and step-by-step procedures for proper trailering.

Another great program for *every type of boater* is **PLEASURE BOATING: THE BASICS OF BOATING** (BMV). This excellent video will teach you in detail how to plan and safely navigate a complete harbor-to-harbor cruise. You'll get information on such essentials as pre-cruise preparations, knots, boating safety, basic navigation, weather handling and rules of the road. So if you have your boat ready and your destination planned, be sure to view this great video first to ensure a most pleasurable cruise.

SAILING SKILLS

A great learn-to-sail video program, **SAILING WITH CONFIDENCE** (COF) was designed to give those with little or no sailing experience the knowledge and skills needed to sail with confidence. Expert instructor Bud Foulke takes you sailing on Lake Ontario as he covers all the basics. Or you may want to take a look at **THE SIXTY MINUTE SAILOR** (BMV). Along with the basics, you'll learn sailing theory and nomenclature. The use of graphics and computer animation as well as footage shot in San Francisco Bay make this a very enjoyable tape to watch.

Another best-selling learn-to-sail video is hosted by Olympic sailor Steve Colgate. In **LEARN TO SAIL** (BMV), he takes the viewer through a complete basic-to-intermediate sailing course. You'll learn all of the language, tips and techniques that will make you a seasoned sailor in no time. Especially for the intermediate sailor is **IMPROVE YOUR SAILING SKILLS** (BMV). This tape is for those of you who know how to get the boat going but aren't sure what to do next. You'll learn all about theory and practice from professional sailors in a step-by-step manner. This is an excellent tape for the whole family.

The **UNDER SAIL SERIES** (BMV) is a great way to bring the pleasure, beauty and sport of sailing into your home. This six-tape program starts with a hands-on introduction in **SAILING FOR NEW SAILORS**, which gets the viewer involved with the language, theory and excitement of sailing. You'll want to go on to learn about **READING THE WIND** for the key elements for sailing a marked course and **RULES OF THE SEA** for guidelines to safely conduct a vessel at sea. For the basics of rigging and sailing, including wind direction, be sure to watch **DAY SAILING** and then go on to **SAILING FOR PLEASURE** for an overview of shopping for and chartering boats. Round out your education with a view of **WINDSURFING**. This informative tape takes you cruising aboard a twenty-nine-foot racer-cruiser and even includes lessons on boardsailing. This is an excellent series for acquiring the background skills and knowledge required to ease any novice into, or reintroduce an old salt to, the exciting sport of sailing.

There are more tapes that will be of interest to the sailor. You can go aboard a forty-foot sailboat for an exciting look at **SAILING IN HEAVY WEATHER** (BMV). This is an essential course in heavy-weather sailing techniques and tactics. The viewer will learn about how to steer in large seas, heavy air sail trim, personal protection, storm tactics and more. To get the optimum in performance from your craft, you'll want to watch **TRIM FOR SPEED** (BMV) from the experts at North Sail. Through a combination of instruction, computer graphics and on-board race footage, you'll learn a wealth of trim and shape tips to increase your speed. And for **GETTING THAT EXTRA KNOT** (BMV), join Peter Isler, former America's Cup skipper, as he reveals the techniques you need to get peak performance from any sailboat. All these videos are top-notch reference guides for your sailing video library.

NAVIGATION

BASIC NAVIGATION RULES OF THE ROAD (BMV) is a perfect introduction for beginners as well as an ideal refresher for advanced boaters. The viewer will be taught about all the basic aids to navigation, such as buoys, lights, structural charts, compasses and more—everything you need to know to navigate the water correctly. Another enjoyable and informative video you'll want to see is **CELESTIAL NAVIGATION SIMPLIFIED** (COF). Join William F. Buckley, Jr. as he simply and clearly explains the theory and practice of celestial navigation using computer graphics to illuminate the finer points. Buckley's unique presentation makes this an exciting video to view.

Another navigation tape that is easy to understand, interesting and packed full of vital information is **MODERN COASTAL PILOTING** (BMV). With this tape, you'll not only learn the traditional methods of coastal piloting but also the modern methods of position determination using electronics. If you're interested in obtaining the internationally recognized navigation license, be sure to view **THE COAST GUARD LICENSE VIDEO** (BMV). This comprehensive tape not only covers the essentials of the license test but also the complete rules of the road, advanced piloting and much more. It teaches in an easy-to-understand manner and is an invaluable aid in getting your license.

One of the more common pieces of electronics on board today is VHF. To learn to use it correctly so you can communicate with clarity, safety and courtesy, you'll want to view **VHF MADE EASY** (BMV). This tape should be a must see for yourself and all your crew. And to learn more about modern marine electronics, **MARINE ELECTRONICS FOR SAILBOATS** (BMV) and **MARINE ELECTRONICS FOR POWERBOATS** (BMV) are designed to help you select the right kind of equipment for your needs and budget. Be sure to take a look at these excellent programs before investing another dollar in marine electronics.

MAINTENANCE & SAFETY

Whether power or sail, sooner or later every boat has problems. **SAFETY BOAT MAINTENANCE** (COF) will give you the knowledge to maintain your own vessel and avoid costly repairs. For that twice-a-year extra measure of attention your craft needs, take a look at two excellent tapes to guide you through the complete processes. **WINTERIZING YOUR BOAT** (BMV) will teach you everything you need to know to protect your boat during the long winter months. For the special attention your boat needs after the winter months, be sure to view **SPRING COMMISSIONING** (BMV). You'll learn the complete spring fitting-out procedures to follow before your boat is launched.

To become thoroughly knowledgeable about boating safety, you and your crew will want to view **THE SAFETY AT SEA** (BMV) series. For the purchase, use and storage of fire-fighting gear, **FIRE PREVENTION** is an excellent tape to start with. Be sure to go on to **PERSONAL FLOTATION DEVICES** to learn the correct selection, usage and storage of these important safety devices, which includes tips on how to utilize ordinary clothing as emergency PFD's. You'll be able to handle emergency situations efficiently if you've had a look at **VISUAL DISTRESS SIGNALS**. This tape shows you all about flares and other devices and also covers Coast Guard regulations regarding their use and replacement. These three tapes cover the most important life-saving topics afloat.

Further beneficial viewing to prepare yourself for any boating emergency is **COLD WATER SURVIVAL** (BMV). This educational program discusses hypothermia, vital survival tips and flotation devices along with recognition, prevention and treatment. For emergency techniques for lifecraft use and survival, **ABANDON SHIP** (BMV) is indispensable. Hopefully, you will never need the advice on this tape, but if you do, this program will teach you all the proven techniques you will need to survive. These tapes are well-produced and should be viewed by all crew members.

MORE BOATING TIPS

Become a better mariner by learning the weather basics that good seamanship demands. **WEATHER, YOU AND BOATING** (COF) will teach the viewer how to read signs of various weather conditions through observation of the clouds, sunsets and sunrises and wind directions. Watching this superb tape will decrease your chances of being a victim of bad-weather boating. A must for East and Gulf Coast boat owners is **MARINE HURRICANE PREPAREDNESS** (BMV). This clear-cut program will show you how hurricanes form, their destructive power and most importantly what steps you can take to protect yourself and your marine property. These are two first-rate programs.

USEFUL KNOTS FOR BOATMEN (BMV), produced by the Coast Guard, is one of the best tapes on the subject. The most common and useful knots for boatmen are depicted clearly and concisely as the viewer is taught the proper usage. For more instruction in proper knot-tying skills, **TEACH YOURSELF KNOTS AND SPLICES** (BMV) lets you learn at your own speed how to tie all the basic knots reliably and comfortably. A unique feature of this tape is a special section for left-handers. Both these programs are valuable aids to enhance your seamanship skills.

If you're in the boat-buying market, you'll want to take a look at either **HOW TO BUY A POWERBOAT (BMV) or HOW TO BUY A SAIL-BOAT** (BMV). These tapes are designed to help guide the viewer through the maze encountered when purchasing either a new or used craft. You'll discover information about the types of vessels and their uses, maintenance, construction, bank financing and the role of dealers, brokers and insurance agents. These tapes are a must if you are planning to purchase the boat of your dreams. For a concise, yet thorough introduction to boat insurance, you may want to view **BOAT INSURANCE MADE EASY** (BMV). This tape will definitely help you save money.

****

*F*or more fun on the water, be sure to take a look at the WATER SPORTS section of this chapter, which follows. Videos are available to help you enjoy water even more, be it diving or snorkeling, skiing or swimming.

WATER SPORTS

There are all kinds of fun to be had on the water, and there are all kinds of videos to help you achieve that fun. Whether your forte is diving and snorkeling, skiing or swimming, take advantage of an expert's advice through an instructional video guide before you hit the water.

DIVING & SNORKELING

There is a lot more to the sport of snorkeling than you think, but you can gain all the knowledge you'll need by viewing **LEARN SNORKELING** (BMV). The in-depth instruction and easy-to-follow demonstrations will show you the techniques of basic snorkeling, advanced skindiving techniques and open water snorkeling. By viewing this excellent program first, you can be sure your next expedition will be a safe and enjoyable one. To go from nervous beginner to "I can't get enough of scuba," be sure to view **THE WORLD OF SCUBA** (BMV). This humorous video will introduce you to a captivating sport. Be sure you sign up for the **SCUBA VIDEO REFRESHER COURSE** (BMV). This complete review of basic scuba diving will be very beneficial to the novice diver as well as the more experienced.

For those who are learning to dive in cold-water areas, **SCUBA: THE FIRST TIME** (BMV) is the official PADI diving instructional video. Hosted by Australia's Paul Mugglestone, it teaches all the techniques used by this expert. For warm-water divers, **THE OPEN WATER EXPERIENCE** (BMV), filmed in Florida, is an excellent introduction for the novice and the perfect way for seasonal divers to keep their skills from rusting. You'll also learn all the techniques needed to get certified as a scuba diver.

Other video guides on this enjoyable sport include **SCUBA GEAR MAINTENANCE** (BMV). The viewer will learn proper upkeep and routine repair of diving equipment. In addition, the knowledge and understanding will allow you to save your money for dive travel rather than spending it all on equipment. To make your dive trip much more enjoyable, be sure to see **PACKING FOR DIVE TRAVEL** (BMV). This excellent video will help you eliminate anxiety as you are taught how to take inventory by your own dive and pack master.

WATERSKIING & BOARDSAILING

To get started in the wild and wet world of waterskiing, you'll want to view **BEGINNING WATERSKIING** (BMV). This is a program for all those viewers who thought waterskiing was too difficult to learn. You'll be able to master all the basics, including equipment options, water starts and hand signals. For more expert instruction, you may also want to view **WATERSKIING FUNDAMENTALS** (BMV). Through the use of multiple-angle photography and slow-motion filming, the pros will show you all the elements involved in this fast-paced sport. After viewing these superb videos, you'll be out of the house and on the water in no time.

To enhance your newfound skill on waterskiis, be sure to take a look at **IMPROVE YOUR WATERSKIING SKILLS** (BMV). Following a short review of basic instruction, the viewer will learn to do the big spray and jump wakes among other more advanced techniques. To master all the facets of this thrilling sport, a view of **WATER SKIING WITH BRETT WING** (BMV) is a great way to go. Everything you need to know is explained in an understandable and entertaining manner that makes learning a pleasure.

If you're interested in the exhilarating sport of boardsailing, you'll want to view some of the tapes from the experts. You can learn the basics from Olympic silver medalist Ann Gardner-Nelson and pro expert Rich Myers in **BEGINNING BOARDSAILING** (BMV). All the hows and whys involved in equipment, starts and jibs are shown through on-the-water demonstrations. And be sure to continue with the experts in **INTERMEDIATE BOARD-SAILING TECHNIQUES** (BMV) as you learn to perfect your starts, turns and freestyle techniques. This video is just the ticket for those of you who set your sights on being the best.

Another excellent video for getting started is **BOARDSAILING I: LEARNING THE BASICS** (ESP). This comprehensive look at boardsailing basics features champion boardsailor Nevin Sayre, who demystifies the challenge of this increasingly popular sport. Once you've mastered the basics, go for the excitement of a shortboard. In **MASTERING THE SHORT-BOARD** (BMV), Sayre takes your boardsailing to the edge as he shows you how to control your board and get the best ride when the waves leave others on the beach.

The hottest new watersport today is ski boarding. This free-spirited sport, also known as wakeboarding or skurfing, derives most of its maneuvers from snowboarding and skateboarding rather than waterskiing. **SKI BOARDING MADE EASY** (BMV) is an excellent video that will show you all you need to get in on the fun. For even more adventures, you may want to try kneeboarding. In **THE KNEEBOARD AUTHORITY** (BMV), expert Ted

Bevelacqua takes you through all the basics, along with fifteen of this sport's most fascinating maneuvers.

SWIMMING

Sue Royston, a certified swim instructor, is available via video to expertly guide you in teaching your child to swim. **SWIM LESSONS FOR KIDS** (COF) uses a unique method that is fun for everyone. This popular video how-to is recommended for children three years of age and up. Or maybe you'd prefer Olympic gold medalist John Naber to do the teaching. In **TEACHING KIDS SWIMMING** (ESP), he covers the basics of swimming and essential skills, then combines them to make a basic stroke. The simple, step-by-step instructions in this program will have your kids swimming in no time.

Swimming lessons aren't just for the young, and **SWIMMING** (COF) is geared to kids of all ages. Learn to swim with confidence as this program takes you step by step through all the fundamentals. Or you can join Olympic swimmers in **BASIC TECHNIQUE: FROM THE FAST LANE** (COF). This program shows the key components of each stroke in live-action demonstrations. In no time at all you'll be ready to go to **ADVANCED TECHNIQUE: FROM THE FAST LANE** (COF) to perfect your strokes and technique. State-of-the-art underwater photography makes these very enjoyable swimming instructional videos to view.

Specially made under the supervision of the Amateur Swimming Association of Great Britain, **SWIMMING STROKES** (COF) is another exciting and informative video. Underwater cameras provide the viewer with a detailed and revealing analysis of swimming strokes. To learn more about the basic swimming techniques that have shaped champions, **BACK CRAWL, BREAST STROKE AND TURNS** (COF) is the tape to watch. This program breaks down the techniques into progressive steps and provides drills to help you develop your style.

To **SWIM SMARTER, SWIM FASTER** (BMV), be sure to watch this first-rate video. Dramatic underwater photography reveals the drills, practice routines and stroke techniques needed to master the fundamentals of competitive swimming. Or you may want to join John Naber, champion of the Montreal Olympic Games, in **GETTING BETTER** (COF). This pro brings to the viewer via video many championship techniques in an entertaining and motivating way. Both these tapes are excellent viewing as well as superb teaching aids to help you swim like a champion.

****

*I*f you've enjoyed one or more of the excellent videos in this section, it's a sure bet you enjoy the water. Maybe one of the great videos detailed in the BOATING section would also be of interest to you. Why not take a look?

OTHER OUTDOOR RECREATION

The great outdoors holds opportunities for many different activities. And videos can help you brush up on your skills or open the door to new adventures. Do your learning at home in front of your VCR and then head on outside for some great fun.

ARCHERY FOR FIELD OR TARGET

Now you can learn the basics of archery from the experts via video. **SELECTING, TUNING, AND SHOOTING GUIDE FOR MODERN COMPOUND BOWS** (PSE) is a comprehensive, basic guide to selecting and fitting modern archery equipment. This program is easy to follow and understand and contains information every archer will find useful, whether novice or veteran. You'll also want to view **UNDERSTANDING ARROW FLIGHT** (PSE). This informative and educational program demonstrates techniques that will improve any archer's understanding of arrow flight and an arrow's relationship to every part of the compound bow.

To learn more about the shooting form, be sure to view **UNDER-STANDING SHOOTING FORM** (PSE). The viewer will see demonstrated the ten basic steps of shooting form that lead to consistent and accurate shooting. You'll learn about stance, breathing, aiming, follow-through and more. And to help you put this knowledge to work in harvesting big-game animals, **MASTERING SHOT PLACEMENT** (PSE) is the tape to view. You'll not only learn how to shoot but, equally important, where to shoot.

For more informative tapes on archery, either for field or target, you may want to take a look at **UNDERSTANDING BOWHUNT SIGHTS** (PSE). This educational program shows the viewer how to select the right bowhunting sight and teaches the basics of sight installation and leveling. Also view **UNDERSTANDING ARROW MAKING** (PSE) to see how and why making your own arrows is a critical step in obtaining consistent accuracy. You'll get the advantage of a pro's techniques for consistent arrow-making results. If you're interested in practicing your new skills with a mechanical release aid, you'll want to view **UNDERSTANDING RELEASE AIDS** (PSE). The viewer is treated to live-action demonstrations on selection, preparation and set-up, step-by-step practice secrets and much more.

SNOW SKIING

Former Olympics winner and veteran instructor Hank Kashiwa can help make your child's first downhill ski experience safe, rewarding and fun. Join this expert in **TEACHING KIDS SKIING** (ESP). This is an outstanding instructional video that will provide parents with advice on proper technique, equipment and preparation in teaching your children this popular sport. Or you can let professional skier Craig Beck teach your child how to ski right at home. By viewing **TEACH YOUR CHILD TO SKI** (COF), you and your children can learn all the fundamentals before hitting the slopes. The learning will be easy and fun with this first-rate instructional tape.

For beginning skiers of all ages, **FUNDAMENTALS OF DOWNHILL SKIING** (COF) is an excellent way to get started. U.S. Demonstration Team instructors Chris Ryman and Jens Husted identify the building blocks for successful skiing. Slow-motion sequences, close-ups and computer-enhanced graphics make it easy to understand the basic ski fundamentals to help you become proficient at this exciting sport. Or you may want to take a look at **DOWNHILL SKIING BASICS** (COF). Expert skier Gordy Skoog hosts this excellent video and shows all the various techniques, from snowplowing to parallel skiing.

Whether you're a beginner or an aspiring expert, **SKI BETTER NOW** (COF) is designed to help you learn exactly what you need to know to ski better. This program will push you to new levels of ability and open the door to new ski experiences as you learn from top teaching pros. For your own pro instructor right in your home, be sure to see **SKIING WITH JEAN-CLAUDE KILLY** (COF). This three-time Olympic gold medalist demonstrates the fundamentals of downhill skiing and shares helpful tips to improve your skiing technique.

If your skiing skills range from intermediate to advanced, a beneficial video for you is **SKIING TECHNIQUES** (COF). The viewer is treated to demonstrations by world ski pro-champion Peter Bogner, who gives valuable tips to help enhance your performance. You'll also learn about pre-season conditioning, injury prevention and ski tuning. To become the skier you've always dreamed of being, be sure to view **SKI WITH ANDY MILL** (COF). This Olympic downhill racer takes the viewer through more than twenty ski techniques. You'll get valuable advice on such topics as balance points on skis, using your brakes, pole plant, turning control, active and passive turns and much more.

Whether a beginner or an expert, the viewer is sure to enjoy **MOGUL SKIING TECHNIQUES** (COF). This program is an exciting visual explanation that makes sense of moguls. You'll learn from Coach Peter Jacobs how every skier can smooth out the bumps and just what the best mogul skiers are really doing. For a comprehensive study of contemporary Alpine skiing techniques, you'll want to watch **ALPINE SKI SCHOOL** (COF). This program is invaluable for alpine skiers who know they can always ski a little better. As you carve and glide down a snow-laden carpet via this video, the spectacular videography makes every turn a unique sensation.

Via **CROSS COUNTRY SKIING FOR BEGINNERS** (ESP), you can travel to Oregon's Mount Bachelor with Olympic medalist Bill Koch for a beginner's course in the fundamentals of this fun and healthy sport. Along with beginning skating techniques, Bill's training includes segments on getting on skis for the first time, learning to walk on skis, the step turn, uphill and downhill methods and more. For more instruction in this athletic skiing form, you can join one of the world's top skiers in **CROSS-COUNTRY SKIING** (COF). Jeff Nowak will teach the viewer every important fundamental of Nordic cross-country skiing, including the perfect diagonal stride, the double-pole technique, telemark position and more. This tape was beautifully filmed in Colorado and reinforced with great music.

ULTIMATE CYCLING

THE COMPLETE CYCLIST (COF) is an exciting program that covers everything a cyclist needs to know. The viewer will learn how to select the proper equipment, riding techniques and more. There is also a special section on road repairs and preventive maintenance tips that is certain to be of use. For all road racers, bi- and tri-athletes, and Tour de France hopefuls, **JOHN HOWARD'S LESSONS IN CYCLING** (NUQ) is a veritable treasure trove of hard-won secrets from a world champion. Ride along with John and discover the best tools for custom bike fitting, energy-efficient body positioning, paceline and echelon tactics and much more. This is an excellent and unique video guide to cycling.

To learn how to select, ride, race and maintain your mountain bike, you'll want to take a look at **THE GREAT MOUNTAIN BIKING VIDEO** (NUQ). This is an excellent program for anyone who ever wanted to know what mountain biking is all about. Be sure to continue your education in this fascinating sport by also viewing **ULTIMATE MOUNTAIN BIKING** (NUQ). This video shows mountain biking at its finest as you learn advanced techniques and winning strategies from the experts. Both these tapes contain useful how-to information as well as exciting race coverage and spectacular visuals.

To gain an understanding of how the parts of your bike work together, you'll want to view either **ROAD BIKE ANATOMY: ASSEMBLY, CARE, UPGRADES** (NUQ) or **MOUNTAIN BIKE ANATOMY: ASSEMBLY, CARE, UPGRADES** (NUQ). Both these tapes will give the viewer the general knowledge needed to recognize and overcome or even avoid mechanical problems. You'll learn to handle basic maintenance and repair, as well as gain a clear overview of bicycle form and function. The unique visuals and concise narratives show how to install, adjust and care for your bike.

MORE OUTDOOR RECREATION

For some great outdoor fun, you may want to learn the **FUNDAMENTALS OF ROWING** (COF). Join your personal rowing coach, Steve Larson, as he teaches you all the basics, from boat selection to proper rowing technique. As a special bonus, you'll also learn the secrets of the pros that turn beginners into experts. If a canoe is your choice of travel, be sure to watch **INTRODUCTION TO CANOEING** (COF). You'll learn to select the canoe and accessories that are right for you, as well as the correct canoe strokes. For further adventure, you'll also learn how to read the current and how to run the rapids.

Many people enjoy vacationing in the wilderness, and there are videos available to help make the experience more enjoyable. **BACKPACKING MADE EASY** (COF) is a beginner's guide that covers all the important aspects of backpacking. The viewer will learn what clothes and food to take, all about tents and sleeping bags, how to cook in the wild and more. To go camping with confidence, be sure to take a look first at **HOW TO ENJOY CAMPING FROM YOUR VERY FIRST TRIP** (COF). This excellent guide will help you plan and carry out a perfect trip.

Another easy step-by-step guide you may want to watch to prepare yourself for an outdoor adventure is **FINDING YOUR WAY IN THE WILD** (COF). This tape will teach you everything you need to know about maps and compasses and plotting your course through the wild. To prepare for any mountains on your course, see **BASIC ROCK CLIMBING** (COF), a video that literally starts at ground zero. Filmed in spectacular Yosemite Valley, this program takes the viewer through all the equipment and techniques essential to rock climbing. The step-by-step coverage is both informative and inspiring.

Playing horseshoes is a popular outdoor pastime, and now there's a video that can help you become more proficient. **HOW TO PITCH MORE RINGERS** (COF), the only instructional tape on the game, is hosted by world champion Carl Steinfeldt. This pro offers the viewer fifty tips on how to pitch horseshoes, from breathing to footwork. If the whole horse, not just the shoes, interests you, **HORSEBACK** (COF) is an introduction to riding hosted by top professional coaches. The carefully chosen sequences explain to the viewer exactly how to master the basic techniques right from the start. Or you might want to take a look at **STEPHANIE POWERS' GUIDE TO HORSEBACK RIDING AND CARE** (FSV). Stephanie and her magnificent horse show the viewer the basics of English- and Western-style riding and how to care for these beautiful animals. You'll learn everything you need to know, including trail etiquette, to get you ready to saddle up.

****

For more outdoor recreation, take a look at the SPORTS, SPORTS & MORE SPORTS chapter. There are some great videos available on outside sports. These tapes can help you brush up on your skills or perhaps interest you in learning a new sport to enjoy outdoors.

SOURCES

(See Chapter 11 for a complete alphabetical listing of all sources with addresses and phone numbers.)

BMV	-	Bennett Video Group
COF	-	Champions on Film
ESP	-	ESPN Home Videos
FSV	-	Fusion Video
NUQ	-	New & Unique Videos
PSE	-	Precision Shooting

RHI	-	Rinehart Industries
TSV	-	Three M Sportsman's Video
VTX	-	Video Textbooks

CHAPTER 6:

ACADEMIA

TEACHING YOUNG CHILDREN - LIFELONG LEARNING - OFF TO COLLEGE - SOURCES

TEACHING YOUNG CHILDREN

Many children, as well as adults, think of the home TV only as a source of entertainment. Even the stores advertise "entertainment centers" to hold your TV and VCR. But with the advent of instructional videos, even the youngest child can be educated at the same time they're being entertained. Take a look at the excellent videos detailed below that are available to make learning fun for your children.

LEARNING ABOUT NUMBERS

One of the most basic skills children can learn about is numbers and math, and many excellent videos are available to make the learning fun. **CLIFFORD'S FUN WITH NUMBERS** (SMV) is a fully animated program from the Scholastic Learning Library that is excellent for preschoolers. Your children will join some delightful characters at a birthday party and learn all about numbers as they count candles, balloons, favors and guests. For more fun with numbers, treat your children to a view of **SCHOOL ZONE: NUMBERS 1-10** (SMV). Even the youngest kids can learn to recognize numbers and to count with this animated program from the School Zone Start-To-Learn Library. And every child is certain to be entranced by Richard Scarry's popular characters in his **RICHARD SCARRY'S BEST COUNTING VIDEO EVER** (SMV). This fully animated program features catchy original songs that will have your children clapping their hands as well as learning their numbers.

From the well-known publishers of Golden Books, more fun learning is available with their Golden Step-Ahead Videos. Developed by educators and educational media specialists, **WORKING WITH NUMBERS** (SMV) combines learning the basics with fun and repeatable entertainment. When the youngsters have mastered that excellent program, they'll be ready to move on to **GET READY FOR MATH** (SMV), another Golden Step-Ahead for skill-building fun. These tapes are especially designed to appeal to ages two to eight. For a change of pace, treat your kids to a video from the Little Schoolhouse Action series. In **ALL ABOUT NUMBERS** (SMV), the Schoolhouse puppets turn solid educational principles into learning fun as they recount the numerous uses of numbers.

123

For more interactive learning experiences for your preschooler, an excellent choice is a video from Bill Cosby's series. In **PICTURE PAGES: WHO'S COUNTING** (SMV) and **PICTURE PAGES: NUMBERS** (SMV), this popular TV father will help your children develop important number skills and entertain them at the same time. Recommended by the National Education Association, each of these outstanding videos comes with two colorful activity books. Another perennial children's favorite, TV host Captain Kangeroo, is also available to come in and tutor your kids. They can join the Captain and his friends, Mr. Moose and Bunny Rabbit, in **COUNTING WITH THE CAPTAIN** (SMV) as they try to count how many cute little puppies there are. A favorite of children and parents for years, "Sesame Street" videos can make learning about numbers fun. The delightful Muppets will entertain and educate as your children enjoy viewing **LEARNING TO ADD & SUBTRACT** (RHV) and **LEARNING ABOUT NUMBERS** (RHV). These live-action programs are sure to be a favorite with the kids, and they also come with a great activity book. Now "Sesame Street" time can be anytime you choose.

Children ages two to five can join Agent 07734 from America's Necessary Numbers and Needed Numerals Department in **HELLO NUMBERS** (SMV). With interactive games, songs and count-alongs, this video makes learning numbers easy and fun. The kids will be educated and delighted as Agent 07734 teaches his video pals to count from one to ten and by tens to one hundred. Agent 07734 then moves on to the three to seven age group in **IT'S A PLUS—LEARN TO ADD** (SMV), which is also loaded with songs and rhymes in a truly interactive format. Both these programs are highly recommended by the Video Rating Guide for Libraries. For more musical math fun, **THE STORY OF NUMBERS** (SMV) is an excellent view. This entertaining musical video introduces children to the meaning of numbers and their relationship to each other. It's a great way to help preschoolers and early graders with arithmetic.

Moving on to math, **WORKING WITH NUMBERS** (SMV) uses musical fun to teach math basics. The kids will join Meggie and her friends in their playroom as they try to solve her math problems with some energetic make-believe songs. For more live-action dancing and upbeat sing-a-long lyrics, a video that is certain to hold your children's interest is **HIP HOP MATH** (SMV). This rap-ability math program also uses captivating graphics to help them master 1200 basic multiplication facts. For learning math the time-tested 3 x 5 card approach, the **LEARN TO: MATH** series provides an entertaining interactive program on understanding mathematics. Children will **LEARN TO: ADD** (SMV) and **LEARN TO: SUBTRACT** (SMV) with the latest in computer graphics. And they'll watch, play along and have fun while they **LEARN TO: MULTIPLY** (SMV) and **LEARN TO: DIVIDE** (SMV).

THE ASSISTANT PROFESSOR SERIES is especially designed to help children grades four and up to conquer the many facets of math. Using colorful animations and graphics, **ALL ABOUT ANGLES** (SMV) and **THE WORLD OF CIRCLES** (SMV) explain these important math concepts in easy-to-follow lessons. **WHICH WAY IS MINUS?** (SMV) introduces and develops the concept of negative and positive, and **WHAT IS AREA?** (SMV) contains excellent simple-to-understand explanations of squares, rectangles, parallelograms and triangles. To round out their math knowledge, be sure to have your children join the Assistant Professor in **WHAT ARE VARIABLES**? (SMV). They'll learn all about mathematical sentences and unknown numbers as they delve further into the fascinating world of math.

HISTORY & GEOGRAPHY

To introduce your child to the intriguing world of history, there are some fascinating educational programs available via the VCR. The **TELL ME WHY** series answers some of history's most intriguing questions while capturing your child's imagination. These tapes are suitable for children of all ages, and parents will enjoy watching along with them. An excellent tape to start with is **BEGINNINGS: CIVILIZATION AND GOVERNMENT** (SMV). This tape takes the viewer on a voyage to the source of our society's customs and most cherished institutions. Children will be entertained as they learn answers to puzzling questions like: Where was the first city? How was cooking discovered? Who wrote the first laws? Who built the first fire truck? **AMERICANA** (SMV) is a great program that covers such topics as: What is the Liberty Bell? When did the Vikings visit America? and much more. It also gives your child the fascinating facts about American symbols, presidential headquarters, branches of government and much more.

For more entertaining education in American history, an excellent choice that will delight children is **SCHOOL HOUSE ROCK: HISTORY** (SMV). This tape is certain to hold your children's interest as they learn through song and animation all about American history. They'll be entertained with facts on the Revolution, the Constitution, passing laws, voting rights and more. For an educational tape that combines history and the latest in computer graphics to entertain and teach kids, see **LEARN TO: PRESIDENTS OF THE UNITED STATES** (SMV). This very well produced program features portraits, photographs and interactive data screens that allow your child to travel through time. Children of all ages, as well as their parents, are certain to enjoy this tape.

Another effective way to have children learn about history is to let them visit, via video, with some of the outstanding people who made that history. Your children can join a lovable cast of puppets and their Magic Time Machine as they travel through the **GREAT MOMENTS IN HISTORY** series learning about the everyday happenings of famous people throughout history. You can start your historical journey with **A VISIT WITH CHRISTOPHER COLUMBUS** (BSG) as he is about to discover the new world, then learn an important historical lesson in speaking up for oneself when you have **A VISIT WITH MILES STANDISH** (BSG). Continue on your journey with **A VISIT WITH PAUL REVERE** (BSG) and get a bit of homespun advice and adventure as you enjoy **A VISIT WITH AN AMERICAN PIONEER** (BSG). Travel back in time for **A VISIT WITH BETSY ROSS** (BSG) as she makes the first American flag and learn the real truth about flying a kite when you have **A VISIT WITH BEN FRANKLIN** (BSG). And don't end your trip until you have had **A VISIT WITH GEORGE WASHINGTON** (BSG) and another exciting adventure during **A VISIT WITH TEDDY ROOSEVELT'S ROUGH RIDERS** (BSG).

SCIENCE & NATURE

The **TELL ME WHY** series is a virtual video encyclopedia designed to capture your children's imagination as they learn about the exciting world of science. **SCIENCE, SOUND AND ENERGY** (SMV) is a great way for children of all ages to learn the facts about modern science. This excellent tape answers all their questions about archeology, physics and chemistry in a fun yet educational way. **HOW THINGS WORK** (SMV) will hold children's attention as they learn the answers to such questions as: What is an electric eye? How are tape recordings made? What is television? What makes a car go? How does a washing machine work? These innovative videos are certain to entertain and educate over and over again.

To let your child see what water is and explain such puzzlers as what makes the weather, you'll want to continue on with the series and view **WATER AND WEATHER** (SMV). Rain, storms, wind, fog and snow are just some of the fascinating subjects covered by this excellent program. To learn where soil and sand come from and why there are so many different kinds of rocks, be sure to view **GEMS, METALS AND MINERALS** (SMV). Information on gems, elements, metals, minerals and coal is presented in a delightful way to entertain and educate. **FLIGHT** (SMV) is another superb video from this series that includes questions like: Why can't man fly? What are satellites? What is the Apollo Program? Then you and your children are certain to want to go on to view **SPACE, EARTH AND ATMOSPHERE** (SMV). You'll see how big the universe is as you learn all about gravity, stars, comets, the solar system, the sun and the moon.

All children are fascinated by space fantasy, and an excellent way to educate them in this vast subject is by viewing the two-tape program **OUR SOLAR SYSTEM.** Take a fun and informative voyage aboard a home-made spacecraft to **THE OUTER PLANETS** (SMV) in our solar system. You and your children will visit Jupiter, the giant of giants, and experience Saturn, the lord of the shimmering rings. You'll encounter the topsy-turvy giant of Uranus, see the intensely cold clouds of Neptune and then view Pluto huddled near its companion moon. Be certain to continue your solar system journey with a visit to **THE INNER PLANETS** (SMV). Packed with spectacular video footage, photographs and animations, this program gives interesting facts about all the inner planets—from the smooth plains of Mercury to the frigid mega-mountains of Mars.

To help kids achieve an understanding of the different kinds of energy, **I LIKE SCIENCE** (SMV) is an excellent choice to watch. Kids will have fun learning how a lightbulb works and the principles of electricity. They'll be entertained and educated at the same time as they learn about the scientific principle of persistence and the varied influences of the sun. To introduce them to the concept of weather, a selection from Mr. Know-It-Owls video school, **ALL ABOUT WEATHER** (SMV), is available for their enjoyment. This live-action program is full of cartoons, puppets and sing-alongs to help even the youngest child discover what makes the temperature change and what causes the wind.

Kids often learn best by doing, and **MY FIRST SCIENCE VIDEO** (SMV) is a colorful, easy-to-follow guide for fun activities using everyday materials found around the home. This fun program covers fascinating topics, with experiments that are easy to perform and fun to do while also being educational. For more simple science projects that can be done at home, **SCIENCE DISCOVERY FOR CHILDREN** (SMV) contains fascinating projects aimed at stimulating the viewer. More than fifteen experiments illustrate capillary action, surface tension, indicator dyes, magnets and more science theories. Your children will want to view these two great hands-on programs time and time again as they have fun while they learn.

The **TELL ME WHY** video encyclopedia series contains some excellent tapes to teach your children about nature and satisfy their curiosity about the world around them. Let your children see what one-celled plants are and just what botany is in **FLOWERS, PLANTS AND TREES** (SMV). They'll also learn about plant growth, seeds and bulbs, flowers, forestry and nature's oddities. **INSECTS** (SMV) will show them just what a moth is and how a butterfly smells, as well as answer all their puzzling questions about other insects they see. Turn your living room into a zoo with the informative and colorful footage of a diverse group of **MAMMALS** (SMV) and the captivating footage of **BIRDS AND RODENTS** (SMV). Then be sure to plunge into the intriguing deep-sea world to discover the innermost secrets of **FISH, SHELLFISH AND UNDERWATER LIFE** (SMV). These well-produced videos will provide you and your children with hours of entertaining and educational viewing.

Even the smallest of children are fascinated by animals, and several excellent videos are available to teach them the value of the animal kingdom. **LITTLE SCHOOLHOUSE: ALL ABOUT ANIMALS** (SMV) is especially for the preschooler to learn how animals affect us, our environment and our attitudes. Bill Cosby's **PICTURE PAGES: ANIMALS** (SMV) is an interactive learning experience geared toward the preschooler and recommended by the National Education Association. For tots as young as one year and up, a unique and delightful video is **FARM ANIMALS: CLOSE UP AND VERY PERSONAL** (SFP). This gem is a unique substitute for hanging around a barn or driving by a pasture and yelling "Moo" at the cows. Children's voices introduce each animal segment, but otherwise the animals make all the sounds. This is a lively, wholesome video that exposes children to live farm animals and the sights and sounds of the barnyard.

For hands-on experience, **MY FIRST NATURE VIDEO** (SMV) is recommended for ages five and up. Kids will discover how much fun nature can be by planting seeds, making creepy crawly traps or growing a miniature garden in a bottle. The award-winning program **SHARING THE JOY OF NATURE** (SMV) is designed to help children of all ages enjoy the beauty of nature. Children's author Joseph Cornell shares eight of his most popular nature-awareness activities and demonstrates nature games. Filmed in the High Sierras and Yosemite National Park, this excellent program is a choice view.

Science and nature very often overlap in the educational process, and a popular PBS series, **NEWTON'S APPLE**, combines these two fascinating subjects. These Emmy-Award-winning videos are all presented through a kid's eye-view. **PLASTIC SURGERY, TORNADOES, BICYCLES AND MORE** (SMV) has the enthusiasm to make learning fun, and **ARTIFICIAL HEART, PENGUINS, FIRE AND MORE** (SMV) is enlivened with demonstrations that are often amusing and always thought-provoking. How Einstein would explain his theories if he could tell you himself is found in

127

BOOMERANGS, MUSCLES AND BONES, BEARS AND MORE (SMV), and interesting facts and ways to explore the world in a new way are presented in **SKIING, BLIMPS, BEAVERS AND MORE** (SMV). You and your children can also learn all about **MUMMIES, TIGERS, HELIUM AND MORE** (SMV) or **DINOSAURS, BULLETPROOF GLASS, WHALES AND MORE** (SMV).

ABC'S & READING

The perfect introduction to the alphabet for young children is **MR. MEN IN THE GREAT ALPHABET HUNT** (SMV). Using the phonetic approach to learning the ABC's, this video provides an educationally sound introduction through story. As the children set off on an exciting Alphabet Hunting Trip they'll discover something for every letter of the alphabet along the way. Children will also enjoy watching the fully animated **CLIFFORD'S FUN WITH LETTERS** (SMV). Along with his friend, this adorable character sniffs out all the letters to get a message across. And more animated animal friends are available to teach your children all about letters in **RICHARD SCARRY'S BEST ABC VIDEO EVER** (SMV). Your kids will join Scarry's animal friends as they introduce each letter of the alphabet through a story.

Children love animals, and the combination of animal and alphabet is a powerful tool for teaching them their ABC's. **THE ALPHABET ZOO: VOLUME ONE** (SMV) uses this technique to perfection as the youngsters master the ABC's and their sounds with the aid of the animals at the Alphabet Zoo. They can then travel along with the Alphabet Zoo's crew via video in **THE ALPHABET ZOO: VOLUME TWO** (SMV). The same animal-ABC combination is used here to teach children basic reading skills. And for more animal/ABC fun, why not join Captain Kangaroo in his **ANIMAL ALPHABET** (SMV). The Captain and Mr. Moose rhyme through the animal alphabet from A to Z as they visit real dancing bears, fishing flamingos and a sea lion who plays frisbee. A trip to the zoo has never been so much fun.

Children of all ages have been delighted for generations with the imaginative characters of Dr. Seuss. These zany characters are now available via video in the classic **DR. SEUSS'S ABC'S** (SMV) to help teach your children basic skills in a fun way. Or maybe your children's favorite characters are the lovable Muppets of "Sesame Street." They can join all of the wonderful "Sesame Street" friends, including the ever-popular Big Bird, in a video that seems to be pure entertainment but is actually teaching them alphabet and reading skills. Big Bird is at his best in **THE ALPHABET GAME** (RHV) as he gets some help from lovable Kermit, while The Cooky Monster uses his own special brand of teaching in **LEARNING ABOUT LETTERS** (RHV). In another video, these adorable characters join together to help the child who is **GETTING READY TO READ** (RHV).

From the publishers of the popular Golden Books, the Golden Step-Ahead series has some outstanding videos designed especially for ages two to eight that combine fun and learning. **KNOW THE ALPHABET** (SMV) and **WORKING WITH WORDS** (SMV) were developed by educators and specialists to teach the basics with skill-building fun. When these two tapes have been played and replayed and their lessons mastered, the kids can

Step-Ahead to **GET READY TO READ** (SMV). Mr. Know-It-Owls is available to teach children ages three to twelve all about nouns, verbs and modifiers in **GRAMMAR AS EASY AS ABC** (SMV). Or take a look at **LETTERS, SOUNDS AND WORDS** (SMV), a delightful musical video that explores the alphabet as it teaches the look and sounds of letters and the simple words they spell. For some fun learning about basic sentence structure and parts of speech, **BASIC GRAMMAR** (SMV) makes use of puppets to teach young children elementary grammar rules.

More videos that will help your child build a solid foundation of reading skills are available from the **LOOK AND LEARN** series. Children as young as two years of age can join Professor Wise Old Owl in **ALPHABET SOUP: LEARN THE LETTERS** (SMV). This interactive, lively tape makes learning letters (capital and lower case) as easy as ABC! They can then follow Professor Wise Old Owl along to **SOUP STORIES: HOW LETTERS BECOME WORDS** (SMV). This program introduces more than 200 new words through six entertaining stories. Each story is designed to teach word recognition and enhance vocabulary with heart-warming stories that reinforce positive values. And for more fun videos from this excellent series, your children can join Kool Kat, the feline story-teller in **BEAR FRIENDS: LEARN TO READ** (SMV) and **BEAR DREAMS: LEARN TO READ** (SMV). In both these tapes, Kool Kat will help them learn reading and word recognition skills as he narrates the adventures of the lovable Barefoot Bear.

For the four-to-nine age group, an exceptionally good instructional video is **UP WITH PHONICS** (BBC). Children will be delighted to travel along with Jo-Ellen and her lovable canine companion Jupiter as they discover verbal sounds in enchanting settings. Through carefully designed lessons, they will be introduced to the vowel sounds and given opportunities to practice them in meaningful ways. This is an excellent video to start your child on the path to the lifelong habit of enjoyable reading.

The **LANGUAGE ARTS LAMPOONS** series is recommended for children in grades two through six. Each video is a separate instructional unit dealing with a specific word attack skill. Delightful and entertaining stories will have your children entranced as they learn all about vowels and consonants in **COOKING WITH CONSONANTS** (SMV), **VINCENT VAN BLEEP** (SMV), **THE STRANGE CASE OF THE VANISHING VOWELS** (SMV) and **DR. DIGRAPH'S HOCUS-POCUS** (SMV). A TV anchorman will teach them the recognition and meanings of affixes and roots in **WORD NEWS ROUND UP** (SMV), and **AL'S PIT STOP** (SMV) will entertain as it teaches correct usage of contractions, possessives and plurals. A tricky rabbit teaches the children about silent letters in **GETTING TO KNOW THE UNKNOWN** (SMV), and Dear Babby, an advice columnist, shows them about accenting syllables in **SOUL TRIP** (SMV). Your children will want to view this entire series again and again as they learn all about grammar.

SOMETHING NEW & EXCITING

LEARNING BASIC SKILLS (SMV) is a lively video packed with bouncy songs, special effects and animation especially for the very young child. Discover how easily your children can learn colors, letters and numbers with this outstanding tape. It also contains a handy guide with lots of creative ideas for learning fun. Or let your children listen to "Rainbow Magic," the first of many enchanting short songs in **COLORS** (SMV) that teach primary colors and their combinations.

Children are certain to enjoy **LEARNING TO TELL TIME/CALEN-DAR** (SMV). They'll learn how to tell time by relating the concept of hours—morning, afternoon and evening—to what is happening around them. By viewing an exciting parade, they'll learn all about days, months and major holidays as they compare the twelve floats in the parade. Or help them learn some very basic skills with **PRESCHOOL POWER** (SMV). This award-winning production, which is filled with songs, dances and jokes, helps your children learn to button, buckle, zip and pour for themselves. In **MORE PRESCHOOL POWER** (SMV), youngsters are taught how to tie their shoes, brush their teeth and even make a fruit salad.

For a very basic but important lesson, let your children join The Telephone Doctor in **TELEPHONE TIPS FOR KIDS** (SMV), who shows children how to take messages and make an emergency phone call. This humorous and delightful program illustrates what can happen when a phone isn't used properly and will be enjoyed by both parents and kids.

****

The preceding videos are designed specifically to teach certain educational skills while also holding the child's imagination. Other videos are available to teach a variety of lessons to even the smallest tot. Take a look at some of the excellent art and craft programs in the HOBBIES, CRAFTS & MORE chapter that are produced especially for children. For your sports-minded child, there's sure to be a video of interest in the kids' section of SPORTS, SPORTS & MORE SPORTS. And to help them become emotionally educated, be sure to look at the videos available in the parenting section of the chapter on SELF-HELP VIDEO GUIDES.

LIFELONG LEARNING

Learning doesn't stop when you get out of school. It's a lifelong process, and videos can be of tremendous aid in a search for knowledge. While they shouldn't be used to replace books entirely, they are an excellent supplemental visual aid to gaining new skills and awareness. If you're interested in brushing up on your academic skills, whether for furthering your education or your own personal achievement, there are videos that are sure to be of interest to you.

IMPROVE YOUR ENGLISH SKILLS

EXPLORING THE ENGLISH LANGUAGE series is an ideal high-tech teaching aid to help students and adults of all ages become more familiar with and proficient at the English language. The series contains eight videos, and it is recommended that you progress through them in sequence. Begin with **VIDEO TUTOR: FUN WITH WORDS** (SMV) and go on to **VIDEO TUTOR: WRITING BASIC SENTENCES** (SMV), **VIDEO TUTOR: COMPOUNDING SENTENCES & PARTS OF SPEECH** (SMV) and **WRITING COMPLEX SENTENCES** (SMV). The mystery of using dictionaries will be thoroughly explained in **VIDEO TUTOR: DICTIONARIES & THEIR MEANINGS—Part One and Part Two** (SMV) and this knowledge put to good use as you view **VIDEO TUTOR: FORMING WORDS & BUILDING VOCABULARIES** (SMV). To round out an excellent and informative course in the English language, complete your lessons with **VIDEO TUTOR: NAMING PEOPLE, PLACES & THINGS** (SMV). This entire series is an excellent reference course you will refer to time and again.

For a comprehensive guide to the basics of learning to read the English language, **READ ENGLISH TODAY** (NUV) is a highly effective video aid for adults and teenagers. Integrated graphics and live-action scenes guide the viewer through fifteen compact, easy-to-follow lessons. Each lesson builds on previous material, and active response is continually invited with immediate feedback provided. With the help of rewind and mute buttons, users of the program can practice until they can answer their video teacher's questions quickly and accurately. This video is also unusual in having persons of many ages and several ethnic groups appearing in live-action scenes throughout the program. This is a superb literacy aid that also encourages viewers to discover the many treasures awaiting them through the printed word.

Another excellent program for improving writing skills is **WRITING FOR RESULTS** (CEP). This informative video teaches how to produce a winning written report by analyzing the reader; determining the purpose; selecting and narrowing topics; gathering, recording and filing information; and organizing the paper. The viewer will also learn the benefits of concrete and specific supporting material, proofreading and revising to produce a well-polished final product. For tips on writing that is geared to the business world, **BUSINESS WRITING SKILLS** (CEP) provides instruction on how to develop basic, tried-and-true skills that will make your writing both accurate and appealing. It includes such topics as structuring a strong opening and closing, formal versus informal writing and the art of writing closings. For dozens of tips you can use right away to avoid embarrassing grammar and usage errors, **BETTER BUSINESS GRAMMAR** (CEP) is an ideal aid for people in the business world as well as students. The program identifies and explains commonly misused words and phrases and gives valuable tips on using words correctly.

BRUSH UP ON YOUR MATH

ARITHMETIC (VAI) is an informative visual study tool designed for those who want a quick refresher course in basic arithmetic. The emphasis is on real-life applications of basic concepts, and the explanations are easy to follow. If you want to delve even further into mathematics, **FRACTIONS-DECIMALS-PERCENTS-CONSUMER MATH** (VAI) is an excellent video to view. Viewers will feel like they are actually in the classroom as they listen to the lively reviews that emphasize mathematical concepts and their daily applications. This is a great way to improve your math skills with your own private tutor.

131

To help students of all ages get more comprehension from their standard algebra courses, **ELEMENTARY ALGEBRA** (VAI) and **INTERMEDIATE ALGEBRA AND TRIGONOMETRY** (VAI) are exceptional supplementary programs. The intensive reviews will prepare students for even the most difficult and challenging problems. **PRE-CALCULUS** (VAI), **CALCULUS** (VAI), **PROBABILITY** (VAI) and **STATISTICS** (VAI) will also be of tremendous benefit to students involved in classes in these mathematical disciplines. The extensive practice provided by these videos is certain to be a valuable study tool.

An extremely useful program for both young and old is **THE HUMAN CALCULATOR** (FSV), which is designed to reach anyone experiencing math anxiety with a simple message....Math can be fun! The program offers unique and enlightening approaches to show the viewer how easy it is to add, subtract, even divide large numbers. This amazing video is also accompanied by a workbook that helps make the learning even easier.

LEARNING ABOUT AMERICAN HISTORY

If you thought history was a dull subject in school, let some outstanding videos change your mind. Via your VCR you can witness the inspiring birth of our nation in **THE REVOLUTIONARY WAR** (TWV). This powerful program begins with the "shot heard around and the world" and ends with the defeat of the professional armies of the most powerful nations to a group of poorly equipped, underfed men fighting for freedom. To extend your knowledge, be sure to take a look at one of the darkest times in our history, **THE CIVIL WAR** (TWV). The viewer will visit Gettysburg, Petersburg, Antietam and Bull Run through footage of early twentieth-century battle recreations and rare still photos.

For an informative and entertaining view of our history, you'll also want to watch **25 YEARS OF NEWS 1941-1965** (TWV). From Pearl Harbor to Vietnam, this is a living history of the people, places and events that changed America. To complete your education, be sure to view the excellent program from the people at *Life* magazine, **LIFE LOOKS BACK** (TWV). This humorous, emotional, inspiring and sometimes heartrending tape will take the viewer on a trip through the sixties, seventies and eighties. For some, it will be a sentimental journey, for others a look at events and places they have only heard about.

For another entertaining and informative way to bring American history into your home, take a look at one or more of the first-rate videos from the **FAMOUS AMERICANS** series. **THE STORY OF G.I. JOE** (TWV) shows the story of the young men in World War II who became "government issue," and the New Deal era that altered American life throughout the twentieth century can be viewed in **THE STORY OF FRANKLIN D. ROOSEVELT** (TWV). You can relive the life of one of the country's most famous aviators in **THE STORY OF CHARLES LINDBERGH** (TWV), from his triumphant solo trans-Atlantic flight to the tragic kidnapping of his son. And you won't want to miss the enthralling life stories of two men who changed America forever. **THE STORY OF THOMAS A. EDISON** (TWV) portrays the inventor who released man from toil and tedium, while **THE STORY**

OF HENRY FORD (TWV) depicts the history behind the man who sparked the twentieth-century industrial revolution in this country.

LEARNING ANOTHER LANGUAGE

With its visual and audio components, video is an extremely effective way to learn another language. The **LANGUAGE ON VIDEO** series is a fun way to learn the basic vocabulary of the foreign language of your choice. Pop the tape into the VCR and view real-life situations—hotel, airport, restaurant, store—with English subtitles on the screen. Foreign words are first spoken at conversational speed and then slower for easier listening and repeating. And don't forget, with a video you can re-wind and repeat a sequence as often as you want. In the privacy of your own home with your own special language tutor, you can soon be speaking **FRENCH** (AOF), **SPANISH** (AOF) or **GERMAN** (AOF) fluently.

Perhaps there's another language you've always wished you could speak and understand. The visual recall method utilized in the **BASIC LAN-GUAGES** series will help you easily learn **BASIC ITALIAN** (RDM) or even **BASIC RUSSIAN** (RDM). The dynamic video approach will introduce you to more than 1,000 vocabulary words as they are spoken, spelled out on the screen and dramatized. Practice at home with your VCR and then amaze your friends as you speak **BASIC JAPANESE** (RDM) or **BASIC POR-TUGUESE** (RDM). Or for the really ambitious, try a program that teaches you to easily converse in **ARABIC** (RDM) or **MANDARIN CHINESE** (RDM). There's sure to be at least one language that will capture your interest and enrich your life.

For native speakers of other languages, there is a unique series designed for those who want to learn English correctly and easily. In **BASIC ENG-LISH/ESL** (VAI), the viewer will learn English as a second language through a grammatical approach that uses easy-to-follow lessons combined with video graphics. When the basics are mastered, the viewer can go on to **INTERMEDIATE ENGLISH/ESL** (VAI), which offers instruction and prac-tice in everyday situations. These excellent videos allow students to individu-alize their instruction and progress at their own speed. And there is a unique program that is of special value to Spanish-speaking people. **BRUSH UP ENGLISH** (RDM) is produced by Linguex, known worldwide for its video-assisted classroom language training. This excellent tape provides a great way for Spanish-speaking individuals to get a refresher course in English con-versation. The program reviews everyday business and social situations that aid the viewers with their comprehension and speaking skills.

STUDY SKILLS

Students of all ages can benefit from some of the excellent videos that address the subjects of good study habits and test-taking. Effective study habits are not only important in an academic classroom but can be of tremendous aid in many varied situations throughout your lifetime. A well-produced video that will help you lay the foundation to good study habits is **THIS WAY TO AN A: EFFECTIVE STUDY HABITS** (CEP). This upbeat program teaches the Empty V System, which stresses the importance and effectiveness of deciding the purpose of each lesson in order to better understand key information. You'll learn proven techniques for studying, reviewing and retaining information that fit into any lifestyle or class structure. Reading and taking notes become easier, more effective and less time-consuming as the viewer learns how to find key facts and ideas. Mastery of this tape will result in excellent skills.

Another high-quality video program that is professional, entertaining and motivational is **EFFECTIVE STUDY STRATEGIES** (CEP). The tape is divided into three segments that cover an organized method of taking notes, an overall look at reading to improve comprehension and retention and step-by-step methods for learning effective study habits. Or you may wish to avail yourself of the two-volume series **STUDY SKILLS** (CEP). This workshop covers all the basic topics related to study skills, utilizing a straightforward format accented with useful, skill-building exercises. Volume I covers procrastination, time management, organization, goal-setting and listening. For proven techniques on memorizing, secrets on how to battle boredom, note-taking, when and where to study and test-taking tips, be sure to go on to view Volume II. Viewers will be able to take the skills they learn in this excellent program and directly apply them to workplace tasks, classroom situations and everyday life experiences.

For many people, the mere thought of taking a test starts adrenaline pumping, perspiration flowing and instant memory loss of everything they have learned. **THIS IS A TEST: THIS IS ONLY A TEST** (CEP) is a humorous and informative video that teaches the art of stress-free test-taking. The viewer will learn how to put test-taking into its proper perspective and will be shown that no gimmick or shortcut can take the place of knowledge. You'll learn how to prepare, organize, study and anticipate with valuable tips for reviewing and retaining information. This is one of the most entertaining and invaluable videos available on the preparation, execution and evaluation of tests. For even more help on performing well on tests, **EFFECTIVE TEST-TAKING** (CEP) covers, among other tips for studying, how to handle different kinds of questions and how to review for maximum retention. This fast-moving presentation keeps even the most inattentive riveted while communicating the essentials of successful test-taking.

EARNING YOUR GED

The GED diploma (general educational development) is generally recognized nationwide as being equivalent to a high school diploma. Passing the GED test can start you down the path to higher education, as well as bring you greater success in your career and personal life. **THE STEP-BY-STEP GUIDE TO PASSING YOUR GED** (EPG) is a fast, easy video course that lets you prepare for the exam in your own home and on your own time. Everything in this program prepares you for success. It will ease you back into the habit of studying and also give you tips on taking the actual test.

The program is organized into three skill levels, and its unique format puts fun into learning. Level A covers basic material, while Level B builds on what you've just learned. To get ready for the actual GED test, Level C gives valuable tips and sample problems.

There are five parts to the complete course, with each tape covering one of the five subjects required for a GED diploma: Social Studies, Writing Skills, Science, Mathematics, Interpreting Literature and the Arts. With each video, you'll receive a study guide with answer sheets and all the information you need to prepare, take and pass the GED—right down to specific information on the requirements for your state. If you're looking for a guaranteed way to get your high school equivalency diploma, be sure to take advantage of this high-quality program. It has everything you need to know.

****

The preceding videos are geared specifically to academic subject matter and are valuable learning tools. For more video learning aids, why not take a look at the PRACTICAL, VOCATIONAL & UNUSUAL SKILLS chapter. The videos in that chapter cover various interests, and there's sure to be one or more you'll want to view.

OFF TO COLLEGE

Whether you're entering college right from high school or have been out there in the world a bit first, there are excellent videos available to ease your journey into the world of higher education. Let these video learning guides help you master the required tests with top marks and then tackle the admission procedures. You'll also find video aid extremely helpful in finding the right college and also in surviving the financial-aid maze that you just might encounter.

PASSING THE TEST

Usually, the first step to getting into college is to pass your SAT or ACT test with high scores. Now you can invite a video tutor into your home to help prepare for these important exams. **SAT*TV** (CEP) is a fast-paced, professionally produced program designed to review academic content, develop test-taking techniques and study skills and build confidence in college-bound students preparing for the Scholastic Aptitude Test. The program is divided into numerous small segments that enable students to study individual chapters and review additional problems in the workbook. The skills you'll master with this program will not only enable you to succeed on your SAT test but will be invaluable to you in college and beyond.

The American College Testing Assessment (ACT) is sometimes taken by high school seniors for college admission, and there is video aid available for this exam also. **ACT MATH REVIEW** (VAI) and **ACT VERBAL REVIEW** (VAI) will help you pass this important test with flying colors. And again, you'll also learn valuable test-taking techniques, multiple-choice strategies and time-saving hints.

High school seniors who are not native speakers of English may be required to take the Test of English as a Foreign Language (or TOEFL) for admission to an American or Canadian college. The **TOEFL REVIEW** (VAI) can be an invaluable aid in this situation. The viewer can work along with the video instructor in this intensive review course, which is designed to increase English proficiency and teach the most effective techniques for success on the exam.

THE COLLEGE SELECTION DILEMMA

College selection can have a tremendous influence on your future career as well as many other areas of your life. **FINDING THE RIGHT COLLEGE** (CEP) presents an organized, rational selection process. This high-quality video utilizes humor, graphics, dramatization and effective communication techniques to show college-bound students how to select a school that is right for them academically, financially and socially. Learn about the many factors involved in this selection, such as type of school (public or private), size (large, medium or small), location, academic quality and social life. The emphasis in this excellent program is on identifying the criteria that are important to the individual and then utilizing an organized, effective selection procedure to narrow down the options. Finally, the program covers the importance of a campus visit in making the final decision and just what to look for when you get there.

An invaluable video aid when you're selecting a school is a **COLLEGIATE CHOICE WALKING TOUR** (CCI). While no video can replace an actual visit to a school, these tapes can help to narrow the field. Each program is a simple, straight shoot of the actual student-guided campus tour offered at each of 300 colleges and universities. While these videos are not produced by experienced filmmakers, they are informative and show just what you would find had you made the trip yourself. Everything is spontaneous, with no script, no actors, no professional narrator. The visuals are completely candid, and the student guides they capture on tape are sometimes far more knowledgeable than the average undergraduate and more forthright than admissions or marketing departments.

Once you've made your selection, videos are also available to help you tackle the admission process. **GET INTO THE COLLEGE OF YOUR CHOICE** (CEP) will help students organize their thoughts, narrow their choices and glide through the college admissions process. This tape starts with a segment on choosing a college and goes on to discuss getting applications, taking tests, filling out applications, writing essays, interviewing and sending "special talent" documents. For more help designed to navigate the college admission process, be sure to watch **THE STUDENTS' GUIDE TO GETTING INTO COLLEGE** (CEP). This unscripted, conversational-style presentation features Harvard students discussing their experiences in choosing a college and gaining admission. Their personal stories offer advice on the admissions process itself, interviews and personal essays that work.

You may prefer another excellent program, **THE EXPERTS' VIDEO GUIDE: GETTING THROUGH THE COLLEGE ADMISSION PROCESS** (CEP). This video guides students through a series of steps toward the goal of selecting and being selected for the right college. The program features straightforward highlights of what to do and when as you maneuver through the admission process. For expert help in an important part of that admission process, be sure to view **THE SECRETS OF WRITING THE COLLEGE ADMISSION ESSAY** (VAI). This entertaining presentation reveals everything needed to write a winning essay, including technique, topic selection and secrets for putting your best foot forward. This tape is certain to boost your chances of earning a place in the college that's just right for you.

How to Wri[te]

Peter S. C[...]

1-56726-149-

J286

THE FINANCIAL-AID MAZE

[...]de, college costs have risen steadily. However, financial [...] worth, is available for students willing to commit the [...] it. Using humor, graphics and effective communica-[...] FINANCIAL PLANNER (CEP) is a live-action pro-[...]rs the information they need to know about financ-[...] Learn the realities and myths of financial aid and [...]al assistance. Learn how to seek out the available [...] monstrate need. This is a comprehensive, straight-[...]d opportunities for prospective college students to

[...]EGE: **MYTHS AND MISTAKES OF FINAN-**[...]er excellent reference source on the subject, as it [...]encountered when pursuing financial aid. An infor-[...] it explores the eight most common problems students run into when seeking to secure a financial-aid package. This tape is entertaining as well as educational. More information on how to pay for your education can be found in the excellent program **HOW TO PAY FOR COLLEGE: A PRACTICAL GUIDE TO GETTING THE MONEY YOU NEED** (CEP). This program brings a team of experts together to explain the do's and don'ts of applying for and receiving financial aid. It covers such subjects as strategies to get more aid, scholarships, innovative payment plans, how much you'll need and lots more.

For an upbeat program that covers all the basics of financial aid, **PAYING FOR COLLEGE: TYPES OF FINANCIAL AID** (CEP) is an excellent choice. Subjects covered in depth include grants, scholarships, part-time employment, military assistance, loans and personal and family funds. This video is an excellent guide to weaving your way through the often confusing world of financial aid.

TIPS ON COLLEGE SURVIVAL & BEYOND

So you found the school of your dreams, aced the admissions test and wrapped up your financial aid. Before you actually get going on your educational journey, take time to view an excellent program called **COLLEGE SUCCESS** (CEP). This video gives prospective college students self-confidence while teaching the skills they will need to thrive in a higher education environment. It covers time management, notetaking, test-taking strategies, study habits, highlighting textbooks, preparing for tests and adjusting to college life. Or turn to the "experts" of today's colleges—actual college students themselves. In the **COLLEGE FRESHMAN SURVIVAL GUIDE** (FSV), sophomores, juniors and seniors will give you great tips on how to adjust to campus life and manage your new freedom. You'll learn from those who have been there all about budgeting your time, successful study techniques, test-taking tips, party-time pitfalls, roommate roulette, money-management tips and a lot more. These are both great prerequisite tapes for any college-bound viewer.

If you've been out of college for one day, one year or more and are considering entering graduate school, video reviews will be an invaluable aid in preparing for the particular examination you'll be required to take. For those taking the Graduate Record Examination for admission to graduate school, **GRE MATH REVIEW** (VAI) and **GRE VERBAL REVIEW** (VAI) will take you through practice exercises and review the skills necessary to become a better test-taker to ensure a higher score on this important exam. Or for an intensive review course in preparation for the **GRADUATE MANAGEMENT ADMIS-SION TEST** (VAI) for entrance to business school, be sure to view **GMAT MATH REVIEW** (VAI) and **GMAT VERBAL REVIEW** (VAI).

Those who are required to take the **MILLER ANALOGIES TEST** (VAI) for admission to graduate school will want to watch **MAT REVIEW** (VAI). This intensive program features an instructor at the chalkboard explaining the analogy concept and the best approach to each type of analogy question. For a comprehensive video review course for those taking the Law School Admission Test, **LSAT REVIEW** (VAI) should definitely be viewed. You'll learn the best strategies for every section of the exam, with numerous sample questions analyzed in detail by your own video instructor.

****

So you've let these valuable video guides help you into the school of your choice and then actually survived the educational experience. Now might be an opportune time to review some of the videos in the PRACTICAL, VOCATIONAL & UNUSUAL SKILLS chapter. You'll find some excellent video guides that will aid you in looking for the right job. Take advantage of these programs for valuable hints on resumes and interviewing.

SOURCES

(See Chapter 11 for a complete alphabetical listing of all sources with addresses and phone numbers.)

AOF -	Audio Forum
BBC -	Better Books Co.
BSG -	Bridgestone Group
CCI -	Collegiate Choice Inc.
CEP -	Cambridge Educational Products
EPG -	Educational Products Group
FSV -	Fushion Video
NUV -	Nuvo Ltd.
RDM -	Rand McNally Videos
RHV -	Random House Inc.
SFP -	Stage Fright Productions
SMV -	Schoolmasters Videos
TWV -	Time Warner Home Video
VAI -	Video-Aided Instruction

CHAPTER 7:

PRACTICAL, VOCATIONAL & UNUSUAL SKILLS

PRACTICAL MATTERS - VOCATIONAL SKILLS - UNUSUAL SKILLS - SOURCES

Just like the ever-popular how-to books that are available in every subject from A to Z, how-to videos abound. Via your VCR you can now get expert practical advice on subjects ranging from babysitting to financial planning to pet care. Programs on civil service exams and job-hunting techniques offer excellent vocational tips from the experts. Just for fun, you can learn all about gold dredging, home brewing or tarot cards. These are just a few of the subjects covered below by some outstanding video productions. So go on and browse. You'll be amazed at what you can learn in the privacy of your own home.

PRACTICAL MATTERS

BABY-SITTING DO'S & DON'TS

BABY-SITTING THE RESPONSIBLE WAY (CEP) is a high-quality program that prepares the viewer to be a responsible baby-sitter. This entertaining video gives in-depth advice on taking care of children safely while being able to handle most emergency situations. Following a humorous dramatization of the worst baby-sitting scenario in history, the program covers information ranging from basic child care to helpful hints on keeping children happy. The viewer will learn what to do in an emergency, how to keep children on schedule, how to deal with mealtime and behavior problems and how to avoid accidents, as well as what a sitter should not do, such as talking extensively on the phone and failing to clean up. This is an excellent preparation video for anyone planning on baby-sitting, as it emphasizes responsibility and deals with baby-sitting as a serious job.

BIKE REPAIR & TRIPPING

For a clear and simple introduction to bicycle repair, you'll want to join host Tom Cuthbertson in **ANYBODY'S BIKE VIDEO** (DIY). You'll learn how to diagnose and fix common bicycle problems, from flats to front-wheel wobbles, and maintain any bike so it will run safely and smoothly. This practical bike repair guide also tells the novice when and how to pick a bicycle shop for expert help.

You're certain to want to ride on with Tom Cuthbertson to his program **BIKE TRIPPING** (DIY), a video about the many ways bicycles can be enjoyed. You'll be introduced to the basics of riding safely and then will learn about the many kinds of bikes available and the specific ways they can be used. Practical tips on planning, packing and preparing both the bike and the rider will make your next bike trip, long or short, much more enjoyable.

BOY SCOUTING

If your child is among the millions of young boys who participate in the challenging world of scouting, you'll be pleased to know that an excellent video is available to help him on the exciting trail toward a tenderfoot badge. **TENDERFOOT: THE BOY SCOUT ADVANCEMENT PROGRAM SERIES** (COF) will help him explore his special place in the environment and his important role in the community. It will teach him how to save a life, pitch a tent, build several types of fires and other skills necessary to earn a tenderfoot badge. Above all, this video shows how boys can have fun together and make lasting commitments to physical, mental and moral fitness.

CAR CARE & INFORMATION

Every day, thousands of dollars are transferred unnecessarily from the pockets of novice consumers to the pockets of professional car salesmen. If you're in the market for a car, whether new or used, you'll be able to make sure each dollar you spend is spent wisely by taking some time first with your VCR and an excellent program called **THE CAMBRIDGE CAR BUYING SYSTEM** (CEP). This informative video teaches the viewer to be a smart consumer. You'll see the value of entering the buying process as an investigator armed with relevant information and a total understanding of the roles played by buyers and sellers. You'll learn such things as what information you need and where to get it, how to take and keep control of the sale and many more tips for driving away with the best car, price and terms available.

Another informative video guide for the car-buying consumer to view is **THE CAR BUYER'S SURVIVAL GUIDE** (FSV). This program, designed mainly for the new-car buyer, shows how to buy the right new car at the right price without getting ripped off. You'll learn how to quickly gain command of the pertinent facts that will give you the confidence to strike a good deal on your new car as well as your trade-in. This program also includes informative interviews with car salesmen and features valuable advice from top consumer and automotive experts.

Car maintenance and repair can be expensive, but videos can help you reduce these costs by teaching you some of the basic repairs and preventive maintenance procedures you can do yourself. **DO-IT-YOURSELF CAR REPAIRS** (EVN) is one such tape you're sure to want for your reference library. Host Norm Wynee gives the viewer simple but thorough advice on brake service, changing oil, preventive maintenance and basic tune-ups and many more tips that will benefit your car and your pocketbook. Additional information you'll want to know can be found in **UNDER THE HOOD AND AROUND YOUR CAR** (EVN). This informative program explains maintenance practices that ensure drivers get better performance from their cars. For a **COMPLETE VEHICLE SAFETY INSPECTION** (EVN), this video guide is an invaluable aid. The point-by-point inspection technique shows how to make sure a vehicle is safe and reliable.

To discover all the skills needed to restore a car to showroom perfection, you'll want to view **AUTOMOBILE DETAILING** (EMG). The video demonstrates how to remove dead oxidized paint, clean and paint the undercarriage, degrease an engine and much more. A great way to learn the profession or just make the inside of your own car look factory-new.

FINANCIAL SAVVY

Creating a personal financial plan and sticking to it is no easy task, but the **GUIDE TO PERSONAL FINANCE** (NGC) is sure to help you get a grip on your finances. Learn how to make your money work for you, how much risk you can live with, what kind of savings and investments best suit your needs, how to protect your assets and where to turn for good financial advice. An in-depth discussion of various financial instruments, including savings accounts, CDs, home equity loans, stocks, bonds and mutual funds, makes this video an excellent "road map" for planning your financial future. If you're getting ready to start a family or already have one, you know how vital financial planning is. For a good place to begin your family's financial plan, take a look at **A GUIDE TO FAMILY FINANCES** (NGC). This step-by-step video provides an overview of appropriate investment strategies, including topics like wills and estates, how to save for college, how to make the best use of credit cards, types of insurance to carry, how to develop both long-term and short-term goals and also how to stick to an effective budget.

If you're interested in acquiring financial savvy when it comes to investing, there are several excellent video guides to get you on your way. In **SYLVIA PORTER'S PERSONAL FINANCE** (CEP), one of America's most trusted financial advisors describes seven winning investment strategies. Using charts, graphs and simple examples, this informative program explains to the viewer the profit potential in home ownership, real estate, mutual funds, stocks and bonds, tax-advantaged investments, high-income investments and growth investments. You'll discover sensible investments geared to your own personal financial objectives. Or you may wish to take advantage of the expertise of America's leading consumer information source with its comprehensive and easy-to-understand video guide, **CONSUMER REPORTS: SMART INVESTING** (CEP). This comprehensive program takes you through the investment marketplace, spotlighting opportunities and pitfalls you can expect to find. You'll learn about all the key principles of investing and how they work.

For a revealing look at what happens in today's financial markets, be sure to view **HOW WALL STREET WORKS** (CCL). Produced for the novice investor, this video follows the stock-trading process from the buyer to the broker to the exchange floor. You'll get the basic do's and don'ts, learn to read a stock listing and gain an understanding of futures and options and the

141

effects of program trading. For more smart investing, an excellent view is **STOCKS, BONDS AND GOLD** (FSV). Louis Rukeyser of "Wall Street Week" and some of the nation's top specialists will provide you with solid investing basics and strategies for successful trading. This program is filled with helpful hints, and it takes the mystery out of money by explaining investments in terms the average person can understand.

Of interest to people of all ages is the exciting video **BUILDING PERSONAL WEALTH** (NGC). Joseph "Jody" Tallal, who became a millionaire at twenty-five, shows how you can build your own personal fortune. In this revealing program, the viewer will learn Jody's techniques for first determining financial goals and then attaining them. This practical system for achieving financial wealth will teach you how to determine exactly how much to save from each paycheck, how to build a retirement fund and much more.

Incredibly, only five percent of all Americans will be able to live comfortably when they retire. To ensure that you're one of the fortunate, begin planning for your retirement now with **A GUIDE TO RETIREMENT SECURITY** (NGC). Specially designed to meet the needs of those in the forty to sixty age group, this video gives practical advice on retirement planning, including in-depth discussions of pension plans, IRAs, annuities and insurance. Or learn how to start saving for retirement now with the advice of *Money Magazine*'s Ed Schurenberg and financial planner Harold Evensky. In the **GUIDE TO RETIREMENT PLANNING** (FSV), they'll show you the way as they provide invaluable insight into investment options, covering how to "watchdog" your company's pension plans, deferred savings plans, early retirement, social security and many other relevant topics. Another excellent choice to view on this subject is **HOW TO STRETCH YOUR RETIREMENT DOLLAR** (FSV). This video is a practical guide to getting more life out of your money in retirement. You'll learn all about financial planning and estate planning, investments and the ever-changing rules of Medicare. This is a straightforward and practical program you'll want to refer to often.

FURNITURE REPAIR/REFINISHING

Rather than throw out that broken piece of furniture or pay an expert to repair it, why not become an expert yourself by viewing **REPAIRING FURNITURE** (TAU) with host Bob Flexner? You'll learn everything you need to know, from choosing glues, disassembling joints, clamping irregular shapes to repairing veneer and mending broken parts. Or you may want to watch **REFINISHING FURNITURE** (BHG), a video guide from the people at Better Homes & Gardens. This is an excellent tape that shows how to repair scratches, burns and dents and then gives all the details you need for stripping and finishing your piece.

For more information on this topic, you may want to join host Avian Rogers in **FURNITURE REFINISHING** (MWP) and learn to disassemble hardware and mirrors, apply stripper, then sand and finish with stain. Or perhaps you'd like to follow along with expert finisher Bob Flexner in **REFINISHING FURNITURE** (TAU) as he covers all the practical and decorative aspects of refinishing, including safety procedures, preventing harm to furniture and modern refinishing systems.

Now that you've refinished that chair and are pretty proud of your results, what about the seat? There are two videos to help you here. **CHAIR CANING** (VVP) is hosted by Jane Nelson, who has more than twenty-five years of experience in wicker repair. In this program she teaches the viewer both types of caning, hole caning and machine caning, and you'll soon be able to cane an heirloom for yourself or even for some extra income. Another way you might want to proceed is to view **SHAKER CHAIR, WEAVING PATTERNS & TECHNIQUES** (VVP). This is a great skill you can put to use to redecorate by changing colors and patterns. The video will teach you true Shaker techniques by working with fabric tape. In addition, you'll get a brief introduction to the history and types of chairs, learn about materials, how to measure and how to weave your own patterns.

PET CARE

To introduce young children to the rewards as well as the responsibilities of owning a pet, the **BEST FRIENDS—PARTS I & II** (SMV) series is a fun and informative program. Part one focuses on dogs, mice, turtles, rabbits and frogs and explains in easy-to-follow instructions the child's responsibilities in caring for each pet. Part two is all about having cats, fish, guinea pigs, ponies and birds as pets and just what is entailed in their care. From this excellent tape, your children will learn their role in caring for each pet.

Another great series on pet care has been produced by Dr. Michael Fox of the Humane Society of the United States. Dr. Fox is America's foremost authority on pet care, and his video series provides pet owners with guidelines for proper and loving pet care. His series includes a video on the care of your **CAT** (SMV), your **DOG** (SMV) and your pet **BIRDS** (SMV), as well as a complete guide to keeping **FISH** (SMV) as pets and the proper care of **HAMSTERS & RABBITS** (SMV). The advice provided by these excellent programs will increase the chances that you will raise healthy and affectionate pets.

YOUR PET, YOUR PAL (SMV) is another good hands-on introduction to a variety of pets, including dogs, cats, ferrets and snakes. This live-action program explains each animal's character and special needs and will be both educational and entertaining to all ages of pet owners. If you're a cat lover, you'll want to join Rue McClanahan of "The Golden Girls" and noted vet Dr. David Griffiths in **RUE McCLANAHAN: CAT CARE** (FSV). They explain how to select, feed, groom, litterbox train, exercise and provide health care for your pet cat. This program covers it all, even visits to a cat show and a shelter and a heartwarming demonstration of the joy cats bring to older people.

To discover a new way to communicate with your pets and get results, you may want to view the unique video **THE TELLINGTON TOUCH VIDEO FOR DOGS** (PAS) or **THE TELLINGTON TOUCH VIDEO FOR CATS** (PAS). These videos are designed to help your dog or cat overcome behavior or health problems through a fascinating technique called the Tellington Touch. This non-verbal communication is something you can use to make a difference in your cat or dog's health and behavior and create a deeper connection with all your pets. For any pet owner who knows that animals can communicate with humans, a remarkable

143

view is **TELEPATHIC COMMUNICATIONS WITH ANIMALS** (PAS). In her unique program, Penelope Smith gives documented proof of her ability to "talk" with all God's creatures. For those viewers who agree with Smith's telepathic theory, this is a video you'll certainly want to view.

REAL ESTATE TIPS

If you're facing the task of selling a home, you'll want to take some time first to view **PREPARING YOUR HOME FOR SALE** (DIY). This program walks the viewer through two homes, one professionally prepared for sale, the other unprepared. Starting at the curb and going through each room, you'll learn what should be considered in packaging and preparing your home to appeal to the broadest range of potential buyers and correcting any shortcomings that might turn them off.

Or if the shoe is on the other foot and you're the buyer, be sure to view **INSPECTING A HOUSE BEFORE YOU BUY** (DIY). This video is designed to instruct you on how to competently assess the physical condition of the house and what you need to look for (or look out for) to be sure there are no serious problems. Both of these excellent programs could save you a substantial amount of money.

SPEED READING

Just think of all the time you could save if you could read faster and still comprehend and retain what you've read. Perhaps if you had that skill, you'd be through this book already and on your way to viewing some excellent and fascinating videos. If you're interested in doubling or even tripling your reading rate, you'll want to take a look at **SPEED EEZ SPEED READING** (BSG). This fun and easy video introduces a powerful speed-reading improvement program that can be easily understood by all age groups. There's also an exercise booklet included to help you on your way to faster, better reading.

TIME MANAGEMENT HINTS

Want to **GET MORE DONE IN LESS TIME** (CEP)? Then this video is for you. Learn the four basic steps you can take to make time work for you. Discover how to control things instead of letting them control you. Learn to overcome procrastination and how to tackle tasks in order of importance. You'll also learn how to deal with time-wasting interruptions, how to devise a time-saving schedule and many more time management techniques to increase efficiency on and off the job.

You might want to use some of that time you freed up to meet time-management expert Susan Freeman from *Inc. Magazine*. In **MANAGING YOUR TIME** (CEP), she presents proven, step-by-step strategies for making your time more rewarding and profitable. You'll learn to think of time as an investment and realize that it's not how you spend it but how you invest it that counts. Freeman also teaches you how to avoid the pitfalls of the "to do" list and how to prioritize the tasks at hand. You'll soon develop tools for managing your busy schedule and be able to take action steps toward improved time management skills.

UPHOLSTERING THE PROFESSIONAL WAY

Upholsterers Ken Bowles and Mike Doyle have used their combined forty years of upholstery experience to produce a series of training videos that show the viewer how to reupholster the way professionals do. Learn at your own pace as you start with **UPHOLSTERY FUNDAMENTALS** (VER) and see close up step-by-step details on how to get the best job done in the shortest amount of time. In no time at all, you'll be moving right ahead to **UPHOLSTERY: ADVANCED FURNITURE TECHNIQUES** (VER) as you gain confidence and personal satisfaction in recovering your own furniture and probably saving hundreds of dollars.

Bowles and Doyle's motto is "Reduce, Reuse, Recycle and Reupholster," and you can do just that with two more of their excellent tapes. **THE SLIP-COVER OPTION** (VER) shows how to make slipcovers that really fit. You'll learn to choose the right fabric, sew boxed, welted and waterfall cushions and fashion pillows. If the seating in your car, truck, boat or RV needs a little sprucing up, be sure to view **AUTO-MARINE UPHOLSTERY** (VER). You'll learn all the secrets and information you'll need. These tapes are well shot and offer many useful tips, both visually and through the narration.

WEDDING PLANS

Here comes the bride...and also some expert help via video. **PLANNING YOUR WEDDING: THE EXPERT'S GUIDE** (TWV) shows the viewer how to plan for a perfect and affordable wedding. Everything you need to know is covered, including bridalwear, catering, music, pre-nuptial agreements and all the trimmings. As a special bonus, the viewer will be treated to an exquisite designer wedding gown show. If a wedding is in your future, be sure to view this informative program first.

If you want to take your newly acquired knowledge further, be sure to view the **WEDDING PLANNING SERVICE** (EMG) video. You'll meet experienced pros who started their business on a shoestring and went on to become tops in the field. When you tag along with these wedding planning experts as they sell their services to new clients, you'll learn the top ten services you must offer to succeed in this interesting business.

WOOD CARVING

Wood carving is an ancient art that is still revered in our fast-paced world. If you've always wanted to try your hand at carving and whittling, an excellent introductory program is **WOODCARVING WITH RICK BUTZ** (MWP). This program will instruct the viewer on selection of tools as well as techniques for whittling, relief and chip carving and sculpting work. For even more skill building, take a look at **CARVING TECHNIQUES AND PROJECTS** (MWP). In this informative instructional tape, Sam Bush and Mack Headley, Jr. show you the fine art of carving letters, monograms, scallop shells and more. Those interested in specialized carving might want to learn how to **CARVE A BALL AND CLAW FOOT** (MWP) or become proficient at **CARVING SWEDISH WOODENWARE** (MWP). These are both great videos for advancing your skills and learning the tricks of the old world craftsmen.

145

For the ultimate carving experience, you'll want to view **CARVING A CAROUSEL HORSE: A STEP-BY-STEP GUIDE** (NOP). This entertaining video exposes the viewer to the wonder and beauty of the carousel, which has thrilled and fascinated people for generations. Master carver Darrell Williams will lead you with step-by-step instructions through an actual carving where you can observe his techniques in action. Be sure to complete your masterpiece with the video aid of **PAINTING A CAROUSEL HORSE** (NOP). These delightful videos can lead you to the creation of a wonderful heirloom by helping you fulfill the dream of producing your very own carousel horse.

VOCATIONAL SKILLS

BUSINESS PLANNING ADVICE

For the first time ever, there is available a practical, step-by-step video guide that shows you **HOW TO REALLY START YOUR OWN BUSINESS** (CEP). Each section of this exciting program presents an essential lesson that is clearly and fully explained, including defining your business, finding the money, starting out on the right foot and everything else you need to know. If you've ever dreamed of starting your own business, controlling your own financial destiny and being your own boss, this program is for you. Or if you're involved in a family-owned business that has been passed from one generation to the next, you'll certainly want to view **HOW TO RUN A SUCCESSFUL FAMILY BUSINESS** (CEP). This live-action program presents ten successful family business owners and management experts who share their expertise on how to run your operation smoothly and efficiently. You'll learn all the particular information you need to run a profitable family business with a minimum of conflicts.

If working at home is right for you, the program you want to view is **HOW TO SUCCEED IN A HOME BUSINESS** (CEP). This practical video guide shows you how to run a business from home and achieve the freedom of being your own boss. You will learn from five successful entrepreneurs as well as a tax expert. You'll find everything you need to know in this informative program to set up, run and prosper in your own home business. Or perhaps you have **FRANCHISE FEVER** (CEP). The growing selection of franchise opportunities has made the dream of owning your own business much easier to attain. This excellent, in-depth program takes the viewer through the process of making an intelligent franchise purchase. You'll learn what to expect and what mistakes to avoid as this informative program helps you take the first step toward owning a successful and profitable franchise business.

Whether you're involved in your own business or employed at the management level by someone else, you can take advantage of some excellent advice offered by the U.S. Government's Small Business Administration. **THE BUSINESS PLAN: YOUR ROADMAP TO SUCCESS** (SBA) teaches the viewer the essentials of developing a business plan that will lead to capital, growth and profitability. It comes with a workbook that provides

146

a checklist of information to include in your plan as well as samples of the income statement, balance sheet and cash-flow forecast. For a step-by-step approach on how to write the best possible marketing plan for your business, the Small Business Administration has produced the excellent **MARKETING** (SBA) program. This informative video details the best methods for determining customer needs and identifying and developing a working profile for potential customers and provides much more information in easy-to-follow examples. For help in putting together a sound promotional plan aimed at targeting new customers, increasing sales and getting the most for your promotional dollar, be sure to take advantage of all the expert advice in **PRO-MOTION: SOLVING THE PUZZLE** (SBA). You'll learn how to choose the best advertising medium for your needs, how to write a press release that grabs attention and much more.

CIVIL SERVICE & GOVERNMENT EXAM PREPARATION

To qualify for federal, state and city jobs, prospective employees must take a civil service exam. If you're interested in pursuing such a job, the best way to start is by viewing the **MATH & VERBAL REVIEW FOR CIVIL SERVICE EXAMS** (VAI). This valuable video aid for test preparation offers a review of the types of math and verbal questions that commonly appear on these exams. This is a great way to increase your chances of qualifying for the job.

Other government jobs also require qualifying exams to be taken. **FIRE-FIGHTER EXAMS REVIEW** (VAI) is an excellent video to familiarize prospective firefighters with the test questions and basic firefighting situations. For aspiring police officers, the video to watch is **POLICE OFFICER EXAMS REVIEW** (VAI). This program summarizes the mental skills and attitudes necessary for police work in city, county, state and other police agencies.

For anyone seeking employment with the post office, the **POST OFFICE EXAMS REVIEW** (VAI) will help the viewer learn strategies for answering even the most difficult questions with speed and accuracy. If a military career figures in your future, you'll want to take a look at the **ASVAB REVIEW** (VAI). Men and women who wish to join the armed forces must take the Armed Services Vocational Aptitude Battery exam, and this video will help sharpen the viewer's academic and technical skills.

COMPUTERS

Computers have become an integral part of nearly everyone's life. Computer circuitry is now found in the cars we drive, the stores where we shop and in most of today's businesses. At least an elementary knowledge of computers is practically a necessity in today's world. If you know little or nothing about computers, you'll want to start with **SQUARE ONE: AN INTRODUCTION TO COMPUTERS** (CEP). This informative video is designed to introduce the viewer to essential computer concepts, the terms used, types of computers and what they are used for. If you're like millions of others who don't know the difference between a mainframe and a mouse, this information-packed program will provide you with the basics in terms anyone can comprehend. Another excellent program is

147

HOW COMPUTERS WORK (EVN), which is not only educational but entertaining to watch. It is based on The Computer Museum of Boston's internationally acclaimed walk-through computer exhibit. You'll join museum visitors as they walk through and learn. This high-quality video is ideal for introducing computers to novices of all ages.

After you have your new system up and running, there is another video you might want to have on hand, **MAINTAINING YOUR PC** (EVN), an excellent hands-on program and reference guide. You'll be able to save hundreds of dollars as you learn to minimize future repair bills. This comprehensive program makes it simple, safe and easy to practice preventive maintenance to make your PC last longer.

To quickly become comfortable with your new computer, be sure to take a look at **GETTING ACQUAINTED WITH YOUR COMPUTER** (CTV). This two-volume set will help you master basic computer lingo so you can hold your own in any situation. Volume I is an introduction for beginners that covers everything you need to know—from diskettes to different function keys to dealing with a computer virus. Volume II gives you step-by-step instruction in hardware and software basics as you learn all about bits, bytes, kilobytes, megabytes, modems, database management and more.

Learning about the disk operating system, which is what makes a computer go, will enable you to become proficient at using any type of computer. There are many excellent videos available to help you get computer friendly that cover the various versions of DOS. For DOS 2.0 - 4.0 or 5.1, you'll want to view **LEARNING DOS** (FSV). For the 6.0 version, take a look at the **DOS 6.X VIDEOS** series. **BEGINNING DOS 6.X** (LNK) will get you started, and **INTERMEDIATE DOS 6.X** (LNK) will build on this basic knowledge. Do go on to view **ADVANCED DOS 6.X** (LNK) and **OPTIMIZING DOS 6.X** (LNK) to ensure your proficiency.

One of the newest innovations in computer technology is the introduction of Windows. Whether you're new in the world of computers or a seasoned veteran just getting into the application of Windows, there are many excellent tapes available to guide your way. **INTRODUCTION TO WINDOWS** (LNK) and **WINDOWS APPLICATIONS** (LNK) are two videos that were created specifically for those totally intimidated by their computer. The style in each tape is warm, entertaining and informative. For a more comprehensive course, you'll want to view **WINDOWS: ADVANCED TIPS AND TRICKS** (LNK) and **OPTIMIZING WINDOWS** (LNK). And for the viewer who utilizes Microsoft Windows, an excellent choice is **LEARNING MICROSOFT WINDOWS** (KYS). This two-volume set starts with beginning basics and moves on to more advanced techniques.

One of the most widely used software programs for word-processing functions in both private homes and business is WordPerfect, and some excellent instructional videos are available to help you learn the basics and more. There are some comprehensive training programs available that will teach you everything you need to know to become proficient in the use of WordPerfect, and they are available for 5.0 and 5.1 WordPerfect software as well as the latest version, 6.0. You'll want to start with **WORDPERFECT: INTRODUCTION FOR DOS** (SFV) to learn all the basic commands and formatting procedures. **WORDPERFECT: INTERMEDIATE FOR DOS**

(SFV) will further increase your knowledge as you gain more confidence and expertise in using this powerful word-processing system. To complete your training and put you at the top of the class, be sure to continue with **WORD-PERFECT: ADVANCED FOR DOS** (SFV). And you'll also want to take advantage of **WORDPERFECT: TIPS & TRICKS FOR DOS** (SFV). This excellent series of tapes can take you from novice to expert at your own pace in your own time and in your own home. The ability to stop, re-wind and review is another advantage of using video for your learning experiences.

Another very popular program is Microsoft Word. If this is your word-processing software of choice, you can dramatically increase your knowledge and productivity by viewing a step-by-step three-volume home-viewing course on this application. **LEARNING MICROSOFT WORD: BEGINNING VIDEO** (KYS) will get you started, and **LEARNING MICROSOFT WORD: ADVANCED VIDEO** (KYS) will help you become an expert. For additional ways to utilize this program, be sure to also view **LEARNING MICROSOFT WORD: POWER APPLICATIONS** (KYS).

For spreadsheet, financial and statistical work, one of the most popular software programs is LOTUS 1-2-3, and a basic understanding of this application can be obtained by viewing **LOTUS 123 LITERACY** (EVN). For a more comprehensive training, you'll want to watch a three-tape series that starts with **BEGINNING LOTUS FOR DOS** (SFV), moves on to **INTERMEDIATE LOTUS FOR DOS** (SFV) and completes the course with **ADVANCED LOTUS FOR DOS** (SFV). If you plan to use Lotus 1-2-3 through your Windows application, be sure to view another three-tape series presented by Judd Robbins. **BEGINNING LOTUS FOR WINDOWS** (LNK) and **INTERMEDIATE LOTUS FOR WINDOWS** (LNK) will teach you everything you need to know to utilize this powerful program, while **ADVANCED LOTUS FOR WINDOWS** (LNK) will ensure your expertise.

There are many other excellent software programs available to the computer user in addition to the ones mentioned above. Whatever program you work with, there is probably a video instructional guide to help you put it to its optimal use. The videos listed below are just the tip of the iceberg and will give you an idea of the excellent home-viewing instructional tapes that abound in this area. For the legal profession, there is the **PERFECTLY LEGAL SERIES** that consists of **LEGAL OFFICE BASICS WITH WP 6.0** (LNK), **LEGAL SHORT CUTS WITH WP 6.0** (LNK), **LEGAL DOCUMENT ASSEMBLY WITH WP 6.0** (LNK) and **BUILDING A LEGAL FORMS LIBRARY WITH WP 6.0** (LNK).

EXCEL users can gain a thorough knowledge by viewing **LEARNING MICROSOFT EXCEL: BEGINNING** (KYS), **LEARNING MICROSOFT EXCEL: ADVANCED** (KYS) and **LEARNING MICROSOFT EXCEL: MACROS, DDE, OLE, NAMED RANGES** (KYS). For EXCEL Windows applications, the two-volume set available for either 4.0 or 5.0, **MICROSOFT EXCEL FOR WINDOWS** (CTV) is excellent viewing.

For graphics applications, you may want to take a look at **BEGINNING FREELANCE GRAPHICS 2.0** (LNK) and **FREELANCE GRAPHICS 2.0 ADVANCED TIPS AND TRICKS** (LNK). Or if Harvard Graphics is your program of choice, be sure to view **BEGINNING HARVARD GRAPHICS** (LNK) and **ADVANCED HARVARD GRAPHICS** (LNK),

149

both available in the 2.0 or 3.0 versions. Users of a desktop publishing program will be sure to gain knowledge and proficiency from **DESKTOP PUBLISHING FOR WINDOWS-WORDPERFECT** (LNK) or **WORD FOR WINDOWS DESKTOP PUBLISHING** (LNK).

JOB-HUNTING TIPS & ADVICE

To take some of the frustration out of job-hunting in the competitive and ever-changing job market of the nineties and to enhance your chances of obtaining employment, several excellent video programs are available to give you the leverage you need. In **WINNING AT JOB HUNTING IN THE 90'S** (CEP), Dr. Mel Schnapper, internationally known career counselor, presents his total job-hunting system to the viewer in this informative, high-quality video. His proven strategies and techniques teach the job-seeker how to translate life accomplishments into a powerful resume, how to get help by networking, how to generate referrals, the right questions to ask during interviews and more.

Whether you're searching for a first or better position, a higher salary or even a complete career change, an excellent video to view is **WINNING THE JOB YOU REALLY WANT** (CEP). From locating jobs, to resumes and interviews, to dressing powerfully for a first impression, this program includes everything you need to know to master the job-hunting process. Especially designed for college students, **A GOOD JOB AFTER COLLEGE: HOW TO GET ONE** (CEP) contains some excellent advice from senior recruiters and vice presidents of some of America's leading companies. These experts will show viewers how to position themselves in the market, how to conduct an interview, what to put in a resume, the importance of post-interview follow-up and how to evaluate a job offer. A great aid to advancing your chances in today's crowded employment market.

Extra help for job-hunters can also be found in **EFFECTIVE RESUME: READING BETWEEN THE LINES** (CEP). This is a comprehensive study on preparing a resume that will grab the prospective employer's attention. You'll learn the different types and formats, what should and should not be included, tips on print and paper, the importance of the cover letter and more. In essence, the viewer is shown how to write a resume that will motivate the reader to dial your number to set up an interview. When that interview has been set up, be sure to take time to view the high-quality, full-motion video program **INTERVIEWING FOR A JOB** (CEP). This program emphasizes four steps in the interviewing process: self-organization, preparation, interview conduct and follow-up. Emphasis is placed on defining your goals, dressing appropriately, researching the company, conveying a good attitude and writing a follow-up letter. This excellent video is appropriate for ages sixteen to adult and can be adapted to various types of positions.

MODELING TIPS

For anyone interested in learning the basics of modeling but not wanting to pay the hefty modeling school prices to learn, a great video to view is **MODELING MADE EASY** (EVN). This video provides the viewer with some excellent step-by-step instruction. Model Jill Donnellan presents basic

r those seeking a career in modeling. She gives
runway work, working with other models and
siness. For more tips to help modeling hopefuls
ELING, COMMERCIALS & ACTING (EVN) is
. You'll get advice from the experts on such top-
riting a resume, finding an agent and more.
ape series gives practical advice to those thinking
areer. The series starts with **HOW TO BECOME**
provides an insider's view of the world of model-
as agents, attitude, positive self-image and persis-
PREPARING FOR PICTURES (CEP) takes the
session that shows you just what to expect and how
e solid and practical information on getting started
w the third tape in the series, **DESIGNING YOUR**
hich will show you how to be creative and put
together a portfolio case to show your pictures to their best advantage.

PHOTOGRAPHY

Photography is a skill that can be utilized strictly for fun or expanded for professional benefit. For a good introduction, you'll want to view **EASY PHOTOGRAPHY** (EVN). This informative program features tips on using a point-and-shoot camera to produce professional-looking photographs. Viewers will learn about different camera types, film types, the use of light and basic photo techniques along with common picture faults and buying tips. This excellent program can teach anyone how to shoot pictures like a pro.

If you're interested in developing a more in-depth knowledge of photography, you'll want to take a look at the **PHOTOGRAPHIC VISION** series, which presents all aspects of this exciting field including ideas for beginners with their first cameras and also experienced photographers seeking to refine their skills. The viewer can learn all the technical aspects involved by watching **THE CAMERA** (CEP), **THE FILM** (CEP), **THE DARKROOM** (CEP) and **THE STUDIO** (CEP) tapes. You can learn to adapt proven techniques to your own situations through the programs on **SEEING WITH THE CAMERA** (CEP), **CONTROLLING EXPOSURE, RESPONDING TO LIGHT** (CEP) and **COLOR** (CEP). You're sure to be able to upgrade your results after acquiring the skills you'll learn from **STRUCTURE WITHIN THE IMAGE** (CEP), **TIME AND MOTION** (CEP), **THE PORTRAIT** (CEP) and **LANDSCAPE AND CITYSCAPE** (CEP). And after you've developed all the excellent skills you'll be taught in this comprehensive course, you may want to view **THE MARKETPLACE** (CEP), which gives an overview of photography as a career.

For some good video instruction on a particular aspect of photography, there are excellent programs available. **ACTION PHOTOGRAPHY** (CEP) teaches the techniques needed to conquer sports photography, and **NATURE PHOTOGRAPHY** (CEP) will teach you how to capture animals in their natural habitat. **SCENIC PHOTOGRAPHY** (CEP) will help you capture spectacular views, and **GLAMOUR PHOTOGRAPHY** (CEP) will teach you how to capture the beauty of subjects and perfect the human form.

151

Or if you're interested in the uniqueness that can be achieved with black-and-white film, you'll want to view **CREATING THE IMAGE** (CEP) and **CREATING THE PRINT** (CEP).

Anyone interested in underwater photography will greatly benefit by viewing **BEGINNING UNDERWATER PHOTOGRAPHY** (BMV). This program is a great introduction to the principles and practices that will help you get the best underwater photos. For more detailed instruction, be sure to take a look at **CATHY CHURCH PHOTO CLINIC** (BMV). This world-famous photography instructor will teach you how to select the right camera, lens, strobe and other accessories. You'll find out how to achieve those brilliant blues and vibrant colors with Cathy's easy-to-follow proven steps to better underwater photography.

PRINTING & GRAPHICS

If you're involved in the production of any type of newsletter or ad, you could benefit from viewing **CLIP ART—USE AND FUNDAMENTALS** (CEP). This program teaches all the fundamentals of designing and producing effective finished artwork by using limited-budget, camera-ready graphics in a variety of applications. Before you take your product to the printer, be sure to view **PRINTING BASICS FOR NON-PRINTERS** (CEP). This guide to printing fundamentals will de-mystify the various steps leading to the printing of both simple and complex projects. You'll learn how to talk to printers in their own language and also how to save money on printing by properly preparing materials for the job.

UNUSUAL SKILLS

BOWS & ARROWS

Whether you have an interest in arrow-making from an archer's point of view or would like to learn the skill as a hobby, **UNDERSTANDING ARROW MAKING** (PSE) is a good instructional video on the subject. Hosts Terry and Michelle Ragsdale, expert archers themselves, offer step-by-step instructions for consistent arrow fletching and building that you can follow along with at your own pace. And once you've mastered these skills, you may want to move on and view **BOWS AND ARROWS OF THE NATIVE AMERICANS** (MWP). In this informative program, host Jim Hamm demonstrates working a bow through the entire process, from tree to finished weapon, and also gives expert tips on strings, arrow shafts fletching and decoration.

CALLIGRAPHY

Fran Strom has taught calligraphy classes and workshops throughout the country, and now you can have her all to yourself in the privacy of your own home via your VCR. Fran's well-produced tapes are an excellent way to learn this fascinating and beautiful style of writing. **POINTED BRUSH**

WRITING (VTX) is a technique that originated with ancient Chinese artists but is still used today by contemporary artists and graphic designers. This video will teach the viewer all the basics as well as showing many examples of using your new skills in commercial and personal applications.

For writing on fabric or making signs and banners, **FLAT BRUSH WRITING** (VTX) is an effective calligraphy technique. The viewer will learn all the basic brush techniques needed to write these gorgeous letter forms, including Roman capitals, serif variations, watercolor "bright brush" and more. Just follow Fran's clear instructions, and you'll soon feel confident enough to execute your own flat brush writings.

COMIC CREATION

If you've ever dreamed of becoming a great comic-book artist, you'll enjoy viewing **HOW TO DRAW COMICS THE MARVEL WAY** (TWV). In this entertaining video, legendary artists Stan Lee and John Buscema reveal the tricks of the trade in comic-book portrayal. This is also a great program for anyone who has an interest in or collects old comic books. A unique and enjoyable video.

DOWSING

Need to find your keys? Want to locate water? Have you dreamed about discovering buried treasure? There's no limit to the mysteries you can unravel when you **DISCOVER DOWSING** (PAS). Host Bill Cox has been dowsing successfully for more than sixty years, and in his interesting video he teaches this unique art with excellent instructions. It's easy to learn and doesn't require any special tools. All you need is your own sensitivity—and Bill even provides tips on developing that. This is an entertaining and informative video that may open up some new doors for the viewer.

GOLD DREDGING FOR FUN

Recreational gold dredging dates back to early 1950's California, where the first enthusiasts had the best of the dredging sites all to themselves. Today, most of the rich sites have been well picked over, but there are still places to be worked just for the fun of it. **BEGINNER'S GUIDE TO GOLD DREDGING** (THU) is a unique video that was designed for novice dredgers who want to get their feet wet without spending a bundle on equipment or devoting years of study to the hobby. This is definitely not a program for the advanced dredger, but if you want to learn the hobby or expand to weekend gold dredging, this is just the video for you.

HOME BREWING

The federal government legalized home brewing in 1979, and now you can learn how to make your own quality beers at bargain brand prices. Designed in the format of a cooking lesson, **HOMEBREWING: AN INTRODUCTION** (PST) was produced by home-brewing expert Joe Sincuk. Joe's career in agricultural research and his love for good beer naturally led to an interest in the process of turning raw grain into a hearty ale.

Let this expert inform you about brewing equipment and ingredients, including where to buy them, and then take you step by step through the process. Your first batch of home brew can be ready in just three to four weeks. In this do-it-yourself age, beer fanciers might want to try a hand at this ancient art.

MARTIAL ARTS

What is commonly known as martial arts is in reality only one part of an entire ancient Chinese culture based on living in harmony with nature and embraces many different forms of movement. An excellent video series that introduces the various martial arts forms was produced by the Long Island School of T'ai'Chi'Ch'uan. Via your VCR, you can now learn along with the master, Bob Klein, as he demonstrates step-by-step instructions for the ancient Chinese movements that serve as the basis for kung-fu. **T'AI'CHI'CH'UAN KUNG-FU** (ASV) will teach the viewer to use internal energy for the application of each movement along with weight distribution, breathing and beginning "push hands." For more instruction in this fascinating art, be sure to continue on with **PUSH-HANDS: KUNG-FU'S GREATEST TRAINING SECRET** (ASV). This unique Chinese form develops fluidity, concentration and the ability to neutralize aggression. You'll learn to sense the other person's intentions before they materialize physically. This is a very important video for all martial arts students. And you'll certainly want to view **SHAOLIN CHUNG HOP KUEN** (ASV), which is a common link among all martial arts. The video will teach you moves from all major martial arts, including kung-fu, karate and tae kwon do.

To learn the skills involved in **THAI KICKBOXING** (ASV), this program shows authentic kickboxing at its devastating best. With actual one-on-one instruction, the viewer can learn theory; stances; footwork; kicks; punches; elbow, leg and arm blocks; and all the combinations. Or perhaps you'd like to try **CHINESE KICKBOXING** (ASV). The complete instructions for full contact include punching, kicking, grappling, groundfighting and the use of animal-style movements. To learn the intermediate fighting form that utilizes graceful sword movements, be certain to watch **T'AI'CHI SWORD FORMS** (ASV). Step-by-step instructions teach fighting applications for each movement, and the viewer will be treated to a demonstration of free-style swordfighting practice.

SIGNING

Now you can learn the basics of Ameslan, the internationally recognized American sign language, through the excellent video guide **SAY IT BY SIGNING** (AOF). Practice at your own rate with your private tutor as you learn greetings as well as how to communicate about time, transportation and more.

TAROT CARDS

Tarot are the oldest cards still in use today and are said to date back to the ancient seers of India and Egypt. **THE ALPHABET OF THE TAROT** (PAS) is a fascinating video that takes the viewer a step at a time through the tarot. You'll gain a complete understanding of the traditional and esoteric meaning of each card. You'll learn what hidden meaning each card reveals about a person, how many ways there are to lay out the deck and how each meaning is affected by the positive or negative influence of surrounding cards. The astrological rulership and intuitive answers to all questions as seen in the cards will be revealed to you. In a short time you'll be reading the tarot yourself and impressing your friends with your mystical knowledge.

To further your knowledge of this fascinating subject, you'll want to view **UNLOCK THE SECRETS OF THE TAROT** (TWV). English psychic Paula Roberts, who has predicted everything from the overthrow of governments to Superbowl winners, shows you how to use the ancient method of tarot cards. She will teach you how to choose your personal tarot pack and how to start reading and interpreting as you learn to unlock the secrets of this ancient art.

TAXIDERMY INSTRUCTION

Via your VCR, John Rinehart, award-winning taxidermist, is available to take you into the exciting world of taxidermy. His **TECHNIQUES IN TAXIDERMY** series of videos will teach you in your own home the secrets of quality and efficient taxidermy. You may also want to view **PANFISH MOUNTING** (RHI) and **BASS/WALLEYE MOUNTING** (RHI). Rinehart will teach you how to skin, scrape, mount, do finwork, set eyes and, most importantly, color your fish. Small-game hunters are certain to get some great ideas from **BIRD MOUNTING** (RHI) and **SMALL MAMMAL MOUNTING** (RHI). Both of these well-produced programs show the viewer step by step how to create an exciting mount with professional results. Deer hunters will want to view **DEER MOUNTING** (RHI) and **ANTLER MOUNTING** (RHI) for great ways to mount and display hunting trophies. These are excellent tapes to learn about taxidermy.

VIDEOGRAPHY

Since this entire book is devoted to instructional videos, why not a video on "how to make videos"? **EASY HOME VIDEOS** (CEP) is a fun program detailing the basic techniques of using a camcorder and includes explanations of video formats, video accessories and pre-production planning. You'll learn about composition, shot selection, on-camera editing, lighting for video and how to tell a visual story. The final segment covers editing, audio dubbing, adding titles and graphics. This easy-to-follow video will guide the viewer through all aspects of making entertaining home videos.

For something really different to show your family and friends, why not learn about **SHOOTING GREAT UNDERWATER VIDEOS** (BMV)? This program was produced by Perry Tong of the "Scuba World" TV show, who will show you everything from O rings to lens covers from concepting to delivering the finished product. Be sure to watch this video if you aspire to be an underwater videographer.

****

*T*he many and varied videos detailed in this chapter are just some of the many instructional video guides available for your enjoyment and education. Be sure to take a look at other chapters in this book, such as *AROUND THE HOUSE* and *HOBBIES, CRAFTS & MORE*, for tapes that can open up new horizons.

SOURCES

(See Chapter 11 for a complete alphabetical listing of all sources with addresses and phone numbers.)

AOF - Audio Forum
ASV - Artistic Video
BHG - Better Homes & Gardens
BMV - Bennett Video Group
BSG - Bridgestone Group
CCL - Chesney Communications
CEP - Cambridge Educational Products
COF - Champions on Film
CTV - Career Track Publications
DIY - Do-It-Yourself Inc.
EMG - Entrepreneur Magazine Group
EPN - Educational Products Group
EVN - Educational Video Network
FSV - Fushion Video
KYS - Keystone Learning Systems
LNK - LearnKey Inc.
MWP - Manny's Woodworking Place
NGC - Nightingale-Conant
NOP - Noble Productions
PAS - Pacific Spirit
PSE - Precision Shooting
PST - Pastime Tapes
RHI - Rinehart Industries
SBA - Small Business Administration
SFV - SoftVision International
SMV - Schoolmasters Videos
TAU - Taunton Press
THU - Thuels Publishing
TWV - Time Warner Home Video
VAI - Video-Aided Instruction
VER - Verano Upholstery
VTX - Video Textbooks
VVP - Victorian Video Productions

CHAPTER 8:

HEALTHY LIVING

GENERAL HEALTH - NUTRITION & WEIGHT MANAGEMENT - DEALING WITH STRESS - EXERCISE FOR HEALTH - ESPECIALLY FOR WOMEN, BABIES & YOUNG CHILDREN - SAFETY & FIRST AID - MORE ON HEALTH - SOURCES

GENERAL HEALTH

Your health is important no matter what chronological age you are. Taking care of yourself by applying healthy habits to your daily routine will make you look and feel your best and contribute toward a longer, healthier life. While the following videos are not a substitute for a doctor's care and advice, they do contain valuable information that you can apply to your own life style right now.

TAKE CARE OF YOUR HEART & BACK

For anyone who has experienced heart problems, there are excellent videos available to supplement your doctor's advice. They can help you learn how to live better and longer with some simple changes to your life style. **STRAIGHT FROM THE HEART WITH MIKE DITKA** (CEP) gives the viewer valuable counsel and information on heart problems. Join Ditka and six leading heart experts as they explain what a heart is, what to do when you first suspect you or someone else is having a heart attack, dietary guidelines for tasteful, healthy eating and much more to improve the quality of your life. If you have had a heart attack or related heart surgery and have received your physician's approval to begin an exercise program, **CARDIAC COME-BACK SERIES 1-2-3** (XJX) is the three-part video series for you. This excellent program will guide you to better health and renewed strength using progressive exercises that build from one videotape to the next.

OH MY ACHING BACK! (COF) is a phrase we hear often and is also the title of a comprehensive educational video that covers the complete spectrum of back problems, rehabilitation and prevention. Valuable information and detailed instructions are delivered by noted orthopedic surgeons in clear, easy-to-understand language along with exercise routines for keeping your back strong, flexible and trouble-free. Or you may prefer a fast-paced, fresh approach to minimize the risks of back pain as presented in **IT'S YOUR BACK (CEP).** This is a hands-on approach to proper lifting, standing, walking, sleeping, yard work and much more that will help you reduce the risks of back pain. Another highly recommended video on back pain also

157

stresses good work habits and safe exercise. **BACK PAIN** (CEP) provides an informative, detailed consultation exploring back pain in a question and answer format. It is invaluable for anyone who wants to better understand this important and common problem.

LIVING WITH YOUR DISEASE

A common health ailment that afflicts millions of Americans is arthritis. To get reliable information and advice on this topic, you'll want to join baseball legend Mickey Mantle and leading national arthritis experts in **FEELING GOOD WITH ARTHRITIS** (XJX). They share with the viewer practical information on diet, medical treatment, positive attitude and exercise. Follow along with a daily program of stretching and strengthening exercises designed to improve mobility. And for those viewers suffering from high blood pressure, **SAY GOODBYE TO HIGH BLOOD PRESSURE** (XJX) is a live-action video emphasizing the ease with which blood pressure can be controlled through proper diet and nutrition. A daily stress reduction and relaxation segment is also included in this excellent and informative video.

For anyone diagnosed as having diabetes, an excellent video to view is **LIVING WITH DIABETES: A WINNING FORMULA** (XJX). The New York Mets' Ed Kranepool shares his personal experiences with the viewer in this information-packed program. Along with actress Gloria Loring, Kranepool covers the total approach to diabetes, including calorie choices, weight control, insulin therapy, easy self-monitoring and more. If you're troubled by hay fever, asthma or food or pet allergies, **COPING WITH ALLERGIES** (XJX) is your guide to quick relief. This excellent program is hosted by Boston Celtics' great Dave Cowens, an allergy sufferer. You will learn what causes your allergies, what tests and treatments are available and how to allergy-proof your home.

Another common ailment many have experienced is headaches. **NO MORE HEADACHES** (XJX), developed in cooperation with the National Headache Foundation, shows you everything you should know if you suffer from occasional or chronic headaches. You'll learn the common and not so common causes and what treatment can work for you. If you experience migraine headaches, you'll want to view **RELIEF FROM MIGRAINES** (XJX). Experts from the American Association for the Study of Headache will help the viewer understand the current theory behind migraine headaches with the latest facts on treatments and what you can do to improve treatment success.

The word "cancer" often evokes images of pain, suffering and death, but it can also mean the first step on a road of treatment toward recovery. **SURVIVING CANCER: THE ROAD AHEAD** (CEP) provides the necessary information needed to understand cancer and its treatments. This excellent program explains the importance of family support, life style and attitude. This is a human story relayed by several patients who have survived cancer.

*T*he above videos are excellent programs for specific situations you may be facing, but don't forget that good health involves many factors. Be sure to look at some of the other sections of this chapter such as NUTRITION & WEIGHT MANAGEMENT and EXERCISE FOR HEALTH.

NUTRITION & WEIGHT MANAGEMENT

Just what is "good nutrition"? Even with all the literature available today, it's easy to be confused about what you should be eating and what you shouldn't. There are some excellent videos available that will help take the mystery out of this important subject and soon have you on your way to sound and nutritional eating. If weight control is a constant battle, be sure to get some expert advice from the programs detailed below.

GOOD NUTRITION

Our health-conscious society is greatly concerned about cholesterol, and **THE NO-NONSENSE CHOLESTEROL GUIDE: GOOD FAT/BAD FAT** (XJX) is an excellent way to educate yourself on the dangers of a high-fat/high-cholesterol life style. You'll learn to define a healthy cholesterol level, reverse cholesterol build-up, prepare healthy meals and decode misleading food labels. Or you may wish to view **THE CHOLESTEROL ZONE** (CEP), an informative program that explains everything you need to know to beat high cholesterol. If you or someone you love is concerned about cholesterol, this video is a must. It will help you reduce your cholesterol level and live a longer, healthier life.

An important video for people who want to know how to make the best nutritional choices is **THE NEW FOOD GUIDE PYRAMID** (EVN). Starting with a brief but entertaining history of nutrition, this tape illustrates how contemporary nutrition can improve how you look, how you feel and how you live. Foods from the major food groups and their relationship to the dietary guidelines for Americans is highlighted. Using a fast-paced format with graphics and informative interviews, this program provides answers to your nutritional questions. Another excellent reference tape for your library.

A specialized nutrition tape geared to the athlete is **SPORTS NUTRITION FOR THE HIGH SCHOOL AND COLLEGE ATHLETE** (CEP). This comprehensive program is a taped video conference on a variety of sports nutrition topics that was held at Old Dominion University. Four of the most widely recognized nutritional experts share their expertise in this field. The viewer is provided accurate sports nutrition information that will replace myths and misinformation. This is an excellent video to ensure proper nutrition for athletic performance and general health.

WEIGHT CONTROL

For a realistic approach to weight management, **TAKE IT OFF!** (XJX) is a doctor-recommended video that will guide you through each phase of the weight-loss process. You will learn the best methods of how to shop, what to eat, how to begin exercising, the best ways to dine out and much more.

This comprehensive tape will get you started now and is an invaluable reference you'll want to refer to time and again. Added bonuses are a complete daily food guide and follow-along aerobic warm-ups for total weight management. Another excellent video choice you may want to view is **LIFETIME WEIGHT CONTROL: DIET FACT AND FICTION** (CEP). This program teaches the viewer the best method of lifetime weight control with a sane, sensible diet of healthy foods combined with exercise. You'll learn to balance exercise and the right eating habits to ensure good health and longevity.

WHAT'S EATING YOU? A GUIDE TO SENSIBLE DIETING (CEP) is geared to teens and young adults but is really a worthwhile view for all ages. This in-depth tape takes a look at how the body works and what it needs to make it function most efficiently. It covers the approaches to losing weight that really work and those that don't. The focus is on a healthy diet, exercise and a positive self-image. Or you might want to learn the secrets to fitness that last a lifetime with **FIT OR FAT** (EVN). This highly informative video presents new information on the physiology of fat cells, the right combination of diet and exercise to lose weight and keep it off, easy and tasty nutrition and much more. This is a really upbeat tape that could change your life.

For those viewers who need some motivation to get them started on a weight-control program, a dynamic program is available. **THE WILL TO CHANGE** (NGC) was developed by top motivational speakers who will help the viewer get on the right path and stay there. This program will help you reach your weight goal by increasing your understanding of the fundamentals of weight control. You'll learn to visualize yourself as a lean, energetic person, and this video can help make that visualization come true.

If you have teenagers in your family, you can help them be prepared for healthy long-term weight control. **FAD VERSUS FIT: YOUR LIFETIME FIGHT AGAINST FAT** (CEP) will teach them effective eating and exercising habits that will last a lifetime. They'll see how their body and needs change with age and develop the ability to control their weight in psychologically and physically healthy ways. This is an excellent foundation for a lifetime of healthy eating. Also geared to the teenage generation is **JUNK FOOD: NOTHING TO SNICKERS ABOUT** (CEP). This live-action video helps teens learn how to read snack food labels to make wiser choices and how fat and calories quickly accumulate in a "meal" of chips and snack cakes. If you're concerned about the alarming trends in eating habits, you won't want to miss this fact-filled presentation.

With the emphasis that our society places on physical appearance, it's not surprising that eating disorders are on a continual and alarming rise. For an informative look at anorexia, bulimia and obesity, an excellent video is **EATING-OUT OF CONTROL** (CEP). This dynamic exploration of the hidden world of eating disorders reinforces the fact that the key to looking and feeling good lies in eating a balanced diet. Another superb tape that helps to explain young adults' eating disorders is **CATHY RIGBY ON EATING DISORDERS** (CEP). This video goes way beyond clinical definitions and examinations to present a highly personal look at the world as seen through the distorted lens of an anoretic.

****

To supplement your new nutritional habits, be sure to take a look at the LET'S GET COOKING section of the chapter AROUND THE HOUSE. There are some great videos available that are based on nutritional but delicious cooking.

DEALING WITH STRESS

If you feel like you're always in the fast lane, take some time out to view one of the instructional videos detailed below. There are programs available that will help you learn to relax and enjoy life more. Relaxation exercises and meditation tapes can be beneficial or perhaps you'll find just what you need in the excellent tapes on massage.

DE-STRESSING YOUR LIFE

Everyone has stress, but it needn't be overwhelming. An entertaining program on stress management is **LESS STRESS IN 5 EASY STEPS** (CEP). The easy techniques demonstrated on this tape work in harmony with your value system as you learn how to make stress work for you, not against you. You'll also learn special exercises for instant relief from tension, how to breathe to calm yourself and how to expand your options and gain better control of your life. You may want to join TV's "Designing Women" star Dixie Carter in **DIXIE CARTER'S UN-WORKOUT** (COL). This is a super-relaxing set of gentle exercises designed to warm your body, tone your muscles and slow you down. Or if you're a fan of the ever-young and vivacious Shirley MacLaine, you can invite her into your home via video. **SHIRLEY MACLAINE'S INNER WORKOUT** (TMV) is a complete guide to stress reduction and relaxation through meditation. This entertaining personality will help you access your inner energy and power using her cleansing, natural methods.

To take advantage of the knowledge of a well-known expert on meditation, be sure to watch Alan Watts' **THE ART OF MEDITATION** (HFF). Watts leads you step by step in the disciplines of body posture, breath control and concentration. This program will help you reach the state of relaxation that is attainable through properly developed meditation. In the informative **SMART COOKIES DON'T CRUMBLE** (CEP), the viewer is exposed to life-changing insights into methods of reducing stress and increasing self-confidence. **HANDLING STRESS—TODAY AND TOMORROW** (CEP), especially geared to students, demonstrates how to identify stressful circumstances and how to manage the pressure they create. By learning how to put events in perspective, students of all ages will possess a vital tool for managing stress.

Stress is not a modern ailment. Stress-reducing techniques have been practiced since ancient times in China, and via video the viewer can take advantage of these time-proven methods. **T'AI-CHI-CH'UAN: CHINESE MOVING MEDITATION** (ASV) will teach you the slow, flowing movements

161

passed down from generation to generation to improve health and lessen stress. Another simple and effective stress-reduction program you may want to view is **STRESS REDUCTION EXERCISES** (ASV) with T'ai-chi'ch'uan master Bob Klein. This program is designed to sharpen your attention, help you drop nervous habits and keep your body youthful and relaxed.

For more instruction in this ancient form of Chinese relaxation, join Nancy Kwan in the well-produced **TAI CHI CHUAN** (COL). You'll learn breathing, balance and how to create the perfect form to achieve T'ai Chi's feeling of "meditation in motion." If you want to experience a unique form of meditation, be sure to view **DEEPENING YOUR MEDITATION** (PAS). This ancient form of meditation is presented by Swami Satchidananda, whose insights will motivate and inspire you to make meditation an integral part of your life as you expand and deepen your own practice.

HEALTHFUL MASSAGE

In addition to the inherent relaxation benefits, massage can be an invaluable aid to general good health. **GO TO MASSAGE SCHOOL IN THE ART OF PRESSURE** (BNS) is a must-see for anyone interested in learning more about the benefits of Japanese massage and acupressure. This hands-on workshop will teach the viewer all about this ancient art. Each segment of the excellent **MASSAGE YOUR MATE** (BNS) tape presents both Swedish massage and Shiatsu acupressure techniques clearly demonstrated with close-up photography.

For a comprehensive education in the art of massage, you'll want to view the **HEALTHY MASSAGE** (FSV) series. These entertaining videos demonstrate how to give a proper massage using easy-to-follow Swedish and Shiatsu techniques. The program is divided into three tapes. You can start with **HEALTHY MASSAGE: THE SCALP, FACE, NECK & CHEST** (FSV) and work your way up to **HEALTHY MASSAGE: THE BACK** (FSV). Be sure to finish your education with **HEALTHY MASSAGE: THE LEGS & FEET** (FSV). The slow-motion and close-up demonstrations will help you gain the skills necessary to give a relaxing and stress-relieving massage.

MASSAGE FOR RELAXATION (NUQ) is still another program that will help you reduce stress and pain at your own pace. This video guide to pampering your body features a variety of techniques, including Swedish massage, Shiatsu and reflexology. You will learn how to relieve tension, locate trigger points for best results, select the best oils for your skin and much more. And you'll relax as you watch and learn from this superb tape set to peaceful music.

For more video education in the area of massage, **T'AI-CHI MASSAGE: RELAXATION ECSTASY** (ASV) gives the viewer complete instructions for a full-body massage based on the ancient Chinese movements. The massage includes acupressure, stretching, loosening joints, face massage, breathing techniques and even massaging with the feet. For a look at a full-body Japanese massage, an excellent program is **SHIATSU MASSAGE** (ASV). The detailed explanation and close-up basic techniques will aid the beginner to release deep-seated tension and dissolve aches and pains. Be sure to go on to **ADVANCED SHIATSU MASSAGE** (ASV) for more detailed demonstrations and an explanation of Oriental medical theory and diagnosis.

The ancient Chinese art of T'ai-chi-ch'uan is also a unique method of exercising for maximum health. **T'AI-CHI-CH'UAN MOVEMENTS OF POWER AND HEALTH** (ASV) treats the viewer to detailed classroom instruction in these ancient health exercises for unleashing the vitality of the body in addition to uniting mind and body with heightened awareness. For easy exercises to aid recovery from illness or injury, **REVITALIZE YOUR BODY** (ASV) is one of a kind. The exercises you'll learn will keep up your levels of energy, enthusiasm and creativity and lead to a more fulfilling life. Instructions are also given for those who cannot stand or have other limitations.

****

*A*dditional videos that may aid you in de-stressing your life can be found in the SELF-HELP VIDEO GUIDES chapter. The tapes dealing with personal growth and motivation can be very beneficial. If your stress is related to a personal situation, you might want to view a program from the section on relationships.*

EXERCISE FOR HEALTH

Exercise tapes are great for losing weight and shaping up, but they're also beneficial for good health in general. Many excellent videos have been produced that will aid the viewer with specific ailments, and programs based on ancient Oriental movements can be extremely healthful. Be sure to take a look at the ones detailed below.

EXERCISE YOUR PAIN AWAY

The value of exercise in maintaining a healthy body as well as aiding recovery from illness is an accepted premise in today's society, and many specialized videos are available. For back pain sufferers, **SAY GOODBYE TO BACK PAIN** (BNS) will guide the viewer through simple routines with progressive, easy-to-do exercises that increase flexibility and strength. The methods shown in this tape have been taught at YMCAs nationwide and have been proven to reduce or eliminate backache in over eighty percent of the cases. For more back pain relief or as a preventive measure, you'll also want to view **JOANIE GREGGAINS' BACK HEALTH** (COL). This program will help you strengthen your back with clearly demonstrated toning exercises. Another excellent view is **RELIEF FROM BACK PAIN** (COL). Instructor Dr. Irene Lamberti demonstrates toning and stretching routines with lots of variety. She explains how to avoid back pain and shows you ways to adapt the workout to your own unique situation.

For a comprehensive program devoted to back exercises, be sure to take a look at the **BACK-CARE-CISE** (NUQ) series. This five-tape guide was developed by sports injury specialist Linda J. Nelson to strengthen and tone

163

weak back muscles and increase flexibility. This is a progressive program starting with Tape 1, which is geared to those viewers who are in pain, recovering or have little exercise experience. You can move on to Tape 2 for increased strengthening and stretching when you experience little or no pain. Tape 3 takes you into total body stretching and toning, and Tape 4 is especially for the neck and upper back. By the time you finish Tape 5 for shoulders, wrists and elbows, you'll feel like a new person. This is also an excellent series to help speed up recovery from injury, to relieve stress and to boost energy.

Do you know that a large number of women over age 60 suffer from osteoporosis? This thinning of the bone tissue is characterized by loss of height, back pain and easily broken bones. To help fight against osteoporosis, be sure to watch **BONE BUILDING WORKOUT** (PAS). It teaches how to use simple, weight-bearing resistance exercises to improve posture, strength and overall health.

If you're recovering from an illness or just starting out on an exercise program, a tape you might find interesting and helpful is **CHAIR DANCING** (COL). This program teaches active, fast-paced chair workouts with unusual moves at three exercise levels. As you get stronger, you'll want to increase the intensity of the workout by adding more advanced arm actions and leg movements. This video is particularly beneficial to those viewers who are, for one reason or another, confined to a chair but still want to exercise.

A most unique exercise tape is **PARKINSON'S—GET UP AND GO** (COL). This tape contains simple, mostly sitting exercises created and led by a group afflicted with this illness. Designed in cooperation with the Parkinson's Disease Foundation, the activities include easy movements, basic massages, breathing exercises and specially designed muscle-toning "floorwork."

EXERCISES FROM EASTERN CULTURE

TAI CHI 3-PACK (FSV) is a three-tape series based on movements originating in China hundreds of years ago. The T'ai-Chi method was designed to condition your body physically and mentally and ultimately lead you to a heightened sense of well-being. This discipline is based on focus, balance and movement. You'll start with the warm-up techniques, posture and movements and then gradually move on to the intermediate level. Working at your own pace in the privacy of your own home, you'll soon be ready to complete the advanced level and reap the rewards of a physically and mentally fit body. This is an ancient treatment for modern problems that you might benefit from for years to come.

Another unique video based on Eastern culture you may want to view is **EIGHT TREASURES** (PAS). The method used in this program was developed by Taoist masters several thousand years ago as a way to attain utmost health on the path of spiritual enlightenment. The simple exercises the viewer will learn not only strengthen the body and mind but energize the spirit as well. You'll learn all thirty-two forms of this ancient method as you work your body from head to toe and unblock your energy channels.

****

There are many exercise tapes available for all levels of fitness and all ages. Be sure to take a look at the FEEL FIT/LOOK GOOD chapter. There's certain to be one or more programs that are ideal for you. For another method of total relaxation plus the health benefits of exercise, you'll want to browse through the yoga section of that chapter.

ESPECIALLY FOR WOMEN, BABIES & YOUNG CHILDREN

Female health problems can be very personal, and there are some videos designed to help you gain the knowledge you want in the privacy of your own home. These tapes, which should be used as a supplement to expert medical advice, can be helpful for health situations that only women face, including pregnancy. To aid you in caring for your children's health, there are some outstanding videos that you'll want to view.

ESPECIALLY FOR WOMEN

The **HEALTH AND HYGIENE** video series was researched and developed by a leading surgeon, obstetrician and gynecologist. **FEMALE HYGIENE** (CEP) is an informative program that discusses necessary hygiene practices for women. To learn the causes of PMS along with ways of controlling and managing it, an excellent program is **PREMENSTRUAL SYNDROME** (CEP). Its companion video is **HOW TO CONTROL MENSTRUAL PAIN** (CEP). For a frank and informative discussion on menopause, you may want to view **MANAGEMENT OF MENOPAUSE-RELATED PROBLEMS** (CEP) or another excellent tape, **MENOPAUSE: WHAT EVERY WOMAN SHOULD KNOW** (XJX). This video, hosted by actress Debbie Reynolds, is a fascinating yet practical overview of a subject that many women choose not to discuss.

Breast cancer is a disease that affects millions of women each year. A very informative and educational video available on this subject is **BREAST CANCER: A CURABLE DISEASE** (CEP). Endorsed by the American Cancer Society, it offers an overview of the entire field of treatment, the importance of cancer prevention, the value of good nutrition and the side effects of prescription drugs. Acting on the information gleaned from this program is the most effective way to control breast cancer. Another excellent choice is **THE BREAST CENTER VIDEO: WHAT EVERY WOMAN SHOULD KNOW** (CEP). This informative program dispels many myths about breast cancer and contains up-to-date information on treatment options along with a step-by-step guide to breast self-examination.

EVERY WOMAN'S GUIDE TO OSTEOPOROSIS (CEP) provides information about the prevention, detection and treatment of this degenerative bone disease. Women of all ages could benefit from this excellent program as it details who is at risk and how to modify your life style and diet to maintain good health.

165

PREGNANCY

WHAT TO DO WHEN YOU ARE DUE: A COMPREHENSIVE GUIDE TO PRENATAL CARE (CEP) blends warm and humorous stories from pregnant women and those who surround them to make this the most entertaining, up-to-date and informative prenatal care program available. The video answers commonly asked questions from mothers-to-be and discusses the importance of healthy habits before, during and after pregnancy. This is an excellent tape for first-time mothers and fathers to view.

Another good program that provides solid information on prenatal diet, weight gain, exercise and more is **EATING FOR TWO: PRENATAL NUTRITION FOR A HEALTHY BABY** (CEP). This award-winning program graphically illustrates the direct relationship between a mother's healthy life style and the subsequent development of a newborn child. It is both dynamic and informative.

A healthy mother requires continuing exercise during pregnancy, and there are tapes available that were especially designed to provide a safe and effective workout during this special time. Mothers-to-be can join fitness expert Kathy Smith in her **KATHY SMITH'S PREGNANCY PROGRAM** (COL) in the privacy of their own home via the VCR. You'll learn how to maintain your energy and strength during pregnancy and get back into shape after your baby's arrived. This program conforms with the guidelines set by the American College of Obstetricians and Gynecologists and includes an exercise guideline booklet.

Another medically approved program is **DENISE AUSTIN'S PREGNANCY PLUS** (COL). This tape contains two workouts: an easy low-impact pregnancy program and a more intense post-pregnancy routine. It's especially designed to build the strength and stamina you'll need (it's called labor for a reason). And for those mothers-to-be who are "steppers," you won't have to stop stepping just because you're pregnant. **STEPPING THROUGH PREGNANCY** (COL) contains medical guidelines combined with special step and floorwork modifications to keep you and your baby in perfect shape. There are plenty of stretches, gentler moves and tasteful music in this serious workout.

TAKING CARE OF BABY

If you have a newborn in your home, you may want to view an excellent tape entitled **YOUR NEW BORN BABY** (SMV). Joan Lunden will answer your questions, calm your fears and build self-confidence. You'll also get invaluable information from Jeffrey Brown, M.D. on such topics as feeding, when to call your doctor, bathing, crying, sleeping and more. This would make a great gift for a new expectant mother. And for when baby gets a little older, **WINSTON'S POTTY CHAIR** (SMV) is a charming, colorful cartoon video that helps children and their parents understand the toilet-training process.

It's been proven that massage improves the emotional communication between parent and child as it helps parents feel more competent in their baby's daily care. The video **TENDER TOUCH: A GUIDE TO INFANT MASSAGE** (HAI) is a unique program that addresses parent concerns, teaches a full-body massage with thirty-two specific strokes and shows how to create a soothing, gentle atmosphere for babies in their new surroundings. Another excellent program on this subject is **BABY MASSAGE AND EXERCISE** (SMV). Endorsed by the International Association of Infant Massage Instructors, this tape shows new parents how to use massage to soothe and relax their baby to reduce stressful crying from colic or teething. This is an excellent reference tape for your parenting library.

CHILDREN'S HEALTH

COMMON CHILDHOOD ILLNESSES (CEP) is a warm and humorous presentation that brings a refreshing approach to the serious subject of childhood illnesses. This entertaining yet informative video addresses common childhood illnesses, their symptoms and possible at-home and professional medical treatment along with how to decide if a doctor should be consulted. This is an excellent reference video to have in any child-inhabited home. Or you may want to see **WHEN TO CALL THE DOCTOR IF YOUR CHILD IS ILL** (CEP). This is another excellent reference tape that helps parents learn what to look for when deciding the seriousness of medical conditions for both infants and children of all ages.

A delightful program designed especially for children from ages three to twelve is **MR. KNOW-IT-OWL'S HEALTH TIPS** (SMV). This award-winning tape teaches kids to be smart snackers, how to eat well and all about dental care. It's an excellent way to get your kids off to a good healthy start.

****

*T*he preceding videos are dedicated to keeping yourself and your children in good physical health. For help in ensuring a positive mental atmosphere for you and your family, you'll want to take a look at the parenting section of the SELF-HELP VIDEO GUIDES chapter. There are many excellent programs available via video to help you and your children handle the inevitable situations that arise during childhood.

SAFETY & FIRST AID

Prevention is, of course, the best way to ensure that accidents don't happen, but unfortunately that is not always enough. To make sure that you are prepared to handle an emergency should it arise, take a look at the excellent videos detailed below. Programs on general first aid and keeping your children safe are sure to be of interest. And don't forget yourself. Videos are available that will teach you to defend yourself in all types of situations.

FIRST-AID TIPS

One of the most important videos you can share with your family and keep in your reference library is a tape on first-aid tips, and there are many excellent ones available. **LEARN HOW TO SAVE A LIFE WITH FIRST AID** (CEP) is a comprehensive program taught by a skilled emergency physician and advanced emergency medical technicians. They show the viewer step by step what to do when faced with a life-threatening emergency. In addition, you may want to view the **AMERICAN RED CROSS EMERGENCY TEST** (CEP), where viewers are taken through a series of dramatic and potentially life-threatening situations followed by demonstrations of the American Red Cross recommended response. You'll join John Ritter and fourteen other stars as you learn the appropriate procedure to follow in an emergency.

The creator of the life-saving Heimlich maneuver offers video viewers an incisive, no-nonsense guide to treating and, when possible, preventing the most common home emergencies. In **DR. HEIMLICH'S HOME FIRST AID** (CEP), the viewer will learn simple but effective techniques for handling choking situations, poisoning, burns, bee stings, black eyes and many more emergency situations. You may want to supplement your knowledge from this excellent program with a view of **THE MEDICAL EMERGENCY VIDEO** (EVN). This program is easily understood by adults and children alike, as it is illustrated with step-by-step, straightforward demonstrations of each maneuver. This is a "must see" video if you have never taken a first-aid course or as a refresher course.

Since heart disease remains the leading cause of death in the United States and many other countries, the importance of knowing proper cardiopulmonary resuscitation techniques cannot be stressed too strongly. If you've been meaning to take a course in this life-saving skill but just haven't gotten to it, now you can do it in the privacy of your own home. **YOUR COMPLETE GUIDE TO CPR** (CEP) is a video that teaches viewers through discussion and demonstration how to identify the early signs of a heart attack and how to administer CPR to infants, children and adults. This could be a "life-saving" video for you to view.

KEEPING OUR CHILDREN SAFE

You can learn how to create a baby-safe home and avoid unnecessary injuries by viewing **THE OUCHLESS HOUSE: YOUR BABY-SAFE HOME** (CEP). The program takes the viewer from the car to the kitchen, up the stairs, into the nursery and then the bathroom as you learn to see each area from your baby's curious and unsuspecting point of view. The important information you'll learn could prove vital to your children's safety. To ensure that your children's play time is safe time, see a helpful video guide for parents and babysitters, **PLAY IT SAFE: MAKING PLAYTIME SAFE FOR YOUR CHILD** (CEP). This informative video will provide explanations of manufacturers' labels, how to test toys for safety, how to child-proof indoor and outdoor play areas and much more. Everyone who cares for children up to the age of seven will find this program of invaluable help in keeping children safe.

There are also safety videos available on the market that are especially geared to entertain your child while teaching important safety concepts. **MR. KNOW-IT-OWL'S SAFETY TIPS** (SMV) features everyone's favorite feathered friend as he teaches some smart and simple safety tips all kids should know related to first aid, electricity, crossing the street and talking to strangers. For a fun, safe way for kids to learn the basic and necessary rules of bicycle, fire and personal safety, **KIDS FOR SAFETY** (COF) is hosted by five energetic kids who guide the young viewers through each safety segment in an upbeat and entertaining format.

You can also enlist the aid of delightful songs and characters in making safety a part of your child's life. **ACCIDENT-PROOF KIDS** (COF) covers such topics as riding in a car, bicycle safety, fire safety and water safety using likeable characters who will teach and entertain your child. One of the most important things you'll want to teach your child is **NEVER TALK TO STRANGERS** (COF). This video provides kids with entertaining dramatic productions designed to help them sort out the big challenges of growing up and developing self-confidence and wise decision-making ability.

Another important video you may want to share with your children pertains to **SCHOOL AND BUS SAFETY** (COF). The purpose of this tape is to increase a child's safety awareness both on the bus and in and around school. Safety is examined at the bus stop, on the bus and in the classroom. The program covers everything your child should know to ensure a safe trip to and from school as well as during the school day. To ensure that afterschool bicycling fun stays fun, you may want to view **BICYCLE SAFETY & GENERAL MAINTENANCE** (COF) with your children. Not only will they learn some basic bike maintenance skills, but they'll pick up key points on bicycle safety.

One of the most important videos you as a parent can share with your children is **STRONG KIDS, SAFE KIDS** (COF). In this powerfully frank video, Henry Winkler and co-hosts discuss the potential dangers children face every day, including sexual molestation and abduction. The program brings all the problems and questions out in the open. The material is frank and to the point but is presented with music and humor and some favorite cartoon characters. This is an invaluable video for the whole family to watch together.

SELF-DEFENSE

Self-defense should be an important aspect of a woman's life style, and via video, many excellent courses are available. **INSTANT SELF-DEFENSE GUIDE FOR WOMEN** (CEP) is designed for today's women who don't have the time to devote to a martial arts program. This tape shows how to instantly create escapes from assaults using natural reflexes and everyday movements that can be used anywhere at any time. For more instruction in this vital area, be sure to view **PROTECT YOURSELF: A WOMAN'S GUIDE TO SELF-DEFENSE** (CEP). This program teaches women how to defend themselves assertively without having to take expensive lessons or carry dangerous weapons. Common sense is combined with a series of effective defense techniques that will improve a woman's mental attitude, self-concept and inner strength. A very effective program.

Other tapes the viewer will find educational in the area of self-defense include **THE WOMAN'S HOW-TO OF SELF-DEFENSE** (CEP). This practical, illustrated video guide shows step-by-step defense techniques and

169

ways to avoid attacks in the office, at school, in the park and while jogging. Emphasis is placed on being assertive and mentally prepared. For that extra conditioning that could be critical if you're attacked, you may want to view **COMMON-SENSE SELF-DEFENSE FOR WOMEN** (NUQ). You will learn essential lessons on protecting yourself and loved ones from potential attacks. This program is presented by national karate champion Garry Wooten in easy-to-learn methods for women of all ages and body types. You'll learn the ten areas to strike to cause pain to an attacker and how to hit these areas with your own natural weapons.

Especially designed for the average person, either male or female, is **PRACTICAL SELF-DEFENSE** (ASV). This tape will show viewers how to defend themselves even if they are not muscular. Master Klein of the Martial Arts School teaches how to use the opponent's force against him. You'll see ways to control your attacker's attention and balance and neutralize his force. This program is also worthwhile viewing for children.

Another excellent self-defense video that can be shared by the whole family is **SAVE YOUR KIDS, SAVE YOURSELF** (CEP). This live-action program presents common, dramatic situations in which an attack can occur involving a child, a woman and a man. The emphasis of the video is on fending off the attack and getting away, and the program is easily watchable for both children and adults. For those who want to learn how to defend themselves against stronger or bigger opponents, a good tape to learn from is **SELF-DEFENSE WITH PRESSURE POINTS** (ASV). Taught by a martial arts master, this program will teach you how to reach pressure points in actual fighting and grappling situations. It is easy to learn and easier to apply.

To ensure that your children have the knowledge and skills they need to defend themselves, you may want to have them watch and learn from the excellent tape **SELF-DEFENSE FOR CHILDREN** (ASV), taped at The American Martial Arts University. Master Robert Lyons will teach your children how to break holds from stronger attackers, out-think the attacker and much more.

****

Because safety and first aid are such important topics, you'll want to have one or more of the preceding videos for your reference library. To further equip your children to be prepared for life's unexpected challenges, you may want to take a look at the FITNESS FOR KIDS section of the FEEL FIT/LOOK GOOD chapter. There are some first-rate programs detailed in the SELF-HELP VIDEO GUIDES chapter that will help your child be emotionally as well as physically prepared for life. If the self-defense videos captured your interest, be sure to take a look at the martial arts segment of the chapter on PRACTICAL, VOCATIONAL & UNUSUAL SKILLS.

MORE ON HEALTH

The subject of healthy living covers a wide range of subjects, and there are many unique videos available for your viewing. If you're wondering just what alternative medicine is all about, be sure to browse through the holistic health section. The tapes on dealing with addictions could be extremely beneficial. In addition, the exciting and insightful videos on health after forty, acupressure and depression could dramatically change your life.

HOLISTIC HEALTH

Holistic health advocates treating the whole person—body, mind and spirit—and is an ancient concept that has gained much recognition lately as an alternative form of medical treatment. For a good overview of this discipline, **HOLISTIC HEALTH: THE NEW MEDICINE** (HFF) shows leading doctors in this field at work and demonstrates their methods for controlling pain, healing cancer and promoting optimum health. To put the concepts of holistic health in practice in your own life, you may want to start with a view of **FITNESS IN THE NEW AGE** (HFF). Dyveke Spino, co-founder of Esalen Sports Center, is the viewer's physical and spiritual guide as she demonstrates progressive and scientific regimens for the body, including relaxation, inner awareness and visualization.

For more insight into the holistic approach to achieving maximum health, you may want to take a look at **QUANTUM HEALING: TOWARD PERFECT HEALTH** (HFF). This video offers a fascinating journey of discovery, from the pioneers of holistic health to the leading edge in today's mind/body medicine. Or join Dr. Bernie Siegel and ECP patients (exceptional cancer patients) as they share their inspiring stories of survival. **HOW TO BE EXCEPTIONAL** (HFF) shares techniques for helping you to cure yourself of almost any disease and for living in the moment. You may be inspired to continue with Dr. Siegel in **INNER VISION: VISUALIZING SUPER HEALTH** (HFF), an excellent video for learning the many uses and varied practices of visualization.

To discover the unlimited energies of your mind and develop your own self-healing powers, you'll want to take a look at **SELF-HEALING CHI GONG** (PAS). This tape shows how to practice mind/body exercises that strengthen and balance each of your five major organs. You'll learn simple and effective techniques that have been practiced by Taoist masters for thousands of years. And for a combination of the best sequences on meditation, medical hypnosis and visualization, **THE HEALING TAPE** (HFF) is a video anthology featuring experts in the field. The program is designed to be beneficial for people with insomnia or stress-related disorders and for those who simply want to effect a change in their lives.

Another unique program available in the alternative health field is **OF SOUND MIND AND BODY** (HFF), a video that explores the healing nature of sound with the leading experts in the field. These experts demonstrate the underlying principles of sound and vibration that make chanting, toning and psycho-acoustics effective healing tools. For an alternative way to deal with addictions, you may want to view **SPIRITUAL HELP FOR ADDICTIONS** (PAS). Swami Satchidananda presents his natural approach to overcoming addictions.

DEALING WITH ADDICTIONS

Cigarette smoking is known to be one of the leading causes of preventable death in this country, but it is an especially difficult addiction to overcome. **BUTT OUT! THE PROVEN QUIT SMOKING PLAN** (XJX), featuring Ed Asner, offers several proven techniques for kicking the habit. The viewer will learn from long-time smokers who successfully quit an array of professional advice for overcoming this powerful addiction.

Two of the most pressing problems facing youngsters today are alcohol and drugs. There are a great many excellent tapes available to educate both parents and their children on the abuse of these substances. **DRINKING...THIS BUZZ IS NOT FOR YOU!** (COF) is an informative tape that illustrates the difficulties and problems encountered by teens who use alcohol to excess and then presents specific techniques to resist the pressures of their peers.

DRUG EDUCATION FOR YOUNG PEOPLE (COF) is another fact-filled series of three programs designed to inform and educate young people about drug abuse, the consequences of different drugs and how they act on the body. It imparts a powerful message to children of all ages. **DON'T SAY YES WHEN YOU REALLY MEAN NO** (COF), also for children of all ages, helps them understand and avoid peer pressure and learn how to say no to drugs.

There are videos available to help parents deal with the problems their children are facing. **KEEP YOUR KIDS OFF DRUGS** (BSG) is a powerful yet common-sense formula to help teenagers lead well-balanced, drug-free lives. **HIGH ON LIFE, NOT ON DRUGS** (BSG) is an outstanding drug-prevention program used by thousands of teachers, clergy and parents.

A very special video is available to help parents deal with their teenage children who have become dependent on drugs or alcohol. **TEENAGE ALCOHOL & DRUG ABUSE** (COF) can help parents cope. And for the first time on video, there is a simple, basic program outlining **STRUCTURED INTERVENTION** (BSG), the first step for recovery from chemical and/or alcohol dependence. **REFLECTIONS: ONE DAY AT A TIME** (BSG) takes the viewer through the Twelve Steps of Recovery of Alcoholics Anonymous.

MATURING

An exciting video dedicated to the health of men and women over age forty is **COMING OF AGE: A LIFESTYLE PROGRAM FOR HEALTHY AGING** (XJX). This remarkable video teaches powerful lessons about staying young. You'll learn how to maintain a healthy heart, skin, bones and muscle tone in order to look your best, feel your best, prevent disease and be treated most effectively. Eddie Albert and the Forever Young Dancers provide inspiration and advice in this superb production that you can put to work today.

For a new perspective on aging, **GREEN WINTER** (HFF) explores the process of aging in all its aspects and helps viewers deal with their own later years as well as those of family members and friends. This program sensitively addresses the merits of retiring versus continuing to work, attitudes toward death, longevity, cosmetic surgery, nursing homes and much more.

Produced by a very active filmmaker in her mid-seventies, this tape offers much to stimulate discussion on the issue of aging.

For a remarkable and inspirational video on the subject of dying, you may want to view **DEATHING: AN INTRODUCTION TO CONSCIOUS DYING** (HFF). This beautifully done program is based on the premise that deathing, like birthing, requires preparation and provides an enlightened view of the transformation called death.

POTPOURRI

For the first time, a unique video tape is available to the public that provides a thorough understanding of the philosophy, science and art of chiropractic. In **HOME CHIROPRACTIC** (OEI), Dr. Karl V. Holmquist, a practicing chiropractor for seventeen years, explains and demonstrates to the video viewer step-by-step cervical, thoracic and lumbar-pelvic techniques that are easy for a family to apply at home. Self-adjusting techniques for total health benefits are also included. This excellent tape makes chiropractic health maintenance available to all families at an affordable cost.

Another unique self-help tape is **HEALING WITH SHAOLIN ACU-PRESSURE** (ASV). This remarkable video teaches you how to heal many ailments that plague modern man, such as migraine, sinus, tension, headaches, ear infection, back pain and more. The viewer will be educated in the history and theory of acupressure and will benefit from the excellent hands-on teaching. This is a must-see for anyone who has an interest in the science of acupressure.

TAKING CONTROL OF DEPRESSION: MENDING THE MIND (XJX) offers valuable insight and support for those who live with depression. Actor Ed Asner and leading national experts explore the causes as well as the treatments and medications currently available that offer new hope for those trying to learn how to take control over depression. The program demonstrates that depression is not a person's fault but a medical condition requiring medical attention.

For an incredible voyage through the human body as a new life begins, **THE MIRACLE OF LIFE** (BNS) is a dramatic breakthrough in science and cinematography. World renowned photographer Lennart Nilsson presents a spectacular look at life from conception to birth.

****

The preceding health-related videos will benefit many viewers and open up new avenues of dealing with life situations. For more instructional videos that can help you lead a better life, be sure to take a look at the array of exercise tapes available in the FEEL FIT/LOOK GOOD chapter or maybe a program to exercise your mind from the SELF-HELP VIDEO GUIDES chapter.

173

SOURCES

(See Chapter 11 for a complete alphabetical listing of all sources with addresses and phone numbers.)

ASV -   Artistic Video
BNS -   Brainstorms
BSG -   Bridgestone Group
CEP -   Cambridge Educational Products
COF -   Champions on Film
COL -   Collage Video
EVN -   Educational Video Network
FSV -   Fusion Video
HAI -   Healthy Alternatives Inc.
HFF -   Hartley Film Foundation
NGC -   Nightingale-Conant
NUQ -   New & Unique Videos
OEI -   One 8 Inc.
PAS -   Pacific Spirit
SMV -   Schoolmasters Videos
TWV -   Time Warner Home Video
XJX -   Xenejenex

CHAPTER 9:

FEEL FIT/LOOK GOOD

*WORK OUT WITH THE STARS - DANCE YOUR WAY TO FITNESS -
ZERO IN ON THE TROUBLE SPOTS - LITE & EASY - STEP IT UP -
BODYBUILDING & WEIGHT LIFTING - ESPECIALLY FOR MEN - FIT-
NESS FOR SENIORS - FITNESS FOR KIDS - YOGA FOR FITNESS -
SPECIAL & UNIQUE EXERCISES - BEAUTY TIPS - SOURCES*

WORK OUT WITH THE STARS

Seems like everybody is getting in the act these days when it comes to physical fitness videos. From sports celebrities to actors and singers, there is a vast abundance of programs just waiting to help you get in shape and stay there. So take a look at the tapes detailed below and pick two or more of your favorites to exercise along with. They will super-charge your life.

CELEBRITIES

One of the first female stars to get into the business of fitness was Jane Fonda. Many of her peers have followed in her footsteps, but she continues to be one of the most popular celebrities invited into countless homes via the VCR. Fonda's fitness programs run the complete gamut from beginner's tapes to those for the truly fit. If you're just getting started on the fitness trail, a good video for you is **JANE FONDA'S LIGHT AEROBICS** (COL). Featuring upbeat music, it starts out with low-impact aerobics to provide conditioning and loosening of those muscles and then follows up with full-body stretching and finally a total body wind-down. As your body gets in shape, you'll want to move on to the intermediate level with **JANE FONDA'S STEP AEROBICS & ABDOMINAL WORKOUT** (COL). This step aerobics and stomach-toning tape will definitely burn fat and shape your body.

For the truly dedicated, an excellent program is **JANE FONDA'S COMPLETE WORKOUT** (COL). This is a solid workout with plenty of variety in both music and routines. This is one exercise tape you won't get tired of. However, you may want to vary your routines with another Fonda tape, **JANE FONDA'S FAVORITE FAT BURNERS** (COL). This easy-to-follow program has lots of variety in movement and music, and Fonda motivates the viewer with her legendary enthusiasm and proven teaching techniques.

Another popular celebrity who has her own following in the fitness media is Cher. **CHER FITNESS - A NEW ATTITUDE** (COL) is a high-quality workout for all levels. The routines are entirely on-bench, with varied aerobics set to Cher's own music and other classic vocal rock. Or you may want to take a look at **CHER FITNESS: BODY CONFIDENCE** (COL). This non-stop dance aerobics program is sure to motivate the viewer with its great '60s & '70s rock-and-roll combined with Cher's special personal approach to fitness.

Another celebrity who has jumped on the fitness bandwagon is super model Cindy Crawford. In **CINDY CRAWFORD: SHAPE YOUR BODY** (COF), she leads you through two comprehensive fitness workouts designed for alternate days and a ten-minute mini-workout to help you revitalize yourself at any time. Her new tape, **CINDY CRAWFORD'S THE NEXT CHALLENGE** (COL), is also full of variety, exquisite MTV-type photography and high-energy dance/club music. This is a great tape for muscle toning.

Two rather unique fitness tapes have been produced by Cheryl Prewitt Salem, Miss America 1980. Pop the video **GET READY** (BSG) into your VCR and start working today to develop a positive, healthy life with this exciting low-impact aerobic workout. And be sure to continue on with a very special exercise program, **TAKE CHARGE OF YOUR LIFE** (BSG). This excellent tape will give the viewer a positive mental, emotional and spiritual awareness through aerobics.

If you're big on country music, you may want to try **TANYA TUCKER'S COUNTRY WORKOUT** (COL). This program combines Tanya's mega-hit music in a solid total-body workout. You'll burn calories to some high-energy tunes in a series of classic aerobic routines. And for an especially fun workout, be sure to take a look at **SWEATIN' TO COUNTRY WITH CHRISTY LANE** (COL). This fast-paced workout features steps from some great line dances, including the archy breaky and the electric slide. Both low- and high-impact aerobic versions are shown, with the floorwork focusing on shaping your legs. For a different type of music, try **LaTOYA JACKSON'S STEP UP WORKOUT** (COL). This is Jackson's first aerobic video, and it's a solid workout set to an upbeat mix of music.

THE FITNESS GURUS

One of the most loved fitness gurus is, of course, Richard Simmons. His **RICHARD SIMMONS - SWEATIN' TO THE OLDIES** (COL) is legendary and presents a live band playing ten hits from the '50s and '60s. The viewer will warm up to "On Broadway," work out to "It's My Party" and "Wipe Out" and then cool down with "Ain't No Mountain High Enough." The easy moves and stimulating beat continue in **RICHARD SIMMONS - SWEATIN' TO THE OLDIES 3** (COL) and **RICHARD SIMMONS - SWEATIN' TO THE OLDIES 4** (COL). The most aerobic of the set is **RICHARD SIMMONS - SWEATIN' TO THE OLDIES 2** (COL), but all of Simmons' tapes are fun to do. They provide a great medley of music and are designed for both men and women of all shapes and sizes and every degree of physical ability. And for a low-key, interesting routine for older exercisers, be sure to take a look at **RICHARD SIMMONS AND THE SILVER FOXES** (COL).

Denise Austin, host of the show "Getting Fit with Denise Austin," has produced a variety of fitness tapes on all levels. An excellent view is **DENISE AUSTIN: STRETCH AND FLEX** (COF). You will learn to relax your mind and tone up your body by stretching. **DENISE AUSTIN: 30 MINUTE FAT-BURNING WORKOUT** (COF) is a highly motivating workout that combines safe, easy-to-follow, low-impact aerobic moves that will keep your body burning fat. And for a super new workout of aerobics and body sculpting exercises, be sure to take a look at **DENISE AUSTIN: STEP WORKOUT** (COF).

If you'd like to concentrate on a particular problem area, Austin probably has a tape to do the trick—such as **DENISE AUSTIN: SUPER STOMACHS** (COF) or **DENISE AUSTIN: HIPS, THIGHS AND BUTTOCKS** (COF), which contain easy-to-do exercises. For a sensational aerobic workout for total body fitness, you're sure to enjoy **DENISE AUSTIN: KICKIN' WITH COUNTRY** (COF). Produced live from the Roy Acuff Theater at Opryland, this program treats the viewer to some of today's most popular country line dances and adapts them to create an excellent aerobic workout.

Another popular TV fitness guru is Kathy Smith. This fitness expert has a variety of programs designed for all levels and interests. Getting started can be tough, but **KATHY SMITH: STARTING OUT** (COF) was created especially for the person who has decided to begin exercising now for a healthier life. **KATHY SMITH: FAT-BURNING WORKOUT** (COL) is one of the best fitness programs ever created for burning fat, toning muscles and getting into shape. And for a very effective program for burning calories, boosting metabolism and eating right, **KATHY SMITH: WEIGHT LOSS WORKOUT** (COF) is an excellent choice.

Designed for the beginner to intermediate exerciser, **KATHY SMITH'S BODY BUILDING** (COF) gets down to basics as every part of the body is worked on. On the intermediate level, **WINNING WORKOUT** (COL) takes the viewer through a complete, goal-oriented, twelve-week fitness program that's fun, effective and easy to follow. And you'll want to continue on to **KATHY SMITH'S ULTIMATE VIDEO WORKOUT** (COF), designed for intermediate and advanced exercisers.

Six-time Ms. Olympia and former host of her own top-rated aerobics television show, Cory Everson has released a series of step and training programs that have been used by many celebrities. Why not take advantage of her expertise and invite her into your home via video? **CORY EVERSON STEP TRAINING VIDEO** (COL) is a good, basic stepping program presented with lively enthusiasm and an exciting Star Wars background. If you're an intermediate-level exerciser, you'll want to follow along with **CORY EVERSON'S TOTAL BODY WORKOUT** (COL). This is a super-comprehensive toning workout to help you burn calories and sculpt your body. And if you're interested in weight training to improve the shape of your body, be sure to look at **CORY EVERSON'S COMPLETE WEIGHT TONING SYSTEM** (COL). This is a three-tape series, one for each body area: Hips, Thighs and Calves; Chest, Shoulders and Triceps; and Back, Biceps and Abs. Cory's "at home" version uses dumbbells and a bench with excellent techniques and clear instruction.

TV fitness expert Charlene Prickett is another prolific producer of fitness videos. For the beginner, **CHARLENE PRICKETT'S HOME STRETCH** (COL) features easy-to-follow moves and deep-stretch/flexibility routines. **CHARLENE PRICKETT'S MUSCLE BUILDING** (COL) tape is a comprehensive total-body toning program on the beginning/intermediate level. **CHARLENE PRICKETT'S STEP RIGHT UP** (COL) is adaptable to many different levels. It's simple and fun and starts with guidelines on how to step. For the more physically fit viewer, Charlene offers **CHARLENE PRICKETT'S REV UP** (COL). This is definitely a challenging, high-energy workout with strenuous, wide-ranging cardiovascular routines. **CHARLENE PRICKETT'S SERIOUS CURVES** (COL) is a tough tape designed to work every muscle to the point of fatigue. And **CHARLENE PRICKETT'S REV UP - THE SEQUEL** (COL) is a super-tough, pure aerobics workout for the most advanced and enduring exerciser.

An exciting newcomer to the TV fitness scene is Susan Powter. In **SUSAN POWTER'S LEAN, STRONG AND HEALTHY** (COL) tape, she takes the viewer through an easy-to-follow program featuring lots of intensity modifications. Susan's no-nonsense motivation will soon have you on the road to better fitness. Or you may want to try a surprisingly challenging workout, **THE NEW LI TEKNIQUE WITH JOAN PRICE** (COL). This fitness expert combines aspects of aerobics, ballet and muscle conditioning to create a distinct style. Often fast-paced, the video does include modifications for less advanced levels.

****

*T*he above videos are excellent and entertaining ways to get into the fitness habit, and there are many more outstanding programs available. Whether you'd like to try aerobics or maybe just something light and easy, there is sure to be a video just right for you.

DANCE YOUR WAY TO FITNESS

Dancing your way to fitness is both fun and full of healthy benefits. Pop the tape into the VCR, turn up the volume and dance away. Your body will feel great, and you'll get to listen to a variety of music and entertainers.

GET FIT WITH THE HITS

The **DANCE AWAY** series is an innovative aerobics workout/dance program that integrates fitness with fun. You will work out to a decade of high-energy songs, sung by their original artists, along with fitness expert Molly Fox. You'll enjoy an invigorating low-impact aerobic routine to a sampling of the dance steps from each particular era. Start your dance to physical fitness with hits from **DANCE AWAY—THE '50s** (COL) and **DANCE AWAY—THE '60s** (COL). You'll soon be high-stepping it into **DANCE AWAY—THE '70s** (COL) and working up a sweat with **DANCE AWAY—THE '80s** (COL). What a fun way to get in shape.

From traditional jazz to urban funk, **VICTORIA'S DANCE STEP FORMULA** (COL) is a unique combination of on- and off-bench dance moves. The viewer receives the benefits of cardio and toning along with the excitement of dance aerobics. Also join this spirited instructor in **VICTORIA JOHNSON'S STEP WITH STYLE** (COL). This is a low-impact exercise/dance tape showing four different workout styles. Have fun with hip-hop and funky and move on to power and dance with vocal rap and club music. Or go all out and tackle **VICTORIA'S HIP HOP SOLUTION** (COL). This is a fast-paced and energetic program that combines funk, hip-hop and jazz steps with some great music.

For more great musical exercises, you may want to look at **JAZZER-CISE CIRCUIT TRAINING** (COL). The viewer will be treated to the excitement of a classic Jazzercise workout blended with the latest interval training and step innovations. The eight-minute aerobic section intermixes jazz steps like "arabesque" or "chasse" with choreographed straddles or step adductions. Between each aerobic set, you'll tone up with five minutes of varied total-body exercises. Or maybe you'd like to change the beat with **DENISE AUSTIN'S SWINGIN' TO THE BIG BANDS** (COL). You'll strengthen your heart and build stamina as you dance and sing along to your favorite big band sounds. This is an excellent tape for beginning exercisers.

If you'd rather dance than exercise, the tape for you to view is **JODY WATLEY'S DANCE TO FITNESS** (COL). This program combines street-style dance moves and a dynamic soundtrack. You'll burn fat while learning the latest dance steps and a series of well-choreographed routines. And for a change of pace, try **HOT COUNTRY AEROBICS WITH KATHY MATTEA** (COL). This is a solid country music/country line dance workout. The tape starts with a discussion of posture and alignment, and then the viewer is taken on a dancercize journey through some great country music. Shape up to classic hits as you dance yourself into shape.

MORE UNIQUE DANCING EXERCISES

To get a challenging aerobic workout and also learn the very latest club dance moves, you'll want to view a tape by Barry Joyce. **STREET JAM TO THE 2ND POWER** (COL) is fast and funky. Each new routine is slowly demonstrated, with every step broken down. Be sure to continue with **BARRY JOYCE'S STREET JAM: THREE TIMES THE FUNK** (COL) for more exercise through new club dances and combinations. These tapes are very well choreographed, with some sliding moves that are best for non-carpeted areas.

Another great dance/exercise tape based on low-impact aerobics is **CHARLOTTE WILLIAMS—FUNK IT UP** (COL). The music is rock/jazz, and the viewer will learn the latest urban funk dance movements through classic low-impact aerobics. As you get into better shape you'll want to move up to **CHARLOTTE WILLIAMS—POWER DANCE MIX** (COL). This is a fun tape with lots of variety and funky/hip-hop music. And for a really fast-paced workout, try a turn at **L.A. JAMMIN' WITH THE LAKER GIRLS** (COL). This is a high-vitality program in both music and workout routines.

For a more gentle series of dance and free-movement exercises, try the unique tape **WOMAN! FREE YOUR SOUL** (COL), hosted by an African tribal dance trainer, Eulyce. This tape is more than dancing exercise; it puts you in touch with your body through movement, sound and breathing.

179

Another experience in exercising to a special type of music is **CAHAL DUNNE'S JIG DON'T JOG** (COL), a delightful video filmed in Ireland featuring favorite Irish folk songs. This tape presents a solid, well-instructed workout along with a visually stunning tour of Ireland.

****

The preceding tapes help you get into top physical shape but also provide lots of musical fun as you dance away the pounds. Once these programs get you in the dancing mood, you'll want to take a look at all the different dancing videos available in THE WORLD OF MUSIC, DANCE & THEATRE chapter.

ZERO IN ON THE TROUBLE SPOTS

Besides a general overall exercise tape, many people also have a need to concentrate on a specific "trouble spot." There are some great videos available that do just that. Take a look at the programs detailed below and pick the right one to zero in on your own personal trouble spot. You'll get results.

ULTIMATE ABS

The most prevalent "trouble spot" is the tummy, and there are many videos available to help. The **29-MINUTE TUMMY TONER** (COF) is a low-impact, three-stage exercise routine designed to ensure a tighter, trimmer tummy in a minimum amount of time. Pop this tape into your VCR just three days a week to reduce your waistline. Or you may want to try an excellent 30-minute-a-day workout program, either **FLATTEN YOUR STOMACH FOR WOMEN** (RHV) or **FLATTEN YOUR STOMACH FOR MEN** (RHV). These tapes are based on the bestseller exercise books from *Consumer Guide*. The professional coaches in these videos will make your exercise program more enjoyable, keep you free from injury and ensure your success. For more help, a complete series of stomach stretches and exercises that puts the emphasis exactly where you want it, **STEEL STOMACHS** (COF), is an excellent choice. Developed by certified fitness consultant Barry Cocheu, the exercises are demonstrated in a step-by-step, easy-to-follow manner and are guaranteed to bring results.

Particularly good for beginners is a tape from the **WEIGHT WATCHER'S EASY SHAPE-UP** series. **WEIGHT WATCHERS: AEROBICS & BACK/ABDOMINAL WORKOUT** (COL) is non-intimidating and easy to follow. The instructors are friendly and supportive to their all-female class, and the toning segments are gentle versions of standard body-shaping routines. Another great program that shows three levels of exercises (beginner to intermediate) is **VICTORIA JOHNSON'S AB LAB** (COL). You'll maximize results by following along at your own level and gradually moving up. In addition to strengthening your stomach muscles, this tape also includes an excellent back and chest workout. Nothing fancy, just good exercise routines set to light club/funk music. A rather unique video designed to firm up and define the abdominal muscles and to strengthen the entire midsection is **SUPER ABDOMENS WORKOUT** (ASV). Taped in beautiful natural surroundings, this video is hosted by T'ai-chi-Ch'uan instructor and physical therapist Jean Goulet-Klein. It is an excellent program for anyone involved in sports, martial arts or dance and will bring results quickly and safely if practiced on a regular basis.

If you're game for trying something a little more strenuous, **KAREN VOIGHT'S FIRM ARMS AND ABS** (COL) is designed for the intermediate level. This tape makes use of a step bench and five-pound dumbbells. The stomach toning features curl variations and quick ab roll-ups performed to invigorating jazz-type music. This tape is a thorough workout using resistance, contraction and controlled movements in unique step routines. If you're really adventurous, probably the toughest ab tape is **JOANIE GREG-GAINS—ULTIMATE ABS** (COL). Every abdominal muscle will get a workout with solid floorwork and lots of variety. You won't be bored, as Greggains' inspiring personality and well-designed program will have you moving from one routine to another with maximum results.

UPPER BODY BEAUTIFUL

If you're interested in firming up your entire upper body, tapes are available that might be of interest. **UPPER BODY BEAUTIFUL—GREAT BODY** (COL) is a unique program that focuses exclusively on your upper body. You'll firm and shape your bustline by strengthening all the underlying muscles and tone your back and arms by utilizing light weights to add resistance. You may want to alternate this program with **WEIGHT WATCHER'S AEROBICS & UPPER BODY WORKOUT** (COL). This program is especially good for beginners, as it presents easy-to-follow routines taught by friendly and supportive teachers. For more help in upper-body toning, be sure to take a look at **TONY LITTLE'S UPPER BODY REDUCTION** (COL). The viewer will firm muscles with a well-planned series of floor and standing isolations. The unique countdown graph will let you control the intensity of the exercises from beginning level to advanced. And Tony's aggressive, one-on-one style will surely keep you motivated.

LOWER BODY

You can pick from several excellent videos if you want to zero in on your legs and lower body. **LEAN LEGS & BUNS** (COL) was produced by the internationally acclaimed Voight Fitness and Dance Center. Top instructor Karen Voight is an excellent teacher to view and follow to reach your goals. The program uses a step bench and light weights to help you maximize results. Or you might want to exercise along with physical fitness specialist Deborah Crocker. Her high-energy program, **DYNAMITE LEGS** (CEP), is from the **ESQUIRE GREAT BODY** series. The specially designed exercises and stretches will help you achieve beautiful results in just thirty minutes a day. And for a complete lower-body workout, **WEIGHT WATCHER'S AEROBIC & LOWER BODY WORKOUT** (COL) is an excellent choice. This video is from the **EASY SHAPE-UP** series and particularly good for beginners.

181

For a complete exercise program that targets different specific areas of your body, the **BUNS OF STEEL** series is one of the best. Get started with **BUNS OF STEEL-1** (COL). Fitness instructor Tamilee Webb will lead you through an intensive workout that will firm, trim and tighten your buttocks, hips and thighs, plus tone and add definition to your upper legs. When you've mastered these routines, you can continue on to **BUNS OF STEEL-2** (COL) for more overall exercises targeted at toning arms and abs and then **BUNS OF STEEL-3** (COL) for a toning workout that concentrates on your lower body. For more workouts that are guaranteed to show results, be sure to continue with Tamilee in **LEGS OF STEEL** (COL) as she leads you in routines to define and strengthen your legs. The truly dedicated will also want to view **BUNS OF STEEL: STEP WORKOUT** (COL). This step-aerobics program features the latest routines and most effective techniques ideal for the intermediate as well as the advanced fitness fanatic.

****

*T*here are many videos available to help with the trouble spots and with overall body toning. For easy-going routines, try a program from the LITE & EASY section or rev it up with a high-energy video from the STEP IT UP section.

LITE & EASY

It's been proven that exercise does not have to be all sweat and groans in order to be effective. Take a look at the following fitness videos for an easier way to get in shape. Stretching and walking are both excellent pursuits on the road to a healthier you. Remember, it's not how tough your exercise program is but rather how consistently you stick to it.

STRETCHING

Stretching helps keep muscles flexible and ready for movement, improves performance and helps prevent injuries from physical activity. It just makes you feel good. To get started on this excellent path to fitness, take a look at **STRETCHING** (COL) with Bob Anderson, America's leading stretching expert and teacher. You can follow along at your own pace as he teaches you the right way to stretch and helps you to begin a regular, life-long program of physical fitness. This great tape concludes with an overall routine for everyday fitness or for specific sports or activities.

For a real treat, Richard Simmons is available via **STRETCHIN' TO THE CLASSICS** (COL), set to well-known classics performed by an orchestra. Simply follow Richard and stretch very muscle from your fingers to your toes. There's not a word of distracting instruction, and there simply isn't a more relaxing way to stretch. You can improve your figure while relieving everyday tension with **ULTRA STRETCH** (COF). The viewer is shown a series of soothing exercises that will prevent sore muscles and also relieve stress. Produced by *Redbook* magazine, this video is an innovative workout designed to lengthen and strengthen the muscles in your legs and upper body and give you a sleeker figure.

Another good program for the beginner or intermediate is **KAREN VOIGHT'S PURE AND SIMPLE STRETCH** (COL). The viewer will increase total-body flexibility and relaxation while listening to a great new-age soundtrack. Using a solid combination of dynamic and static stretches, Voight demonstrates three different intensity levels and gives precise tips on technique. Or you might want to join another fitness expert in **JOANIE GREGGAINS—SCULPT AND STRETCH** (COL). This is a well-planned, safe, easy-to-follow tape for beginners and intermediates. The stretches usually work two body areas at once for effective body sculpting. One of the exercisers performing in this excellent program is sixty-seven years old, so you know that anyone can be motivated by Greggains' overwhelming enthusiasm.

WALKING PLUS

With the aid of a video, you can walk your way right into physical and mental fitness, and one of the best programs to start with is **HEALTH-WALKING** (COF). This health walking training system was designed by Nike and SyberVision. It's an easy program that combines efficient, low-impact exercises with motivational ideas to keep you putting your best foot forward. Even if you don't follow a regular fitness program, you'll enjoy this video and feel great in no time at all.

For another program to help develop the proper walking stride and techniques, you'll want to take a look at **YES! WE'RE WALKING** (CEP). You will learn how to establish a walking program that meets your individual needs and benefit from a fitness walking warm-up and stretch section. You'll also receive a copy of the sixteen-page Rockport Fitness Walking Test with your video. This is the perfect low-impact exercise program for better overall fitness. And for even more instruction in this great activity, the **WALKING WORKOUT** (COF) is an easy-to-follow, step-by-step tape hosted by Cynthia Costa. You'll learn all the fundamental skills necessary to reach your goals and become healthier and more fit.

If time is your enemy, you can get help from Ann Peel, one of the top-ranked racewalkers in the world. In **WALKING FIT** (CEP), she'll show you how to set up a fitness program that you can squeeze into your busy schedule. Along with demonstrations on proper walking, this comprehensive walking video presents information on walking shoes, avoiding injury and pain and walking as a competitive sport as well as tour walking and hiking. If weight loss is your goal, be sure to see **LESLIE SANSONE: WEIGHT LOSS WALK** (COF). This is a great exercise program that will allow you to walk up to four miles—indoors. The pace is just right, the music is terrific and it's a great way to get into shape.

When your body and mind are ready, you may want to increase your speed and try **RUNNING FOR FUN AND FITNESS** (COF). Marathon winner Bill Rodgers is available via video to guide you through a running program that covers attire, avoiding injuries, short- and long-distance running and much more. To really stay in shape, use Marty Liquori as your personal trainer and coach. **MARTY LIQUORI'S RUNNER'S WORKOUT** (COF) is good for beginning and accomplished runners alike, and his advice will help you become a better athlete.

****

The preceding videos may be "lite and easy," but if you incorporate their advice into your everyday life you're sure to reap many beneficial and healthful results. For more non-aerobic fitness programs, take a look at the YOGA FOR FITNESS section.

STEP IT UP

There are some great videos on aerobic exercises, from light-and-easy low-impact routines to high-energy workouts, that are sure to capture your interest. Or if you're into steppin', be sure to browse through the excellent tapes that can help you step your way up to maximum physical fitness. For the ultimate workout, there are some very demanding programs that will present you with a challenge. So take a look, pick a tape and get started on the road to optimum physical health.

AEROBIC WORKOUTS

Aerobics is a popular way to get into shape, and a good video to start with is **LIGHT AND EASY WORKOUT** (COF). From the **ESQUIRE GREAT BODY** series, this program will help you get noticeable results in just thirty minutes a day. The special controlled-movement exercises will take you from a gentle warm-up to a refreshing cool-down with a great workout in between. You'll soon want to move on to Esquire's **LOW-IMPACT AEROBICS** (COL), which is also based on getting results in just thirty minutes a day. This program will teach you a safe, fun and fast way to lose weight and get into shape. For the perfect routines to sculpt muscles without high-impact stress, Esquire's **LOW IMPACT AEROBICS WITH WEIGHTS** (COL) is the tape to view. Using light hand weights, this program will guide you through moderately paced aerobics and no-strain hand-weight exercises for all the major muscle groups.

For more aerobic instruction, **SUPER SLIM DOWN** (COF), produced by *Redbook* magazine, is a great way to drop a few pounds or a few dress sizes as you get into shape. This excellent video was designed to show you how to burn calories and condition your heart as you achieve your weight goal quickly and safely. For another aerobics program that will have your whole body in constant motion, try **KARI ANDERSON'S SWEAT EXPRESS** (COL). This Seattle fitness expert will show the viewer how to really burn fat with innovative, continuous aerobic action. The workouts, the warm-ups and the cool-downs are all extensive and fast-paced. Or you might want to join Len Kravitz in **ANYBODY'S EXERCISE** (COL). As a "Dance Exerciser of the Year," he brings intelligence and an upbeat personality to this video. He's tough, but his manner is polite, graceful and even a little "dancey." The tape combines a unique blend of aerobics with some "double toning."

Another exciting aerobics fitness program you'll want to view is **SLIDING: ULTRA SLIDING WORKOUT** (COL). In this well-produced video, Sandy Lewis demonstrates a range of invigorating aerobics with movement styles ranging from basic to advanced, from Latin to funky. For **AEROBICS WITH SOUL** (COL), join Maria Nhambu Bergh, a native of Tanzania, in a unique program featuring tribal dances and original African music. Maria's all-female group demonstrates three different levels so you can increase the intensity as you learn the moves. This is a really fun way to get into shape and stay there.

For a rather different but practical way to get into shape via aerobics, take a look at **DEFENSE-ROBICS** (COL). This tape is a solid self-defense-oriented aerobic workout followed by a practical instructional segment on protecting yourself. Created especially for women, it also explores women's feelings about men and taking care of themselves. This is an invaluable tape for your fitness library. Another unique program you may want to add to your aerobics collection is **YOGA-ROBICS** (COL), hosted by Larry Lane. This creative workout combines modern dance techniques and aerobics with yoga breathing. From the quiet music to the instructor's low-key style, you'll work out without a struggle.

STEP WORKOUTS

Once you've gotten yourself into moderate shape, you'll want to step up your aerobic routines, and a great tape to go on to is **STEP REEBOK: THE VIDEO** (COL). This is an ultra-high-tech production with MTV-style photography and great music in a solid basic-step workout. Despite the quick video cuts, instructor Gin Miller is easy to follow as she progresses from simple to more complex movements. If you are really brave, follow Gin Miller into **REEBOK-POWER STEP** (COL). This is the toughest, most complex Reebok tape ever and is filled with unique, explosive propulsion moves. This video could be a worthwhile goal to shoot for.

A good beginning-intermediate tape for step-aerobics you might want to view is **JOANIE GREGGAINS—ULTIMATE STEP WORKOUT** (COL). Greggains' great motivation and video close-ups will really help the viewer learn the basic steps in very easy-to-follow moves. This is a great toning program and does require the use of dumbbells. Another approach to step aerobics, **NUTS & BOLTS WITH A SPRING** (COL), contains basic steps with lots of build-on combinations. The upbeat music, interesting graphics and creativity of this tape make it a fun and interesting program to follow. Or you might enjoy **POWER STEPPING WITH LYNNE BRICK** (COL). This fitness instructor of the year coaches the viewer in a solid program with explicit cuing and clear guidance. You'll pick up new moves while getting a great workout.

If you've moved up to the intermediate/advanced level, be sure to take advantage of the expertise of athlete Gilad Janklowicz. **GILAD'S STEP AND TONE WORKOUT** (COL), filmed on a stunning Hawaiian beach, will give the viewer a thorough total-body workout that incorporates dumbbells into the aerobics. Gilad's an athlete, not a dancer, so he concentrates on basic shaping routines to burn calories and tone your body. For more of his strong, friendly personality, be sure to go on to **GILAD'S STEP AERO-BICS** (COL). This tape is a little more advanced, and as usual with Gilad, you'll be exercising outdoors on a beautiful Waikiki beach. For a more chore-ographed step video, take a look at **STEP ON IT WITH ANDRE HOULE** (COL). After a dancey warm-up, the viewer will move into some interesting sequences, including movements that have your back to the TV.

Two videos featuring ESPN's body-shaping team were designed to aero-bically train the viewer using the new step method that shapes the body and contributes to weight loss. **THE AEROBIC STAIR—INTERMEDIATE** (ESP) and **THE AEROBIC STAIR—ADVANCED** (COL) both use a step and hand weights to help viewers get in better shape. And you may want to top off your aerobic training with the **SUPER STEP WORKOUT** (COL). Hosted by instructor Charles Little, this choreographed program mixes the newest steps and top-of-the-bench hops and jumps with proven classic rou-tines. You'll burn calories, tone your body, get in shape and never, ever get bored with this excellent video.

TOUGH STUFF

You don't need leg warmers or fancy running suits for the **ARMED FORCES WORKOUT** (CEP). All you need is discipline and desire. This is a complete training course, including warm-up, aerobics, physical readiness training, stretching and cool-down exercises, done by the men and women of the armed forces, including the "daily seven." Consistent use of this tape will see you in tip-top shape. If you desire to go even further, the **TOUGH STUFF WORKOUT** (CEP) is based on the advanced training system devel-oped in the Soviet Union called Plyometrics. This dynamic program is an explosive power and speed workout that will give you better results in less time than most other programs. Follow along only three times a week, and you'll soon be looking and feeling great.

To add some fun and variety each day to your exercise program, be sure to take a look at the **ROTATION AND MOTIVATION EXERCISE** series. While all three of these videos can stand alone, rotating the tapes provides a more effective total conditioning program. **THE CALORIE BURNER WORKOUT** (CEP) will take the viewer from a solid warm-up into aerobic exercises and then a comfortable cool-down. Designed to flatten the stom-ach while shaping and firming the mid-section, **THE NO FLAB WORK-OUT** (CEP) includes standing exercises and floorwork for maximum results. And for muscle firming and toning routines that add definition to your body and muscle groups, you'll also want to try the **TIGHTEN UP WORKOUT** (CEP).

More high-paced workouts can be found in the dynamic video **PLAT-FORM OF POWER** (COL). Using a step, the viewer will mix propulsions, repeaters and straddles with some unique bench moves. A challenging seg-ment of the video will really have you burning the fat. You can keep on going with instructor Barbara McDermott in **HIGH ENERGY STEP** (COL). This is definitely an intense workout, and you'll spend a lot of time in the air. McDermott's superb instruction and dynamic personality will help you tone your entire body with proven routines.

For a really tough, fast-paced workout that blends interval step aerobics with solid muscle toning, **KAREN VOIGHT'S ENERGY SPRINT WORK-OUT** (COL) is especially challenging. You will maximize calorie burning and excitement as you follow Voight's seven "sprints" and well-structured body-shaping routines. And for the apex of fitness, the tape to do is Teri Wexted's **ALL OUT—THE TOTAL BODY WORKOUT** (COL). Great choreography and exciting music combine with a wide variety of moves by a high-energy instructor. Wexted demonstrates superb form while using graphics and reverse-angle video insets to show movement details. Execution of this certified fitness program should be any serious exerciser's ultimate goal.

****

The preceding videos can help you get in tip-top shape and increase your endurance. Why not use that endurance and take your healthy body outdoors with one of the excellent tapes from THE GREAT OUTDOORS chapter? Your great new body will make any activity, whether snow skiing or water skiing, canoeing or camping, more enjoyable.

BODYBUILDING & WEIGHT LIFTING

In addition to an improved physical appearance, bodybuilding and weight lifting provide many more beneficial results. Use the videos detailed below to improve your overall body conditioning, strength and flexibility as well as cardiovascular development.

The bodyshaping plan of fitness expert Cory Everson goes beyond aerobics. Her series of videos will teach you how to reshape, tone and firm your body. Her **CORY EVERSON: BODYSHAPING** (ESP) is geared to all skill levels. The video zeros in on the specific muscle areas you need to trim and mold to have the exact shape you want. For the next step in your program, be sure to move on to **CORY EVERSON: BODYSHAPING FOR SLENDER THIGHS, HIPS & STOMACH** (ESP). In this program, Everson takes you step by step to the shapely and sexy body you've always dreamed about. For an instructional video specifically for use with her BodyShaping Home Gym, take a look at **CORY EVERSON BODYSHAPING HOME GYM & WORKOUT VIDEO** (ESP). When used together, the workout and the gym can help you change the shape of your body, lose fat, burn calories and strengthen your muscles.

Another fitness and bodyshaping expert, Anja Schreiner, is available to come into your home via video. She will guide you through her personal fitness routine using both circuit-training and free weights. Her **ANJA SCHREINER'S UPPER BODY WORKOUT** (ESP) will help to tone your arms, define shoulders and back and strengthen your chest. To slenderize your thighs and tone your buttocks, **ANJA SCHREINER'S LOWER BODY WORKOUT** (ESP) is sure to do the trick.

187

For a unique way to shape and tone at home, why not take advantage of Gold's Gym, a recognized leader in the world of optimum fitness and conditioning. In **PERSONAL TRAINER: LEVEL ONE** (COF), professional trainers will introduce the viewer to easy weight-training routines using available household items or free weights. You can expect great results from only three sessions a week. For more advanced exercises and weight-training routines, **PERSONAL TRAINER: LEVEL TWO** (COF) is the way to go for the body you've always wanted.

An excellent video program for both men and women is **KEYS TO WEIGHT TRAINING** (COL). Bill Pearl, professional weight trainer and winner of five Mr. Olympia titles, will guide you step by step through three progressively challenging free-weight routines. You'll also benefit from his expertise on safe lifting techniques, motivational tips and guidelines for creating your own custom routine. You might want to supplement this program with **MARGARET RICHARDS' HIGH VOLTAGE WORKOUT** (COL). Nothing fancy, Margaret's easy-to-follow program ranges from squats and lunges to push-ups and basic dumbbell routines. Each thirty-minute section is complete, but you can alternate days or go for the entire one-hour workout.

****

*A*lthough today many women also participate, bodybuilding and weight lifting have traditionally appealed more to men. Other videos that the male viewer may find interesting can be found below in the *ESPECIALLY FOR MEN* section.

ESPECIALLY FOR MEN

There are some excellent videos designed especially to appeal to the male viewer and to aid him in achieving the body he desires. Those who really want to develop their bodies as well as condition and strengthen them but don't have the time or the money for trips to the gym should browse through the videos detailed below. There's sure to be one or more that can be used to create an in-home gym via the VCR.

Athlete Gilad Janklowicz has developed an exceptional workout program especially designed for men's natural strengths and physical abilities. **GILAD INTERVAL TRAINING FOR MEN** (ESP) includes warm-ups, cardiovascular intervals and cool-down/stretching routines. With this exceptional workout program, you'll also be introduced to strength circuit training with weights and floorwork circuits. Or let the Hulk show you how to achieve body perfection by viewing **LOU PERIGNO'S BODY PERFECTION** (COF). Along with L.A. Lakers stars Kurt Rambis and Michael Cooper, Perigno will show you his personal program of exercise and health, including weight training, calisthenics, aerobics and proper nutrition.

If you're interested in weight lifting, see **WEIGHTLIFTING TRAINING & CONDITIONING** (COF). Starting with a warm-up for ligaments and tendons, the viewer will progress to slow stretching exercises, all designed to prepare the body by loosening up the joints, muscles and tissues. You'll continue on to a series of exercises utilizing barbells, dumbbells and the weight bench. This is a great program to get you started in weight lifting while providing beneficial conditioning along the way.

Seven-time Mr. Olympia, Lee Haney, has produced a series of videos to share his secrets for building a great body. In **LEE HANEY'S WORKOUT** (ESP), he takes you through his day-by-day routines as he shows you how to develop your legs, abs, back, shoulders and arms. In addition to the excellent demonstrations, you'll get Haney's personal tips on motivation and a posing demo by Lee himself.

This popular former Mr. Olympia has also produced three very specialized video workouts especially for men. In each video, he focuses on a specific body area and demonstrates the routines and repetitions necessary to develop muscle. **LEE HANEY: POWER ARM WORKOUT** (ESP) is a comprehensive arm routine that will add mass and power to your biceps and sculpt and define your triceps. Or learn to pump those pecs to develop a titanic chest by following the routines in **LEE HANEY: MASSIVE CHEST WORKOUT** (ESP). And for the ultimate training to develop massive and powerful legs, be sure to work along with Lee in **LEE HANEY: EXPLOSIVE LEGS WORKOUT** (ESP).

****

The preceding tapes are especially for men, while many of the tapes in previous sections have been designed mainly for the female exerciser. Be sure to look at the SPECIAL & UNIQUE EXERCISES section for more specialized fitness videos designed with a particular viewer in mind.

FITNESS FOR SENIORS

As the country becomes more "fitness aware," the benefits of exercise are becoming more and more evident. One of the fastest growing groups of people to embrace physical fitness regimens is senior citizens. And one of the fasting growing market areas for fitness tapes is seniors. Following are tapes for mature adults that are appropriate for a wide range of ages and levels of physical ability.

One of the first exercise tapes geared to the mature exerciser to come on the market was the **DANCIN' GRANNIES** program. **DANCIN' GRANNIES: EASY START** (COF) is especially for beginners and is full of safe, easy dance exercises. The great music in this program makes exercising fun, and you'll find the stretches designed for the mature woman to be an excellent way to tone up your body. You'll also want to dance on to another tape, **DANCIN' GRANNIES: TRIM & TONE** (COF). After following this program for just a few weeks, the mature viewer will feel stronger and more vital.

The **SENIOR STRETCH** series is another unique program aimed at helping seniors remain young and free of pain through physical fitness. Produced by seventy-five-year-old fitness expert Terry Robinson, the video demonstrates simple body movements the viewer can perform daily at home, in the office or while traveling. You can pick from **SENIOR STRETCH FOR WOMEN** (COF) and **SENIOR STRETCH FOR MEN** (COF). And to add a different dimension to your exercising program, you may want to try **SENIOR STRETCH FOR COUPLES** (COF). These are all excellent tapes to get you started on your own physical fitness regimen.

While **20/20 TOTAL BODY FITNESS** (COF) is aimed at men and women over fifty, it is effective for exercisers of all ages. It is a safe, carefully crafted program that requires minimal time for maximum results. You will utilize relatively inexpensive equipment as you work out in the privacy of your own home via your VCR. Or you might want to try the **GOLDEN WORK-OUT** (COF), which was developed for mature adults. The safe and effective dance step exercises in this program will help you develop your muscles, attain postural alignment and prevent hypertension and locked joints.

FIT AFTER 50 (TJP) is a unique exercise video tape that truly caters to the needs and abilities of those over fifty and the sedentary. This tape was inspired by a marvelous fitness course given as part of an Elderhostel program and features "elders" as they go through a gentle, fun-to-do workout. The warm-ups are done seated, and all the exercises are stress-free. You'll enjoy a stimulating workout regardless of age and wind up feeling great. Or you may want to take a look at **MORE ALIVE AFTER 55** (TWV). This safe, non-aerobic fitness program was designed to help the viewer build flexibility, strength and endurance. These special exercise routines are for mature adults who are truly young at heart.

Even the celebrities have become involved in exercise tapes for the seniors market. Now you can invite lovable Angela Lansbury into your home via video and follow along with her personal program for fitness and well-being. In **ANGELA LANSBURY'S POSITIVE MOVES** (COF), she guides the viewer through her easy-to-follow routine of simple stretches, exercises and enjoyable activities for a very pleasurable workout. Or you might want to join one of TV's "Golden Girls" in **ESTELLE GETTY'S YOUNG AT HEART** (COL). You'll be motivated by Getty's encouragement and gentle humor as you follow along at your own level.

Probably the easiest to follow seniors program is **WALK AEROBICS FOR SENIORS** (COF). This video takes the viewer through four low-impact steps. You'll march, kick, knee-lift and side-step as you walk along to big band instrumental music. The walking movements will get your heart rate to a moderate level so you get all the health benefits of an aerobic workout without jumping around. The program is equivalent to a brisk two-mile walk outdoors, but you never leave your living room.

****

190 *To expand your physical fitness routine even further, be sure to take a look at the stretching and walking programs in the LITE & EASY*

section of this chapter. Or you might want to try one of the excellent yoga tapes in the YOGA FOR FITNESS section.

FITNESS FOR KIDS

It's never too early to get the little ones started on the path to physical fitness. Videos are available to teach even the smallest tots fun yet beneficial exercise routines that they'll enjoy doing. Many of these tapes will seem like playtime to your children, but they really will be helping them develop physically fit bodies.

LITTLE TOTS' TUNE-UPS

SING, STRETCH AND SHAPE UP (SMV) is a fully animated program especially for the little tots. They'll join delightful cartoon characters Casey Rabbit, Albert Possum and Omar Owl as they explore new ways to move like different animals. The fun, child-appealing music will hold their interest as they sing, stretch and shape up. Or introduce the youngsters to huge, lovable Enufsenuf in the interactive video **TEENY TIME TUNE-UPS** (BSG). This program is designed for body and character building using fun songs to help children grow physically, mentally and socially. They'll learn some new catchy tunes that reinforce positive values as they tune up.

Two well-produced videos for kids two to five years old provide an ideal way for parent and child to exercise and play together. **WORKOUT WITH MOMMY & ME** (COF) is a blend of games, exercise, make-believe and songs that will start your child toward a life of fitness. You and your child will join Olympic coach Barbara Davis plus two mothers and their kids as you chase elephants in Africa, walk on the moon and get involved in some exercise games. There are also some educational segments, such as the one on counting in a foreign language, that combine learning with workouts. And **WORKOUT WITH DADDY & ME** (COF) is based on the same unique format that is both educational and entertaining.

A fun indoor exercise tape for kids ages three to eight is **KINDER KICKS** (SMV). The program shows safe and creative ways for children to exercise indoors. Basic components of large and small muscle movement are included plus safety rules, imagery development, balance, coordination and flexibility. And for more aid in developing good exercise habits at an early age, **TIP TOP** (SMV) is a program that kids will have fun with. The tape, designed by fitness expert Suzy Prudden, features a carefully coordinated series of progressive exercises and warm-up activities. Volume 1 is geared to exercises for children from three to six years of age, while ages seven to ten will enjoy the routines in Volume 2.

MORE KID-PROOF EXERCISES

For kids five to ten years old, a high-energy, creative and playful video is **HIP HOP ANIMAL ROCK WORKOUT** (COL). The animated characters and high-energy music will get your kids moving. This program is a low-impact workout led by an enthusiastic fifteen-year-old girl, and all the moves

191

mimic animal motions. The kids will love the "enchanted rain forest" setting and the hot dance tunes they've heard on TV. And for a spirited "serious" workout, treat five- to ten-year-old Barbie fans to a **DANCE WORKOUT WITH BARBIE** (COL). Through the California Raisin animation team, Barbie comes to life to motivate and inspire and get your kids in shape. This program is fast and dancey and has great vocal pop/rock sound. The kids will want to exercise over and over again.

Instead of just letting your kids watch TV, make it possible for them to get a genuine aerobics and toning workout. The **FUNHOUSE FITNESS** series, designed by child development experts, provides kids with an all-around workout plus information on nutrition and exercises. For the four- to eight-year-olds, **SWAMP STOMP** (COL) combines a playful blend of high-energy music and "real" exercises with action, dance and fantasy moves. Kids eight to twelve years old will especially enjoy **FUNHOUSE FUNK** (COL). This fast-paced program combines MTV-style music and non-stop dance moves with funky, high-energy exercise routines. Both of these excellent videos are hosted by Jane Fonda and led by J.D. Roth and his Saturday morning Fox TV crew.

For the pre-teener, you may want to take a look at **AMERICAN JUNIOR WORKOUT** (COF). This video will help children discover their talents and learn how their bodies work while they also learn the value of physical fitness. For the teenagers, **THE COMPLETE TEEN WORKOUT** (COF) is an excellent aerobic workout tape. Susan Zaliouk, youth fitness teacher and dance instructor, structured this video specifically to the physical requirements of the developing teenage body.

Another great program to start children of all ages on their way to healthy habits is **WALK AEROBICS FOR KIDS** (SMV). This easy-to-follow beginner's-level walk aerobics video was produced by aerobic instructor Leslie Sansone. It is specially designed to encourage kids to get in shape with walk aerobics. For a change of pace, a video you may want your children to view is **YOGA FOR CHILDREN** (PAS). This unique program is hosted by Swami Satchidananda, who has been teaching yoga to children the world over since 1949. His method of yoga helps children to develop strong, flexible, healthy bodies and clear, focused minds.

To ensure that your kids get in shape both physically and spiritually, you may want them to take a look at **CHILDREN'S FITNESS FUN** (SMV). The easy-to-follow exercises were designed just for kids ages four to twelve and include warm-ups, workouts and cool-downs. Your children will want to play the original music score over and over again for hours of fitness fun. This special program is based on the theory that kids can give their praise to God while establishing great habits for a lifetime of fitness. It's a positive, Christian video that builds up children's physical ability as well as their self-esteem.

****

*K*ids can have hours of fun with the preceding videos while getting into shape physically. For more physical activities for the youngsters, be sure to take a look at the programs in the kids section of the WORLD OF MUSIC, DANCE & THEATRE chapter. The dance instruction tapes can also afford your children a good physical workout while teaching them some great dance routines.

YOGA FOR FITNESS

An excellent way to shape up both your body and your mind is to learn yoga. Yoga exercises focus on your breathing, your body alignment and your self-awareness. This classical discipline has been around for centuries and is currently growing in popularity as a fitness medium. There are excellent videos available to guide viewers through the graceful movements of yoga, from beginner to advanced and regardless of age.

Produced by the people at the *Yoga Journal,* **YOGA FOR BEGINNERS** (COL) is a good way to get started. This extraordinarily well-produced program is an introduction to Hatha yoga. The viewer will learn to execute twenty-three different poses and receive guidance on body position, balance point and even where to focus "mental awareness." From the "inverted dog pose" to eyelid relaxation, this video will soothe every part of your body. For more exposure to yoga, be sure to take a look at the three-volume program **YOGA JOURNAL'S YOGA PRACTICE**. This exciting series covers all levels of yoga from beginner to advanced. Each tape emphasizes a specific yoga benefit so you can choose your own exercise goal. This series is well produced, and the instruction is friendly and reassuring. You can take your pick of **YOGA FOR FLEXIBILITY** (COL), **YOGA FOR STRENGTH** (COL) or **YOGA FOR RELAXATION** (COL). Each video has two complete workouts along with a booklet listing the exercises. You may want to try all three.

Another good beginner's tape is **RICHARD HITTLEMAN'S YOGA COURSE I** (COL). You'll get private, one-on-one lessons from this thirty-five-year-old yoga veteran. Starting with the basics, you will learn everything from choosing the most comfortable sitting position to easy breathing routines and much more. You'll soon be ready to move on to **RICHARD HITTLEMAN'S YOGA COURSE II** (COL) for higher-intensity movements for the intermediate or advanced viewer. This series is considered one of the most serious and most instructional of all yoga videos. To round out your knowledge, be sure to avail yourself of **HITTLEMAN'S GUIDE TO YOGA MEDITATION** (COL), a perfect tape to relax to.

Another non-mystic, fun-to-learn introduction to Hatha yoga is **LILIAS, ALIVE WITH YOGA - I** (COL). Lilias's down-home style and sincere, friendly approach will appeal to many viewers and help them achieve the inner peace that yoga brings. This program focuses on stretch/muscle-toning yoga movements, which enable you to discover what your body actually feels like. The mellow music complements Lilias's one-to-one teaching technique. You'll want to go on to **LILIAS, ALIVE WITH YOGA - II** (COL) for more toning-oriented movements on an intermediate to advanced level. And to really open up and invigorate your body, be sure to view **LILIAS: ENER-GIZE WITH YOGA** (COL). This is an excellent series of tapes for all levels of yoga devotees.

To add to your repertoire, be sure to view **YOGA MOVES** (COF). This is a step-by-step approach to yoga starring yoga master Alan Finger. He guides you through an array of yoga exercises that will tone, strengthen and aid you in developing suppleness and energy. For those viewers familiar with basic yoga, **PRISCILLA PATRICK'S YOGA MAINTENANCE ROU-TINE** (TWV) is an ideal tape to watch. You will be revitalized by this solid yoga workout designed to develop strength, tone and flexibility. And for an easy, stress-reducing yoga workout that fits into the busiest schedule, take a look at **PRISCILLA PATRICK'S 15 MINUTE YOGA ROUTINE** (TWV). This video will leave you feeling relaxed and refreshed.

For a dynamic program designed as the fitness of the future, you'll want to see **THE ULTIMATE STRETCH & WARRIOR WORKOUT** (PAS). Based on the doctrine of Kundalini yoga, this video is a blend of movement, stretching, postures, meditation and relaxation to empower you on all levels. You will learn to begin the day with dynamic breathing and stretching, then on to a non-stop, no-holds-barred energy-building routine. After winding down, you'll be guided through a meditation segment and finish up feeling good and looking great. Or you might want to **LEARN YOGA FROM A MASTER!** (PAS). Swami Satchidananda is one of the most well-known instructors of Hatha yoga in the world today. In his video, he individually guides each viewer in a number of different postures that will both relax and energize the body and mind.

****

Yoga is just one of many ways to keep physically fit. Another way is dancing, and there are some great videos available in the DANCE YOUR WAY TO FITNESS section of this chapter. Or for something more aerobic, try one of the excellent tapes detailed in the AEROBIC WORKOUTS section.

SPECIAL & UNIQUE EXERCISES

As you can see from the preceding sections, there is a vast array of fitness videos available for the home viewer. In addition, many tapes have been produced that address special and unique situations. If you are looking for that special fitness program that will accommodate your own unique needs or those of someone you know, be sure to look below at the outstanding tapes available.

A truly inspiring fitness program is **REACH FOR FITNESS** (CEP). In this unique video, Richard Simmons offers advice about nutrition and daily exercises designed especially for the disabled. The exercises are suitable for individuals affected by a range of disabilities and health conditions. This extremely motivating program teaches viewers to believe in themselves and have a positive attitude.

For those viewers with special fitness needs, leading occupational therapist Nancy Sebring has produced two remarkable videotapes. **NANCY'S SPECIAL WORKOUT: FOR THE PHYSICALLY CHALLENGED** (COF) is a unique workout that starts with easy warm-ups, moves to a cardiovascular routine and then ends with a cool-down period. This entire program is done while sitting down, either in a wheelchair or in a standard chair. It is a fun and beneficial workout for the disabled. And for a new, creative exercise program for the learning disabled, **NANCY'S SPECIAL WORKOUT: FOR THE DEVELOPMENTALLY CHALLENGED** (COF) is an extraordinary video. Nancy works in the field daily with people who have special needs, and her program is filled with great exercises and fun for the learning disabled.

For another program that is exceptionally motivating, take a look at the **LARGER WOMAN'S WORKOUT** (COL). This is a well-produced workout tape based on the premise that success means progress, not perfection. This is a solid but less-structured workout showing a class of larger women and geared to their special needs. This video demonstrates the need for fitness programs geared to all types of body structure and levels of ability.

Just for the fun of it, take a look at **BOXOUT** (COL) with Sugar Ray Leonard and Jill Goodacre. Sugar Ray and Goodacre, a fashion model, team-teach and even spar together. The viewer will learn a workout that blends boxing moves into a great routine without the need for gloves or punching bag. This is a fun tape.

If you have access to a pool, there are two exciting videos you'll want to view. **AQUASIZE** (COL) combines aerobics and calisthenics that use every muscle with the natural buoyancy of water for a productive workout. Learn the moves by watching on land and then move to the pool to practice, taking along your waterproof instructional guide. Or join Candy Costie, 1984 Olympic gold medalist, in **WATER WORKOUT** (CEP). This water workout tape adds new dimension to traditional aquatic exercise and provides a new source of exercises that will appeal to all ages. Instead of bringing the VCR outside, the viewer can take the accompanying audiotape to the pool.

If your exercising equipment is gathering dust in the corner, it's time to get it out and get going with a video especially designed for using exercising equipment. For an interesting diversion while you get a cardiovascular workout on your stationary bicycle, pick a tape from the **VIDEO CYCLE** series. Pedal along on a realistic trip complete with riding companions and authentic itinerary. Each carefully planned workout/tour features a musically programmed warm-up, an aerobic section and a cool-down. You can take a trip to **MAUI** (COL), tour **BRITISH COLUMBIA** (COL) and pedal through **SWITZERLAND** (COL). Or maybe you'd like to witness a **VERMONT AUTUMN** (COL) or the exciting city of **SAN FRANCISCO** (COL). What a great way to "take a trip" and exercise, too, without ever leaving home.

Other videos geared toward exercising equipment include the **SKI MACHINE: ST. MORITZ** (COL) by NordicVision. Again, this is an excellent way to exercise as you ski through the Swiss Alps and tour this world-famous winter resort. To hike from the Alpine village of Zermatt to the glacier fields of Grindelwald in Europe, get out your Stairstepper and pop a tape in the VCR. **SWISS ALPS FOR STAIRSTEPPERS** (COL) will make you forget you're even exercising as you enjoy the energetic music and spectacular visuals. And if you own a rowing machine of any kind, you'll want to work out with members of the U.S. Olympic team. The **ROWING MACHINE COMPANION** (COF) is perfect for both men and women no matter what shape or level of fitness. You'll tone your whole body and burn calories as this video puts you in the same boat as the world's finest rowers.

****

Whether you're just beginning your fitness program or have already gotten into tip-top shape, don't forget that there is more to being healthy than physical fitness. Be sure to take a look at the videos in the HEALTHY LIVING chapter. You'll find some great videos on nutrition and on exercising for special physical ailments.

BEAUTY TIPS

While we all know that being in good health is the first step to looking your best, there are videos available that can help you improve on what you have. The tapes detailed below are full of helpful tips and techniques that are easy to put to use.

For a fun and easy way to apply foolproof makeup, learn from the Queen of Color, Carole Jackson, in **COLOR ME BEAUTIFUL MAKEUP VIDEO** (RHV). She shows you how to choose and use the makeup colors that will make you look your best. An added bonus with this great tape is a take-along color chart for makeup shopping. For more of the latest makeup techniques, see **HOW TO MAKE-UP** (CEP). You'll learn professional tips for different facial structures, hair colors and skin tones.

The older face can benefit from David Nicholas's **40 & OVER MAKE-UP TECHNIQUES** (BFV). This well-known makeup artist will help the viewer learn to accentuate the positives of aging to look more glamorous. The beauty of various racial characteristics is demonstrated in **ETHNIC MAKE-UP TECHNIQUES** (BFV), which is aimed at the black, Hispanic and Oriental viewers. **RUBENESQUE MAKE-UP TECHNIQUES** (BFV), inspired by Rubens paintings of larger women, helps the heavyset woman develop her full beauty potential.

Complete your new look with a view of **HOW TO DO NAILS & NAIL CARE** (CEP). The viewer is taught step-by-step techniques of manicure and pedicure by a professional nail-care specialist. You'll also want to watch the great contemporary video **HAIR CARE** (CEP) to help you put your best head forward. Designed by a hair-care specialist, the video teaches step-by-step washing and conditioning techniques and provides tips for special types of hair and treatments for hair-related problems. You might also be interested in looking at the **GORGEOUS BRAIDS VIDEO** (VVP). In this interesting tape, beautifully braided hairstyles are modeled and then recreated for the viewer. You'll learn how to do the basic braid, the under braid, the French braid and many variations. Tips for dealing with a variety of hair types are included.

If you'd like to stimulate and tone your skin to make it more supple and youthful looking, you'll want to view **THE ACUPRESSURE FACELIFT** (COL) hosted by Lindsay Wagner. In this wonderful restorative tape, Wagner shows the viewer how to use the Oriental massage system on a daily basis or when you need a special lift. Or you might want to join a professional skin-care specialist in **SKIN CARE** (CEP). You'll be introduced to the latest procedures in skin care for more beautiful, youthful-looking skin.

To really look your best, don't miss **FLORENCE HENDERSON'S LOOKING GREAT—FEELING GREAT** (TWV). This informative and entertaining video shows how to bring out your face's natural beauty and potential. Florence Henderson, star of "The Brady Bunch," will also teach you what fashions work for you along with "do anywhere" exercises to improve posture and toning. This is a great video you won't want to miss.

****

*T*he preceding videos provide great tips on looking your best. But don't forget, the foundation of looking good is good health. Be sure to take a look at the excellent videos available in the HEALTHY LIVING chapter. And to keep your mind healthy, too, browse the programs detailed in the SELF-HELP VIDEO GUIDES chapter.*

SOURCES

(See Chapter 11 for a complete alphabetical listing of all sources with addresses and phone numbers.)

ASV - Artistic Video
BFV - Butterfly Videos
BSG - Bridgestone Group
CEP - Cambridge Educational Products
COF - Champions on Film
COL - Collage Video
ESP - ESPN Home Videos
PAS - Pacific Spirit
RHV - Random House Inc.
SMV - Schoolmasters Videos
TJP - Three J Productions Ltd.
TWV - Time Warner Home Video
VVP - Victorian Video Productions

CHAPTER 10:
SELF-HELP VIDEO GUIDES

GOALS & SELF-IMPROVEMENT - SUCCEEDING IN BUSINESS - PARENTING: AN INEXACT SCIENCE - ESPECIALLY FOR CHILDREN - PERSONAL ADULT RELATIONSHIPS - SOURCES

GOALS & SELF-IMPROVEMENT

Self-help books abound in a variety of subjects including motivational and goal-achieving advice. Now you can get this same help from the experts via video. Viewing a motivational tape can be a very productive experience as you watch some of the world's most dynamic speakers addressing you right in the privacy of your own home. It's certainly less expensive than attending a seminar, and the added bonus is that you can re-wind and watch over and over again.

MOTIVATIONAL DYNAMICS

Motivational tapes are as varied as the many different disciplines of motivation. One philosophy, **THE SILVA METHOD IN ACTION** (NGC), is based on mind-power techniques for developing personal and professional success. The program builds on the premise that the viewer can learn to function at an inner-conscious level—the alpha brain frequency—by using the right-brain hemisphere to enhance mental abilities. This is an exciting, live instructional video that will teach you how to gain access to the realm of your mind where your imagination works most creatively. Seven key Silva techniques are presented in this program to help the viewer solve problems faster and achieve goals more easily. You'll learn how to make every aspect of life more productive and less stressful as well as how to revitalize the power of memory and remember things quickly and easily. With the exciting graphics, animation and audiovisual reinforcements, this program is truly user-friendly.

Another widely used motivational method teaches how to develop life-transforming powers. It is called neurolinguistic programming, or NLP. **NLP IN ACTION** (NGC) is a dynamic video that shows the viewer how to model human excellence for personal and professional growth. You'll learn to make your present actions a resource for positive results in the future and to create and utilize your own natural states of excellence. Two of the country's top NLP trainers are your guides in this powerful program. You will learn to use the technique of path-building toward your goal and to seize your opportunity to create a compelling future for yourself. This could be just the video you need to make dramatic changes in your life.

199

Multi-talented author, psychotherapist, lecturer and TV personality Dr. Wayne Dyer has produced a video based on his own life experience and the stuff that goes into making a strong, secure, no-limit person. His witty and charming style in **HOW TO BE A NO-LIMIT PERSON** (NGC) makes sense, stressing reality, not fantasy. You and your family will laugh at Dr. Dyer's great stories and be touched by his simple but profound truths. He demonstrates how serenity is more important than acquisitions and that the quality of your life, rather than the outward appearance, is what matters. This is a very enjoyable and motivating program that you will value more each time you watch it.

Another very successful author and lecturer on motivational theory is Brian Tracy. In his **10 KEYS TO PERSONAL POWER** (NGC), Tracy shares the ten qualities that he feels are the basic ingredients to career and personal success. You will learn how to introduce or reinforce these qualities in your life and become the success you've always dreamed of. You might also enjoy Tracy's **SUCCESS SECRETS OF SELF-MADE MILLIONAIRES** (NGC). You'll discover the twenty-one qualities that rocketed self-made millionaires to the top—qualities you won't have to develop the hard way like they did. All you have to do is pop the tape into the VCR and take advantage of Tracy's expertise.

For another ten-step formula that gives you the do's and don'ts for rising to the top, you'll want to join nationally prominent lecturer Zig Ziglar in **HOW TO BE A WINNER** (NGC). Just a brief exposure to Mr. Ziglar's brand of logic and enthusiasm is enough to make a fan of the viewer. Long after you've made all his suggested changes in your life, you'll want to see this tape again and again. It has an amazing afterlife and is a great video to view when you hit a "downer" and need to be revitalized. To see more of this dynamic speaker, be sure to view **GOALS: HOW TO SET THEM, HOW TO REACH THEM** (NGC). In this powerful program, Ziglar presents the seven steps of goal-setting used by top achievers to help you get from where you are to where you want to be faster and more confidently. He'll show you how to set your goals properly and then follow his rules for goal achievement, including what to do when you get there.

Another excellent tape is **THE GREATEST SECRETS OF SUCCESS** (NGC). In this unforgettable video, Og Mandino takes the viewer on an odyssey of joy, laughter and tears that reveals all the compelling "secrets" of success that he discovered in his rise from poverty to worldwide recognition as a best-selling author and dynamic speaker. You'll learn the vital art of living in the present and why self-education is the only real and lasting success. Every copy of this video carries the label: "Warning! Watching this video tape may change your life...for the better!" And a program that is sure to inspire and motivate the viewer is **THE TOP 5%** (NGC), produced by veteran motivational speaker Earl Nightingale. In this powerful and practical presentation, Nightingale reveals the six all-important principles to follow to join the leaders in career and personal achievement. He will show you how to overcome self-imposed limitations as you acquire the correct mental tools to create a positive outlook. Nightingale is a pioneer in motivational theory, and his easy-to-follow road map can put you on the path to prosperity and happiness.

Jerry Gillies, author of the best-selling book *MoneyLove,* believes that if it isn't fun, it isn't worth doing. His video **GETTING READY FOR A PROSPEROUS 21ST CENTURY** (CCL) was recorded before a live audience and is chock-full of ideas on how to prosper in the twenty-first century by focusing on what you really love doing. For a collection of leading motivational speakers all on one tape, be sure to view **SEVEN MAGNIFICENT MOTIVATIONAL SPEAKERS** (CCL). This power-packed video presents segments from renowned speakers Mark Victor Hansen, Rita Davenport, Jack Canfield, Terry Cole-Whitaker, Les Brown, Dan Burrus and Donald Jolly. The presenters bring their own unique motivational techniques to the forefront.

KEYS TO PERSONAL GROWTH

It's a basic fact of nature that confident people attract success in all areas of their lives and that the foundation for that kind of confidence is self-esteem. **THE POWER OF POSITIVE SELF-IMAGE** (NGC) is literally an "owner's manual" on developing self-esteem. Host Mike McCaffrey teaches the viewer the keys to breaking free of negative thought patterns and replacing them with positive, life-enhancing habits. This exciting video will give you the priceless ability to see yourself in a positive light, which means that the world will have a new look, too. If you truly want to make your life more positive, start with this video.

For further development of self-esteem, you may want to view the marvelous blend of humor and motivation of Jack Canfield in his **BLUEPRINT FOR WINNING** (CCL). Canfield is one of the world leaders in the self-esteem movement. His excellent video teaches the value of developing self-esteem in our lives and, more importantly, how to achieve it. You may want to follow a different path to confidence and self-esteem by viewing **THE DYNAMICS OF SELF-ESTEEM** (CCL). In this inspiring tape, Dr. Nathaniel Branden helps you recreate your childhood and build the self-esteem you may never have developed. Or you might want to view the renowned Barksdale Self-Esteem Program that people from all walks of life have used since 1958 with spectacular results. Based on this popular motivational method, **BUILDING SOUND SELF-ESTEEM** (BSG) will help you tap into your inner resources and overcome the obstacles in your life.

Regarded as "the coach's coach" in the field of personal growth, Tim Piering is available to you through his presentation **HOW TO LIVE AN EXTRAORDINARY LIFE** (CCL). Taped before a live audience, this program imparts a clear message on developing personal growth that will inevitably lead to success and make your life more enjoyable and productive. Be sure and go on to view **QUANTUM LEAPS IN PERSONAL GROWTH** (CCL). Learn from best-selling author Dr. Vernon Woolfe all about "holodynes," those thousands of mental images that totally run our lives. In this excellent video, Dr. Woolfe exposes these holodynes and teaches how to deal with them to achieve success, happiness and prosperity throughout life. This is another remarkable program you'll want to view again and again.

Do you dream about joining the ranks of life's consistent winners? If so, stop dreaming and take advantage of the expertise of lecturer Denis Waitley.

201

In his inspiring video **DYNAMIC SELF-DISCIPLINE** (NGC), Waitley introduces the viewer to the key discipline-building habits that can put whatever you want from life solidly within your grasp. You'll learn to set easily attainable, short-range goals that can lead to long-term objectives for creating personal and professional fulfillment.

UNDERDEVELOPED & OVEREXPOSED: PUTTING YOUR SELF-ESTEEM IN FOCUS (CEP) is an excellent program that is especially effective for young adults. This positive and upbeat video acquaints them with the problems caused by low self-esteem and teaches techniques for creating a more positive self-image. This is a highly effective motivational tool not only for young adults who need to improve their self-image but also for those who feel up one day and down the next. A good informative companion tape is **READY, SET...GOALS** (CEP), which discusses setting and achieving goals. Viewers learn about the different types of goals they might work toward and people and things that might help or hinder. Stress is put on the importance of setting realistic and measurable goals and the resources available to help achieve them.

COMMUNICATION SKILLS

The art of successful negotiation isn't confined to the boardrooms of corporations. In fact, it takes place everywhere, every day, and you have a part in it. The entertaining video **GUIDE TO EVERYDAY NEGOTIATING** (NGC) is a how-to program that clarifies the fundamentals as well as the finer points of negotiating techniques. Top negotiator Roger Dawson will teach the viewer the "flinch," the "reluctant buyer" gambit and the "vise" technique, plus many more easy-to-learn and quite effective methods of negotiating. They will help you save money just as often as you decide to use them.

We spend a great deal of effort developing reading, writing and speaking skills, but we often ignore the most essential communication tool of all: listening. **EFFECTIVE LISTENING SKILLS** (CEP) discusses the habits and traits that keep us from being good listeners. The viewer will learn improved listening skills based on the D.R.I.V.E. process: Deciding to listen, Reading all stimuli, Investing spare time wisely, Verifying what you hear and Expending energy. This tape could make a big difference in the lives of people of all ages.

No matter what your job, it's a sure bet you can benefit from better public-speaking skills, and **CONQUER YOUR FEAR OF PUBLIC SPEAKING** (CEP) could be a valuable investment in your future. Nationally known management trainer Gloria Goforth is a powerful teacher. She shows how to identify personal strengths and other useful techniques you can put to use in relating to one person or a large group. Or you can learn **HOW TO SPEAK WITH CONFIDENCE** (NGC) from Bert Decker, one of America's leading communications consultants. Decker explains the four stages of any public-speaking experience and shows the viewer step by step how to pass through them successfully. You'll also learn about the three major factors that can make or break a speech and how to skillfully use humor. To carry your newly learned skills of speech even further, be sure to go on to the excellent video **POWER TALKING** (CCL). If you've ever had the feeling you could accomplish anything if you could only find the right words to express yourself, this tape is definitely worth the view. Host George Walther points out that power talking isn't inherited; it's learned. He'll introduce you to successful people in all walks of life who have enhanced their vocabularies to include phrases that induce a positive response. This enlightening program presents fifty ways to say what you mean and get what you want. It is sure to be a boost to both your professional and your personal life.

Good public speaking is only the first step to succeeding in the business world. You also have to communicate with the people you're addressing to ensure they both hear and understand what you're saying. **PERSUASIVE SPEAKING** (CEP) is a very effective program that gives the viewer expert tips on such things as how to size up an audience, how to use eye contact and body language to your advantage and many more great communication techniques. For more advice on being persuasive, whether through speaking or writing, you'll want to view **POWERFUL WAYS TO PERSUADE PEOPLE** (CEP). This video offers the viewer dozens of ideas on presenting and clinching arguments, effective ways to get someone to do something for you, when to use humor to persuade, writing persuasive proposals and much more.

TIME MANAGEMENT

Everyone suffers from procrastination at some time or another, and **OVERCOMING PROCRASTINATION** (CTV) helps the viewer learn how to "just do it." This program will help you develop "get-it-started-and-get-it-done" thinking that will light your fire when all else fails. For another beneficial change in your life, try viewing Brian Tracy's **PERSONAL TIME MANAGEMENT** (NGC). This informative and dynamic video can help you gain extra hours every day. You'll get proven and practical advice on overcoming procrastination, what to do at the start of any project, easy steps for higher productivity and how just a little time spent on planning can have big returns.

****

*T*he preceding videos can improve the quality of your life. For more self-help guides in special areas, you might want to take a look at the great videos available in the SUCCEEDING IN BUSINESS section and the segment on PERSONAL ADULT RELATIONSHIPS in this chapter.

SUCCEEDING IN BUSINESS

Whether you're self-employed or report to a boss, there are videos that will enhance your chances of succeeding in the business world. Why not take a look below at the outstanding tapes available. There's bound to be one or more that fit your particular needs and situation.

SURVIVING THE BUSINESS WORLD

Surveyed employers named a positive attitude, adaptability, dependability, loyalty and interpersonal skills as the most important traits new employees can bring into their organizations, all traits that are seldom taught in a school curriculum. The exceptional video **TAKE THIS JOB AND LOVE IT** (CEP) prepares the entry-level employee for the realities of the workplace. Viewers will learn about appropriate attire, how to address and deal with their new bosses, how much socializing is acceptable and much more on adapting to individual work environments. This entertaining program stresses that when starting a new job, preparation can make the difference between a smooth take-off and a crash landing.

Once you're in that job, be sure to view the informative tape **IF YOU REALLY WANT TO GET AHEAD** (CEP). You'll get hundreds of ideas to help you move up the ladder and help your company forge ahead. Learn about getting along with others, promoting yourself, gaining and using power and coping with criticism. A great companion tape you'll want to view is **WHAT THEY STILL DON'T TEACH YOU AT HARVARD BUSINESS SCHOOL** (CEP). Mark McCormack, founder and CEO of International Management Group, based this video on his very popular success manual. His "applied people sense" theory can turn you into a streetsmart executive as you follow along with this live-action video. This motivational yet practical program can be an invaluable aid in advancing your chosen career.

To re-enforce all the tips and techniques you've learned about public speaking and being persuasive, an excellent program to watch is the **GUIDE TO BUSINESS NEGOTIATING** (NGC). This information-packed tape will teach the viewer proven strategies and tactics specifically for the business environment. Learn the perfect way to deal with an overbearing boss, angry associate or irate customer. Whether you're dealing for a multimillion-dollar corporate buyout or are in a one-on-one personal confrontation, host Roger Dawson will show you how to enter any business negotiation and come out on top.

THE WOMAN ENTREPRENEUR: DO YOU HAVE WHAT IT TAKES? (CEP) was produced specifically for the fastest-growing segment in the small business community, the female-owned business. This tape is based on a best-selling book by Dr. Robert Hisrich and Candida Brush. Several successful women entrepreneurs share their feelings about starting their own businesses. You'll be able to test yourself on your abilities to start a business and evaluate your feelings of independence and control. Discover the importance of a sound business plan as well as your willingness to take risks. This video will point you in the right direction for success and help you find out if you have what it takes to operate and succeed at your own female-owned business.

THE WORLD OF SELLING

Getting customers to purchase a product or service involves much more than simply leading them to the checkout counter. **SELLING SKILLS** (CEP) is a live-action program that uses interviews with professional sales personnel to present strategies for enhancing business transactions. While the program uses specific examples from the fashion merchandising industry, the techniques presented are applicable to sales positions in any type of business. The viewer will learn how to prepare for a sale, approach customers and determine needs to ensure making a successful sale. To find out where you can and should improve your sales strategy, be sure to join the seven sales experts in **HOW TO MANAGE YOUR SALES STRATEGY** (CEP). In addition to basic selling techniques, this program covers such topics as value-added selling, telemarketing operations and knowing your competition. You'll gain advice and tips on how to achieve maximum sales and how to make sure you are meeting your customer's needs as well as those of your company.

If you want to learn the secrets of selling from one of the country's greatest salespeople, join Zig Ziglar in **5 STEPS TO SUCCESSFUL SELLING** (NGC). This motivating and dynamic speaker takes the viewer through the five basic steps that cover every aspect of the selling process. In this exciting video, you'll see Ziglar demonstrate each step in the money-making process of qualifying, selling and closing a prospect. You'll discover how to create satisfied customers and a thoroughly satisfying income for yourself. If your goal is to become a mega-star of professional selling, the experts to help you along are Jim Cathcart and Tony Alessandra with their excellent tape **THE MILLION DOLLAR SALES STRATEGY** (NGC). Reach for the pinnacle of the sales profession with their proven principles of time management, prospecting, closing techniques and customer relations. The viewer will learn how to develop the refinements and professional pride that are the real hallmarks of top-earning sales pros.

To cover some of the specific points of selling, there are several other videos you may want to view. You can spend time with three top sales professionals as they share their secrets of success in **HOW TO FIND NEW CUSTOMERS** (NGC). You'll discover new methods for prospecting, qualifying and following up leads, providing exceptional service, growing new business from current clients and much more. **UPSIDE DOWN SELLING** (CCL), which is hosted by best-selling author George Walther, focuses on another aspect. In this exciting live presentation, Walther demonstrates how to increase sales by directing a greater percentage of sales efforts toward existing customers rather than prospects. Another highly motivating and fast-paced program has been produced by the dynamic speaker Brian Tracy. **24 TECHNIQUES FOR CLOSING THE SALE** (NGC) will give you proven and powerful closing techniques that can help you turn any prospect into a buyer.

****

*T*he preceding tapes can help make a big difference in your business life. You might also want to take a look at the videos in the PRACTICAL, VOCATIONAL & UNUSUAL SKILLS chapter. There are many excellent videos detailed there that could also prove to be beneficial.

PARENTING: AN INEXACT SCIENCE

Although parenting is the most important job that many adults will ever have, it is an inexact science that requires no formal training, no degree, no certificate of achievement or even interviews to determine qualifications. In the past, trial and error was often the only avenue open to new parents. But now, there is help via video. The programs detailed are designed to increase your success rate in the job of parenting.

BABY BASICS

NEWBORN BASICS (CEP), written and hosted by qualified physicians, presents an invaluable lesson to new parents about babies—from a few days old to a few months. You'll get a first-hand look at the needs, common physical traits and proper care of infants. The most complete and accurate infant-care program available, this informative video answers a multitude of questions asked by new parents and makes it possible for these topics to be addressed before crucial moments arise. You will learn about the proper care of infants, including feeding methods, hygiene, taking temperatures and much more. You'll find out how to create a safe home environment, how to hold the newborn and when to go to the doctor. This comprehensive program is a must for the reference library of all new parents.

Another excellent program that takes the new parents from the day they leave the hospital through the often frightening and apprehensive first few months is **BABY'S FIRST MONTHS: WHAT DO WE DO NOW?** (CEP). The viewer is guided step by step by the twelve board-certified pediatric specialists who developed this informative, authoritative video. You'll cover such topics as colic, diaper changing, bathing, feeding, crying and much more. Or you might want to join TV personality Joan Lunden in **YOUR NEW BORN BABY** (SMV). She'll answer your questions, calm your fears and help you become confident about handling your newborn. You will also get invaluable information from Dr. Jeffrey Brown on a variety of topics.

For some additional baby aid, take a look at **BREASTFEEDING YOUR BABY** (CEP). This program, designed in conjunction with the LaLeche League, helps the new mother learn the techniques and positions for successful breastfeeding. New and experienced parents alike will want to view **HELPING YOUR BABY SLEEP THROUGH THE NIGHT** (SMV). This award-winning video will show you how to help your babies soothe themselves to sleep and how to enhance your children's sleep environment.

BASIC PARENTING SKILLS

Parenting is an acquired skill that can be taught or improved upon, and videos are available to help take the guesswork out of this important life-long job. **TEN WAYS TO BE A BETTER PARENT** (CEP) is a live-action program that will benefit parents, educators, babysitters or anyone involved in child care. Viewers of this excellent tape will learn methods for building positive self-esteem and positive attitudes and feelings in their children. The proven consistent guidelines for behavior and safety also stress the importance of keeping a sense of humor to help cope with the challenges and failures frequently facing parents. This is an excellent foundation program for both new and experienced parents. Searching for solutions to common problems incurred in child-raising can leave parents extremely frustrated. The entertaining video **SOLUTIONS TO TEN COMMON PARENTING PROBLEMS** (CEP) provides simple and realistic solutions to such challenging situations as thumb-sucking, bed-wetting, temper tantrums, sibling rivalry and toilet training. This informative and entertaining program can make parenting more enjoyable and rewarding as you learn how to interpret and respond to a child's behavior.

Another excellent video series on parenting is the **BOY'S TOWN PARENTING SERIES**. These tapes are packed with concise information and lively, true-to-life vignettes that illustrate key points. While the tapes are rather short, only fifteen minutes in length, the valuable lessons they contain make them a bargain purchase. **A CHANGE FOR THE BETTER** (CEP) will help parents with frustrating behavior problems, while **CATCH 'EM BEING GOOD** (CEP) shows parents how to concentrate on the good things their children are doing. To help your youngster sort through problems and also develop a healthy sense of self-esteem, both **I CAN'T DECIDE** (CEP) and **IT'S GREAT TO BE ME!** (CEP) are excellent choices to view. And **I'M NOT EVERYBODY** (CEP) is invaluable in learning to guide your child to deal with peer pressure. **HOMEWORK? I'LL DO IT LATER** (CEP) and **YOU WANT ME TO HELP WITH HOUSEWORK?** (CEP) address two subjects that often cause havoc between child and parent. For a method to handle children's and teens' defiance and temper flare-ups, **NO I WON'T AND YOU CAN'T MAKE ME** (CEP) shows parents how to improve their relationship with their child. And to help cement a good family foundation, be sure to view both **TAKE TIME TO BE A FAMILY** (CEP) and **NEGOTIATING WITHIN THE FAMILY** (CEP). These excellent programs are ones that parents will want to refer to time and again.

For parents with children in the often difficult pre-adolescent and teenage years, the **COMMON SENSE PARENTING** series contains two very good videos. **HELPING YOUR CHILD SUCCEED** (CEP) shows how to prepare children for new or difficult situations they will encounter every day. By guiding them in solving problems and making responsible decisions, you help reduce the power of peer pressure and greatly increase a child's self-esteem. To help your children set and achieve realistic goals, **TEACHING RESPONSIBLE BEHAVIOR** (CEP) is an excellent tool. Learn how to correct children's inappropriate behavior and help them accept responsibility for homework and household chores by negotiating positive changes in behavior. For parenting skills your children will appreciate, be sure to view **HOW TO RAISE HAPPY, CONFIDENT KIDS** (CTV). This excellent tape will give you sound, practical advice for facing the most common parenting challenges and guide you in creating and maintaining high self-esteem in your children.

Another set of videos on the subject of parenting has been developed by a group that produces all of its videos on a solid Christian foundation and stresses products with integrity. **JOY OF FAMILY** (BSG) is a two-video program hosted by Dr. Denis Waitley, who uses his professional training and ability to communicate in understandable terms to discuss love, responsibility, purpose and faith within a family setting. **POSITIVE PARENTING** (CEP) is designed to help parents instill strong self-esteem in their children, with individual segments covering self-esteem, role models, self-determination, self-discipline and optimism.

PARENTING PRESCHOOLERS (CEP) is a practical, fast-paced visual presentation of the challenges and rewards of being a parent of a preschooler. The program covers such topics as sibling rivalry, meal time, public behavior, toy management and more. Parents will see practical approaches for building self-esteem in their children as well as in themselves as parents. Chapters for single parents and dual-career families are certain to be of interest to viewers in those particular situations. An excellent program designed specifically for fathers is **FOR DADS ONLY** (CEP). Both instructive and entertaining, this video has some humorous segments on stopping baby's crying, feeding and burping, the dreaded diaper change, proper bath procedures plus much more. This is the perfect video aid for teaching males the basic skills necessary for becoming a "professional" dad.

If you're the parent of a hyperactive and/or inattentive child, you'll want to view the video guide **WHY WON'T MY CHILD PAY ATTENTION?** (SMV). Dr. Goldstein, a noted psychologist who has lectured nationally on attention problems in children, provides an easy-to-follow explanation of why some children have so much trouble paying attention, sitting still and controlling themselves. His practical advice on what parents can do to successfully manage the problems these behaviors cause will be welcomed by any parent in this situation.

A new baby in the house can be a traumatic experience for the children already there, but you can help alleviate these confusing feelings the older children may be experiencing. Try sharing with them the excellent video **HEY, WHAT ABOUT ME?** (SMV). By watching the kids in the program together with their baby brothers and sisters, they'll find out just what to expect with a new baby at home. The tape also features games, lullabies and bouncing rhymes children can do with their new brother or sister that will make all family members feel important. To introduce the concept that sharing can be fun, have your youngster watch **PLAYSKOOL'S MINE AND YOURS** (SMV). This video is in a story format and uses live action, animation and clay animation to show children that sharing can be more fun than playing alone.

From a children's TV workshop comes a video that many parents will want to have on hand, **WHAT KIDS WANT TO KNOW ABOUT SEX & GROWING UP** (PAA). Viewing this program together is an excellent way to help your child learn the facts about sex and growing up. The tape frankly answers the urgent questions young people have about puberty, sexuality and reproduction. You and your child will join an informal group of both boys and girls as they discuss the facts and feelings of sexual development. The discussions are led by adult counselors who approach this sensitive subject with warmth, humor and compassion. This outstanding video makes dealing with a tough subject a whole lot easier.

An excellent video is available for that large segment of the population known as "working moms." **THE WORKING MOM'S SURVIVAL**

GUIDE (XJX) is both informative and entertaining, providing lots of practical advice. This "survival kit" will appeal to the working moms who are caught in the trap of trying to do it all—being a good parent, partner and professional. With time as the worst enemy, these struggling moms need to learn what's important and what's not, and this video is an excellent guide to distinguishing between the two.

****

*T*he preceding videos are excellent reference aids for dealing with the responsibility of parenting. For more help, you'll want to take a look at the valuable guides to childhood illnesses that appear in the HEALTHY LIVING chapter. And be sure to take a look at the videos in the next section that are especially for children to view.

ESPECIALLY FOR CHILDREN

There are excellent programs available that are specially designed for viewing by children of different ages, from the youngest tot to the teenager. These videos are both entertaining and informative and can help your children cope with the wide world around them. The tapes detailed below, covering everything from character-building to handling peer pressure, may be of interest to both you and your children.

CHARACTER BUILDING

An exceptional animated series for children is **THE HUMAN RACE CLUB** by children's author Joy Berry. Each video presents a story that teaches children an essential character-building skill. **THE LETTER ON LIGHT BLUE STATIONERY** (CHE) is a story about self-esteem. It encourages kids to value themselves and others by learning to appreciate every human being. **THE LEAN MACHINE** (CHE) is an excellent video on learning to handle emotions and uncomfortable feelings. Featuring a cast of characters children can relate to, **CASEY'S REVENGE** (CHE) is a story about fights that inevitably occur between brothers and sisters. The program shows kids why revenge doesn't work and how everyone wins when brothers and sisters respect one another.

A HIGH PRICE TO PAY (CHE) teaches a valuable lesson on earning money and having possessions. Kids will learn how they can find satisfaction in the choices they make and also how to respect the choices of others. In **THE FAIR WEATHER FRIEND** (CHE), kids learn valuable lessons on making and keeping friends. This video will help them understand that being a friend takes special effort and that friends are chosen for who they are, not what they have. Another powerful lesson can be learned from **THE UNFORGETTABLE PEN PAL** (CHE), a story about prejudice and discrimination. This video will help kids learn the negative effects of prejudice and the importance of forming their opinions about others intelligently.

Your children can have lots more fun, too, while learning to cope with the challenges of growing up through the stories in the character-building series by Anthony Paul. Delightful animated stories will hold their interest as they join Weatherbee the Duckling to **LEARN MORE ABOUT CONFIDENCE AND LOVE** (SMV), and Benny Bear is available to help them **LEARN MORE ABOUT SHARING AND KINDNESS** (SMV). They'll be able to visit the circus as they **LEARN MORE ABOUT PATIENCE AND PEACE** (SMV) and take a trip to the zoo while they **LEARN MORE ABOUT OBEDIENCE AND SELF-CONTROL** (SMV).

The honey bee Nzzzzz family stars in the fun-filled story that will enable your children to **LEARN MORE ABOUT GOODNESS AND FAITH** (SMV). As they **LEARN MORE ABOUT HONESTY AND RESPONSIBILITY** (SMV), they'll be enthralled with the antics of Thunder the Puppy and Bouncer the Rabbit. Two entertaining stories impart valuable lessons as they **LEARN MORE ABOUT THANKFULNESS AND GENTLENESS** (SMV), and Bouncer the Rabbit is sure to become a favorite character as they **LEARN MORE ABOUT POLITENESS AND JOY** (SMV).

It's never too early to teach your children about the importance of good character and conduct. Entertaining videos have been developed for ages three and up to help them grasp new skills and ideas. The musical escapades of the New Zoo Revue friends will help youngsters understand and control **TEMPER TANTRUMS** (SMV). **FEELINGS** (SMV) will help them build self-esteem while dealing with different kinds of feelings. They'll learn about sharing, honesty, what to do when feelings are hurt, controlling emotions and respecting others.

An outstanding video for kids of all ages is **PREJUDICE: ANSWERING CHILDREN'S QUESTIONS** (SMV). This special presentation scrutinizes some of the influences that shape children's ideas about the world and examines stereotypes based on race, sex, religion and disability. News correspondent Peter Jennings leads an audience of young children as a team of experts conducts several experiments designed to help the children better understand the roots of prejudice. This is an excellent program for parents to share with their children.

LEARNING SKILLS TO LIVE BY

You can help even the youngest toddler cope with the big, wide world by introducing them to delightful videos that both entertain and educate. **DOING THINGS** (BOP), for those eighteen months of age through the preschool years, looks at activities from children's daily routines, such as eating, washing and playing, and compares how a variety of animals go through the same simple processes. This program will stimulate conversation and reinforce involvement with similar events.

MOMMY, I CAN LEARN MYSELF is a delightful series geared to ages three and up. Your children can learn all about **MANNERS** (SMV), including answering the telephone, please and thank you, dining, common courtesy and acceptable behavior. To help them feel more comfortable in their expanding world, **NEW EXPERIENCES** (SMV) is a worthwhile view. Through animation and fun characters, they'll learn about new additions to the family, a new pet, going to the doctor, going on an airplane, moving to a new place and eventually going to school.

Children are often frightened by the unknown, and a move to a new home can be a terrifying experience. **LET'S GET A MOVE ON** (SMV) is a program to help kids and their parents survive the impact of moving, saying good-bye and adjusting to new people, new situations and new spaces. This Parents' Choice Award video will help your children get ready and actually enjoy the adventure of the move itself. If the big change in your children's lives involves divorce, an excellent video to share with them is **SURVIVING YOUR PARENTS' DIVORCE: IT'S NEVER EASY** (CEP). The information provided in this tape will give your children specific coping techniques and help them through a confusing and trying experience.

THE DOORWAYS PROJECT—SURVIVING THE TEEN YEARS is a Christian series developed by award-winning author and speaker Winkie Pratney. Some of the issues teens face daily are discussed in **FRIEND-SHIPS** (BSG) and in **SEX AND DATING** (BSG). Pratney's messages are always relevant and often humorous as he provides young people **GUID-ANCE** (BSG) and a blueprint for meeting their **PSYCHOLOGICAL NEEDS** (BSG). Teenagers can be difficult to reach, and watching these videos together is an excellent way to bridge the communication gap.

Another well-produced video dealing with the difficult issues facing teens today is **TEENAGERS & TOUGH DECISIONS** (CEP). Featuring interviews with teens across the country, this lively program is divided into ten brief segments, each covering a special topic such as peer pressure, money management, families and divorce, sex and pregnancy or substance abuse. This is a very helpful tape to guide your teenager through tough times. For a terrific program that will stimulate thoughtful conversation about self-esteem and values, share with your teenager the video **DATING IN THE 90'S: FEELING GOOD ABOUT YOURSELF!** (CEP). The story in this program deals with the ongoing coercion from peers to be sexually active and examines the importance of developing self-esteem and values to negate the pressure. This video grasps the attention of young people while exploring the issues and problems involved in dating.

****

The videos in this section are excellent tools for bridging the generation gap and opening the pathway to good communication. For more helpful videos related to parent-child relationships, be sure to take a look at the programs available in the PARENTING: AN INEXACT SCIENCE section.

PERSONAL ADULT RELATIONSHIPS

Whether you are single or married, female or male, young or old, relationships can at times be a frustrating experience. From handling an existing relationship to starting a new one, there is help available via your VCR. The videos detailed below contain some invaluable advice.

DEVELOPING A RELATIONSHIP

Flirting is as old as time, and everybody does it in one way or another, including you. But are you doing it for the right reasons and are you getting the desired results? Why not invite relationship therapist Dr. Rachel Grant into your home via video to teach you **THE FINE ART OF FLIRTING** (CCL)? This lively and informative tape will show you, step by step, how to meet interesting new people and put some sparkle in your life. Or you may want to join Don and Mary Kelley in **FINDING EACH OTHER** (CCL). Now a happily married couple, they present interesting and timely information on this fascinating topic before a live audience. This video would also make an ideal gift for people consistently picking the wrong mate.

If you're looking for ways to make an existing relationship more successful, relationship counselor Dr. Deborah Cooper has a great tape for you to view entitled **AVOIDING REJECTION IN A LOVE RELATIONSHIP** (CCL). Dr. Cooper feels that the best and longest-lasting relationships are between opposite personality types and that the key is understanding these opposite characteristics. Learn what rejection is not and how passive and assertive types can be compatible. You may want to join best-selling author and psychiatrist Dr. David Viscott in **I LOVE YOU, LET'S WORK IT OUT!** (CCL). This live seminar video contains dozens of sure-fire techniques for bringing a soured relationship back to its original sweetness.

THE POLITICS OF LOVE (NGC) is a very warm and uplifting video presentation. In this extraordinary production, author and lecturer Leo Buscaglia shows you how to turn every area of your life into a source of joy. He'll guide you along as you learn to accept the challenge of life and build lasting, mutually rewarding relationships. Dr. Buscaglia offers his own style of personal encouragement to people of all ages to fully develop their human potential and enjoyment through mature love. In **LOVING RELATION-SHIPS** (PAA), he examines the myths and magic of intimacy. He'll guide you through an exploration of the differences between sex and affection and suggest ways in which you can become more lovable and caring in all your relationships. Dr. Buscaglia's ideas are universal in concept and application and can create more joy in life for yourself, members of your family and everyone you meet.

You'll also want to join the remarkable Buscaglia in his program **TOGETHER** (PAA). In this heartfelt tape, he explains to the viewer how to break down the barriers of loneliness. You'll learn how the benefits of sharing can overcome the risks and how you can use relationships to foster growth and positive change in both yourself and your loved ones. In the inspiring program **SPEAKING OF LOVE** (PAA), through personal stories and observations Dr. Buscaglia considers the idea of love in all its many meanings. He raises a host of provocative and helpful questions that will challenge and encourage you to express your important feelings.

SEXUAL ENCOUNTERS

Playboy Enterprises has some exciting videos for lovers that are tastefully produced in a sensitive and mature style. They are, however, recommended for adults only, as nude models are used. The **SECRETS OF**

MAKING LOVE I & II VIDEOS (PLB) will keep the excitement alive in a committed relationship. Written by a psychologist and therapist, these videos will help both partners learn to communicate sexual needs and desires. Also designed to enhance every aspect of a sexual relationship is the three-volume **THE BETTER SEX VIDEO SERIES. BETTER SEXUAL TECHNIQUES** (PLB), **ADVANCED SEXUAL TECHNIQUES** (PLB) and **MAKING SEX FUN** (PLB) are all geared to helping you find more pleasure and excitement in your sexual relationship.

A unique tape for guiding you and your mate to full sexual health is **INTIMATE WORKOUT FOR LOVERS** (PLB). Pump up together, pamper each other and experience heightened pleasure. Or view an exercise video unlike any you have ever seen. **FIT FOR SEX: THE EXERCISE GUIDE FOR LOVERS VIDEO** (PLB) demonstrates a complete workout designed to strengthen all the major muscles you use during lovemaking.

Also produced by Playboy Enterprises are three exciting massage videos for lovers that are beautifully and tastefully produced. Pop in these videos on a Saturday night and let professional models teach you the secrets of massage. You can enjoy the all-consuming experience of **SENSUAL PLEASURES OF ORIENTAL MASSAGE** (PLB), or let **ULTIMATE SENSUAL MASSAGE** (PLB) teach you and your mate how to turn a simple caress into a work of art. For the grand finale, **SECRETS OF EUROMASSAGE** (PLB) combines the pleasure principle with the sensuality and style of European masters of massage. Again, these tapes are for adults only.

For tastefully produced video guides on the sensitive subject of lovemaking, you might consider watching **INTIMACY AND SEXUAL ECSTASY** (PAA). For an adult audience only, this sophisticated video is a course in conscious, caring lovemaking. Drawing from both Eastern and Western traditions, this insightful program presents the most powerful ways of creating deep levels of love and sexual fulfillment in an intimate relationship. To learn awareness techniques in the art of lovemaking that are based on the sexual teachings of Chinese Taoism, consider viewing **SECRETS OF CHINESE LOVE MAKING I & II** (PAA). This unique two-volume program takes the viewer through several different sets of exercises designed to enhance the flow of chi (the subtle energies in the body). You'll also learn proven techniques, including meditation, foreplay and pleasure-enhancing exercises for both you and your partner. These are tastefully done videos for the adult couple to view in the privacy of their own home.

****

The preceding tapes are both inspiring and informative in dealing with relationships. Other important tapes related to this subject can be found in the FEEL FIT/LOOK GOOD and HEALTHY LIVING chapters.

SOURCES

(See Chapter 11 for a complete alphabetical listing of all sources with addresses and phone numbers.)

BNS -	Brainstorms
BOP -	Bo Peep Productions
BSG -	Bridgestone Group
CCL -	Chesney Communications
CEP -	Cambridge Educational Products
CHE	Celebrity Home Entertainment Inc.
CTV -	Career Track Publications
NGC -	Nightingale-Conant
PAA -	Pacific Arts
PLB -	Playboy Videos
SMV -	Schoolmasters Videos
XJX -	Xenejenex

CHAPTER 11

<u>SOURCES</u>

    Sources for all the videos detailed in this book are listed below in alphabetical order, along with their addresses and phone numbers. Many of these companies have an 800 number, and you can contact them directly if there is a particular video you want to order or for pricing information (all the videos presented are under $100.00, with the average price being $29.99). You may want to request their catalogs in order to browse through their entire collection of programs. In most cases, the catalogs are free or cost a very nominal amount.

    All the companies included in this book were very cooperative in providing the necessary information to ensure the reader wide coverage of the thousands of instructional videos available. When contacting them, it would be greatly appreciated by the author if you would mention this book.

****

<u>CODE</u>	COMPANY	<u>ADDRESS</u>	<u>PHONE NO.</u>
ACB	A.C. BURKE & CO.	2554 Lincoln Blvd Marina Del Rey, CA 90291	310/574-2770
ACN	ACORN MEDIA	7910 Woodmont Ave Bethesda, MD 20814	301/907-0030
ACV	ARTIST'S CLUB	5750 N.E. Hassalo, Bldg C Portland, OR 97213	800/845-6507
ALW	ALWHIT PRODUCTIONS	3784-B Mission Ave Oceanside, CA 92054	619/966-1085
AOF	AUDIO FORUM	96 Broad St Guilford, CT 06437	800/243-1234
ASV	ARTISTIC VIDEO	87 Tyler Ave Sound Beach, NY 11789	516/744-5999
AVP	ARTISTS' VIDEO PRODUCTIONS	32 Narrow Rocks Rd Westport, CT 06880	800/845-6507
BBC	BETTER BOOKS CO.	P O Box 9770 Ft. Worth, TX 76147	817/335-1853

BFV	BUTTERFLY VIDEOS	P O Box 184-C13 Antrim, NH 03440	800/433-2623
BHG	BETTER HOMES & GARDENS	P O Box 11430 Des Moines, IA 50336	800/678-2699
BMV	BENNETT VIDEO GROUP	2321 Abbot Kinney Blvd Venice, CA 90291	800/733-8862
BNS	BRAINSTORMS	8221 Kimball Ave Skokie, IL 60076	800/621-7500
BOP	BO PEEP PRODUCTIONS	P O Box 982 Eureka, MT 59917	800/532-0420
BSG	BRIDGESTONE GROUP	300 N. McKemy Ave Chandler, AZ 85226	800/523-0988
BWV	BARB WATSON VIDEO	P O Box 1467 Moreno Valley, CA 92556	909/653-3780
CCI	COLLEGIATE CHOICE INC.	41 Surrey Lane Tenafly, NJ 07670	201/871-0098
CCL	CHESNEY COMMUNICATIONS	2302 Martin St, Ste 125 Irvine, CA 92715	714/263-5500
CEP	CAMBRIDGE EDUCATIONAL PRODUCTS	P O Box 2153 Charleston, WV 25328	800/468-4227
CHE	CELEBRITY HOME ENTERTAINMENT INC.	22025 Ventura Blvd Woodland Hills, CA 91365	818/595-0666
COF	CHAMPIONS ON FILM	P O Box 1941 Ann Arbor, MI 48106	800/521-2832
COL	COLLAGE VIDEO	5390 Main St, NE Minneapolis, MN 55421	800/433-6769
CPP	CPP MEDIA GROUP	15800 NW 48th Ave Miami, FL 33014	800/628-1528
CTV	CAREER TRACK PUBLICATIONS	P O Box 18778 Boulder, CO 80308	800/334-1018
DHV	DANCE HORIZONS VIDEO	P O Box 57 Pennington, NJ 08534	800/220-7149
DIY	DO-IT-YOURSELF INC.	117 Creekview Carrboro, NC 27510	800/285-7776
DVU	DANCE VISION USA	2005 W. Carson St Torrance, CA 90501	800/851-2813
EMG	ENTREPRENEUR MAGAZINE GROUP	P O Box 50370 Boulder, CO 80321	800/421-2300

EPG	EDUCATIONAL PRODUCTS GROUP	1000 Centerville Turnpike Virginia Beach, VA 23463	800/288-4769
ERG	ERGO MEDIA INC.	P O Box 2037 Teaneck, NJ 07666	800/695-3746
ESP	ESPN HOME VIDEOS	P O Box 2284 South Burlington, VT 05407	800/662-3776
EVN	EDUCATIONAL VIDEO NETWORK	1401 19th St Huntsville, TX 77340	800/762-0060
FIN	FINLEY-HOLIDAY FILMS	P O Box 619 Whittier, CA 90601	800/345-6707
FSV	FUSION VIDEO	17311 Fusion Way Ctry Club Hills, IA 60478	800/959-0061
HAI	HEALTHY ALTERNATIVES INC.	P O Box 3234 Reston, VA 22090	703/430-6650
HFF	HARTLEY FILM FOUNDATION	Cat Rock Road Cos Cob, CT 06807	800/937-1819
JPV	JOHN PATRICK PRODUCTIONS	P O Box 289 Short Hills, NJ 07078	800/254-3210
KUL	KULTUR VIDEOS	195 Highway 36 West Long Branch, NJ 07764	800/458-5887
KYS	KEYSTONE LEARNING SYSTEMS	125 East 300 South Provo, UT 84606	800/748-4838
LNK	LEARNKEY INC.	1845 W. Sunset Blvd St. George, UT 84770	800/865-0165
MWP	MANNY'S WOODWORKING PLACE	555 S. Broadway Lexington, KY 40508	800/243-0713
NGC	NIGHTINGALE-CONANT	7300 N. Lehigh Ave Niles, IL 60714	800/525-9000
NNL	NANCY'S NOTIONS	P O Box 683 Beaver Dam, WI 53916	800/833-0690
NOP	NOBLE PRODUCTIONS	P O Box 8261 Cedar Rapids, IA 52408	800/221-8273
NUQ	NEW & UNIQUE VIDEOS	2336 Sumac Drive San Diego, CA 92105	619/282-6126
NUV	NUVO LTD.	P O Box 1729 Chula Vista, CA 91912	619/426-8440
OEI	ONE 8 INC.	P O Box 2075 Forks, WA 98331	800/504-1818

217

PAA	PACIFIC ARTS	11858 LaGrange Ave Los Angeles, CA 90025	800/538-5856
PAS	PACIFIC SPIRIT	1334 Pacific Ave Forest Grove, OR 97116	800/634-9057
PBC	PRINCETON BOOK COMPANY	P O Box 57 Pennington, NJ 08534	800/220-7149
PLB	PLAYBOY VIDEOS	P O Box 809 Itasca, IL 60143	800/423-9494
PSE	PRECISION SHOOTING	P O Box 5487 Tucson, AZ 85703	800/825-9080
PST	PASTIME TAPES	529 W. 42nd St, #4 New York, NY 10036	212/563-9219
RDM	RAND McNALLY VIDEOS	P O Box 182257 Chattanooga, TN 37422	800/234-0679
RHI	RINEHART INDUSTRIES	P O Box 5010 Janesville, WI 53547	800/367-3337
RHV	RANDOM HOUSE INC.	400 Hahn Road Westminster, MD 22157	800/726-0600
SBA	SMALL BUSINESS ADMINISTRATION	P O Box 30 Denver, CO 80201	800/827-5772
SDA	SODANCEABIT	15550 Carfax Ave Bellflower, CA 90706	800/643-2623
SFP	STAGE FRIGHT PRODUCTIONS	P O Box 373 Geneva, IL 60134	800/979-6800
SFV	SOFTVISION INTERNATIONAL	1240 East 800 North Orem, UT 84057	800/748-4746
SMV	SCHOOLMASTERS VIDEOS	P O Box 1941 Ann Arbor, MI 48106	800/521-2832
TAU	TAUNTON PRESS	P O Box 5507 Newtown, CT 06470	800/888-8286
THU	THUELS PUBLISHING	P O Box 202151 Minneapolis, MN 55420	No Phone
TJP	THREE J PRODUCTIONS LTD.	P O Box 30 White Plains, NY 10603	914/592-6033
TSV	THREE M SPORTSMAN'S VIDEO	3M Center, Bldg 225 St. Paul, MN 55144	800/525-6290
TWV	TIME WARNER HOME VIDEO	P O Box 3925 Milford, CT 06460	800/224-9944

VAI	VIDEO-AIDED INSTRUCTION	182 Village Road Roslyn Heights, NY 11577	800/238-1512
VER	VERANO UPHOLSTERY	P O Box 128 El Verano, CA 95433	800/635-3493
VTX	VIDEO TEXTBOOKS	P O Box 503 Ashland, OR 97520	800/628-4541
VVP	VICTORIAN VIDEO PRODUCTIONS	P O Box 1540 Colfax, CA 95713	800/848-0284
XJX	XENEJENEX	29 Sawyer Rd/1 Univ Pk Waltham, MA 02154	800/228-2495

INDEX

Adventures in Video

makes a great gift.

Additional copies are available
at a 15% discount if ordered on this form.
Orders of 10 or more copies
receive a 30% discount.

ORDER FORM

PRINT OR TYPE *(Please attach this form if using your own p.o.)*

Please send me **Adventures in Video**.

Quantity	Price	Total
_____	$38.00	$ _____
_____	$24.00 paperback	_____
	Less 15% discount	_____
	Less 30% discount for 10 or more	_____
	+ postage & handling ($2.75 for single-copy orders; $.50 for each additional copy)	_____
	TOTAL of enclosed check or money order	$ _____

Name _____

Company/Institution _____

Address _____

City _____

State _____ Zip _____

Complete
order form
and send with
your payment to:

**Arden Press Inc.
Dept. A
P.O. Box 418
Denver, CO
80201**

(303) 697-6766